WHY PEOPLE DIE BY SUICIDE

WHY
PEOPLE
DIE
BY
SUICIDE

Thomas Joiner

Harvard University Press

Cambridge, Massachusetts, and London, England
2005

Library of Congress Cataloging-in-Publication Data

Joiner, Thomas E.
    Why people die by suicide / Thomas Joiner.
        p. cm.
    Includes bibliographical references and index.
    ISBN 0-674-01901-6 (cloth : alk. paper)
        1. Suicide.   2. Suicide victims—Psychology.
    3. Suicide victims—Family relationships.
    4. Children of suicide victims.   I. Title.

    HV6545.J65 2005
    616.85′8445—dc22   2005051347

This book is dedicated to those who have lost someone to suicide, and especially to those who have been supportive of survivors like me, including, for example, my friends from high school, who did all the right things.

CONTENTS

WHY PEOPLE DIE BY SUICIDE

PROLOGUE

In 1990, close to a million people died by suicide worldwide. My dad was one of them.

Of course my dad's death has deeply affected both my feelings about suicide and my understanding of it. My feelings about suicide stem partly from people's reactions to my dad's death. Some friends and family reacted in ways that I still treasure—the sorts of things that make you proud to be human. Others' reactions were not quite up to this very high standard.

My intellectual understanding of suicide evolved along a different track than my feelings. Informed by science and clinical work, I came to know more than most about suicide—on levels ranging from the molecular to the cultural. But here too, my dad's death never left me, for the simple fact that I could evaluate theories and studies on suicide not only by formal professional and scientific criteria, but also by whether they fit with what I know about my dad's suicide. As I will point out, a nagging fact about my dad left me unsatisfied with existing theories of suicide and pushed me to think in new ways about his death and about suicide in general. All of this will become

1

clear throughout the book, but first, let me turn to the details of my dad's suicide.

In Atlanta in the early morning hours of August 1, 1990, my dad was sleeping, or trying to, in the bed that was mine as a teenager. He wasn't sleeping with my mom; I think his snoring had become too much of a problem. I was a graduate student in Austin, Texas at the time.

It was summer, so my dad must have been alternately cold and hot in that bed—cold when the air conditioning kicked in (because the vent was right next to the bed), hot when it turned off (because that room was not well insulated). My dad rose from the bed. I wonder if he made some silent gesture, like putting his hand against the wall that separated my old bedroom from his old bedroom, where my mother lay asleep. He walked past the room he had shared with my mom, and then past my younger sisters' rooms, where they lay asleep. Here again, did he hesitate as he passed their rooms, I wonder? Was he prepared with a cover story in case my mother or sisters woke up and asked him where he was going?

He went downstairs. Before going out the door, he must have pulled open a drawer or two in the kitchen, looking for a large knife. Or maybe he got the knife from his fishing tackle in the garage. It surprises and distresses me even now when I can't remember or never knew a key detail like this about my dad's death.

He walked outside, got into his van, and drove a half-mile or so to the lot of an industrial park. He prepared no note. At some point before dawn, he got into the back of the van and cut his wrists. His self-injury escalated from there—the cause of death from his autopsy report is "puncture wound to the heart." These details remain very painful for me, but they are important—as will become clear, people appear to work up to the act of lethal self-injury. They do so over a

long period of time, by gradually accumulating experiences that reduce their fear of self-harm; and they do so in the moment, by first
engaging in mild self-injury as a prelude to lethal self-injury.

My dad's body was not discovered until about 60 hours after his
death, which necessitated a closed casket funeral. So the last time I
saw my dad was in June of 1990 when I joined the family on a beach
trip. We fished and talked about the NBA finals and a large stock deal
my dad was proud to have recently pulled off. We played board
games in the van on the way home—the same van in which my dad
died. I am still stunned to think that six weeks later he would leave
the house and walk away from us forever. He never said goodbye to
my mother, my sisters, or me.

In the months before his death, my dad had parted ways with the
company in which he had formed his professional identity and, indeed, much of his identity as an adult. The position with this company was one of influence, and after leaving, he struggled to regain
his former feeling of effectiveness. I think this struggle was exacerbated by some callous and self-serving behaviors by those remaining
at the company, who my dad believed were friends.

The first family member I saw after my dad was found was my
Uncle Jim, my dad's older brother. He met me at the gate at the Atlanta airport. He must have been heartbroken and incredibly con-
fused about how his very successful little brother could have suddenly died by suicide. He shouldered this shocking burden and put
it aside, at least for a while, to pay attention to how I was feeling
and, in the days following, to how my mom and sisters were feeling.
Jim didn't understand much about suicide—I think he would have
said that himself—but some people don't require understanding in
order to act right. They just let compassion take over; that's what my
Uncle Jim did.

The relation of understanding suicide and "acting right" about it is
interesting to explore. In thinking back over people's reactions to my

dad's death, my sense is that no one understood it, really. To some people, like my Uncle Jim, understanding didn't matter and wasn't a barrier to acting with real generosity of spirit. To others, the lack of understanding seemed an insurmountable barrier, so that instincts toward compassion were short-circuited. They were caught up in their minds about how to understand this shocking death and what to say to me and my family. One contribution of this book, I hope, is to provide understanding, so that those who need it in order to unleash their caring and generosity will have it.

Ironically, those whose reactions were the least helpful were those who might have known better—those who, unlike my Uncle Jim, got tripped up by intellectual lack of understanding. All that was needed was eye contact and phrases like, "Man, I'm real sorry about what happened to your dad," as well as a willingness to interact with me like I was the same person they always knew. My friends from high school all did this by instinct, both at the time of my dad's death and in the weeks and months following. For instance, at my parents' house after my dad's funeral, one of my high school friends told a story about how his girlfriend had recently "dropped him like a rock." The phrase probably is not very funny to read, but there was something about his tone and facial expression that was extremely funny—I'm sure that was the first time I had laughed in the several days since my dad died. As another example, a few weeks after my dad's death, I went to dinner with a girl I had admired very much in high school, but with whom I had lost touch. She was among the first people I told about the exact details of my dad's death, and her understanding and composure encouraged me to talk to others.

By contrast, my peers and professors in psychology—yes, psychology of all things—struggled to get it right. A girlfriend seemed more concerned about tainted DNA ("suicide's genetic, right?") than about how I was coping. Peers and professors ignored my dad's death altogether. One professor, a psychoanalytically oriented clinical supervisor of mine, was particularly inept and seemed unable to say anything at all in response to my dad's suicide. He tried to hide his inability behind a psychoanalytic stance of neutral silence, but never was that charade more apparent and more pitiful. These people, I think, needed to intellectually grasp suicide before they could do anything else . . . and since they couldn't grasp it intellectually—few can—their otherwise good hearts were hampered. It is also possible they were just too scared to deal with the topic. I hope this book frees good hearts in those with a need for intellectual understanding and steels those who need courage to help the bereaved.

Among my psychology peers and professors, there were people who, like my Uncle Jim, just did what was right. A different psychoanalytic supervisor was among the most understanding and helpful of anyone I encountered in the difficult days and weeks following my dad's death. A week or two after my dad's death, still another person, my professor Jerry Metalsky, paused as we were working on a manuscript, looked me in the eye, and said with real feeling, "I'm just so sorry about what happened to your dad." These simple words choked me with tears at the time, and can still bring tears to my eyes to this day.

One of my peers, Lee Goldfinch, found my parents' phone number in Atlanta and called me, as it turned out, on the day of my dad's funeral. This alone set him apart, but as we talked for a few minutes about what happened and how my family and I were doing, Lee wept in a very quiet and selfless way. That brief conversation with Lee represented one of the times in my life that I have felt most understood, most listened to.

Some experiences within my family exacerbated the pain of my dad's death. Just as some of my psychology peers and professors struggled for understanding and thus couldn't quite hit the right note, some in my family faced the same difficulty. For example, one relative counseled another to tell others that my dad died from a heart attack. The instinct to lie about suicide is not rare. In one study, 44 percent of those bereaved by suicide had lied to some extent about the cause of death, whereas none of those dying from accidents or natural causes lied.[1]

Indeed, those who die by suicide will occasionally advise in suicide notes that others lie about their deaths. Edwin Shneidman[2] gave this example: "Please take care of little Joe because I love him with all of my heart. Please don't tell him what happened. Tell him I went far away and will come back one of these days. Tell him you don't know when." This example shows why it is not rare and why it is understandable that people sometimes lie about suicide.

Lying about suicide is just one form of misunderstanding it. Another, more pernicious form is blame, and in this regard, my own experiences were quite mild—I am aware of no one who blamed my mother, my sisters, or me for my dad's death. Unfortunately, others are forced to go through this particular form of hell. In Shneidman's case example of Ariel, Ariel's father had died by self-inflicted gunshot wound in what was very likely a suicide (but there was some possibility of the death being an accident). Ariel wrote, "Well, my aunt . . . told me that I had killed my father, and he had committed suicide because of me." Almost exactly three years after her father's death, Ariel herself nearly died by setting herself on fire.

Misunderstanding and even taboo about suicidal behavior are rampant. Karl Menninger[3] said, "So great is the taboo on suicide that some people will not say the word." The staff of the magazine that promotes prominent research at my university wanted to run a story on my suicide research. They pondered featuring the work on the magazine's cover, but decided against it—they could not imagine prominently displaying the word "suicide," although they ran the article itself.

These same attitudes are common among family members of those who engage in suicidal behavior. Decades ago, Menninger,[4] in describing relatives' reactions to the hospitalization of depressed and potentially suicidal patients, commented, "Patients committed to our care in the depth of a temporary depression in which they threatened suicide would begin to improve, and relatives thereupon would seek to remove them, utterly disregarding our warning that it was too soon, that suicide was still a danger. Frequently they would ridicule the idea that such a thing might be perpetrated by *their* relative." Menninger collected a large file of newspaper clippings reporting the deaths by suicide of such patients.

I understand why people tiptoe around suicide or even lie about it outright. This has never been clearer to me than when my oldest son, Malachi (named after my dad's ancestor who was the first in our family to come to America), asked me why my dad was not alive. He was three years old at the time. Luckily, I had anticipated this question, but I thought I'd have another two or three years to think about my answer. I took a deep breath and said something like, "Well, you know how people can get sick, like when you have a cough or your stomach hurts. People can get sick like that in their bodies, and they can also get sick in their minds, sometimes very sick. My dad got very sick like that in his mind; he got to where he was so sad and lonely that he didn't want to live anymore. When people feel like this for a long time, they sometimes think about hurting themselves or even killing themselves. That's what my dad did."

Malachi's reaction was similar to the many times he had learned a surprising fact about nature from me. With the same sense of innocent surprise, not tinged much at all with negative emotion, he said, "You mean he killed him*self*?" much as if he were saying, "You mean there are fish that can taste things with their *skin*?" (which there are and which we had just read about). I answered (to the first question), "Yes, he did. That can happen sometimes when people feel so sick in their minds."

I was ready for fallout. For example, I imagined what I would say to a teacher or parent connected with Malachi's preschool who might approach me and say, "Malachi's been telling the other children about people killing themselves." I prepared for what I would do if Malachi became worried or upset about this (might his own dad kill himself?) or had bad dreams. None of this occurred, but it worried me, and so I understand why people lie about suicide, though the disadvantages far outweigh the advantages.

Every now and then Malachi will surprise me with a comment or a question related to my dad's death. Perhaps the one that touched me the most occurred about a week after our first conversation. We were about to go outside to play when he abruptly turned and said, "When *you* were a little boy, *I* was *your* dad." More than just the timing of the comment, there was something in his expression and tone that made me see that he understood that it was painful that my dad was gone, and he wanted somehow to lessen the pain. He did.

When he was four or five, he asked me how my dad died by suicide, to which I replied that he cut himself. In another conversation when he was six, in which I mentioned the specific cause of my dad's death, Malachi pointed out, in a somewhat playful tone he uses when he believes he's discovered something that I didn't want him to know, that earlier I had only said my dad cut himself—I had never been more specific. Had I lied altogether, Malachi eventually would have caught me in my lies.

Allow me to emphasize that approximately one millionth of the conversations between us are about my dad's death. The topic ranks far, far behind topics like school, friends, various sports, the antics of his charismatic little brother Zekey, science, nature, his mother's ability to do magic tricks, and things like fish that can taste with their skin. But I have been open about it with him, as I will be with Zekey, and I have not regretted it at all. And now, when I talk about the topic with others, it's really very easy; if I can tell the three-year-old that I love most in this world (along with his brother and mother), I can tell anyone.

The idea that suicide is a shameful act of weakness nagged at me in the years following my dad's death. My dad was not weak in any sense of the word. On the contrary, he had a stoic toughness about him that seemed to inure him to physical pain. The anecdotes are numerous—and I'm confident that there are more I never knew about or have forgotten. When he was three, he tried to balance by standing on an upright milk bottle, which broke and severely cut his Achilles tendon (and which the babysitter packed with chimney soot and wrapped). As an adult, he was a Marine sergeant. When I was seven, my dad took our family skiing. I'm not sure, but I think it was the first time he had ever skied. He broke his leg. A few years later he was jogging with our family dog Jupiter. Jupiter cut in front of my dad, who tripped and ruptured his Achilles tendon. Still later, he was badly injured in a boating accident.

The idea that suicide requires a kind of courage or strength has implications not only for the causes of suicide—a focus of this book—but also for the public view of those who die by suicide. The truth about suicide may prove unsettling—it is not about weakness, it is about the fearless endurance of a certain type of pain. Perhaps this view will demystify and destigmatize suicide and perhaps even the mental disorders associated with suicide, like mood disorders.

There is no question but that my dad had a mood disorder, and one of relatively long duration. I remember being puzzled as a young child that my dad spent most of the day in bed once, but wasn't physically sick. Later, I imagined that he may have had too much to drink the night before. But that didn't fit. I never knew him to drink to excess. I now understand that he was in the middle of a depressive episode.

Near the end of his life, he seemed to have even more obvious depressive episodes, especially around the Christmas holidays. When I would come home from college for the holidays, my dad would sometimes pick me up from the airport, and his depression was often palpable the moment I saw him. On the drive home from the airport,

I would think of whatever I could to draw him out, but would get only monosyllabic replies. Though I'd keep trying, I was relieved when the twenty-minute drive was over. And I was glad—no, saved is more like it—by the relief provided by seeing my old friends from home.

My dad and I often watched sports together when I was a child. Some of my earliest and fondest memories of him are when he and I would lie next to each other on a sofa watching football or basketball games. He'd have to pull the sofa out from the wall so we would both be able to see. We'd be under the same dark red wool blanket, with a Bulldog on it and GEORGIA underneath the Bulldog in big block letters. Years later, home from college for the holidays, I'd often arrange for or be given tickets by friends and family to various sporting events. I'd invite my dad, again in an attempt to draw him out, and again with no success. The twenty-minute ride from the airport became the three-hour stay at a football game.

He also had what I now see as frequent episodes of what is called hypomania, a milder form of what is known as a full-blown manic episode. Manic episodes are discrete periods of symptoms; the episodes are phasic—they come and go—and they include grandiose, often delusional ideas, expansive planning, elated mood, and boundless energy (e.g., going without sleep for days). The sleep symptom in bipolar disorder is notable. People experiencing manic episodes are too busy to sleep. Irritability also can characterize manic episodes. The combination of severe manic phases and severe depressive phases is known as bipolar I disorder in the psychiatric nomenclature.

My dad never had frank manic phases, but he did experience episodes of hypomania, which can be viewed as an attenuated form of mania. Someone with hypomania may sleep every night (but for a shorter time than usual), may express quite positive self-views (but not seem frankly grandiose), and may have a noticeably upbeat mood (but not seem extremely elated). The combination of hypomania and severe depressive phases is known as bipolar II disorder in the psychiatric nomenclature, and I now see that this was what my dad had. Bipolar II disorder is a serious condition; approximately as many people with bipolar II die by suicide as those with bipolar I. Some estimate that up to 10 percent of those with bipolar disorder of either type die by suicide.

I believe most of my dad's hypomanic episodes occurred in the spring, which is one of the most common times for manic or hypomanic phases to occur. The clearest example was from the spring of 1989—about fifteen months before his death by suicide—when my dad visited me, somewhat unexpectedly, in Austin, Texas. I accompanied him all day as he met with various officials of state and local government to discuss things related to real estate, taxes, and the like. These busy people all saw my dad on very short notice—a testimony, I now know, to his truly considerable talents and ingenuity. To a person, they were also perplexed about just what my dad was talking about (not to mention why his long-haired son in high-top basketball shoes was accompanying him)—evidence, I now see, of his hypomania.

On this trip, my dad also saw the hovel that my friend and I were living in. It was truly bad, but the rent was incredibly low and I didn't mind. I figured my dad wouldn't mind it too much either. He didn't seem to; all he said was something like, "don't tell your mother." But it occurred to me later that this may have been a real disappointment to him; he may not have understood that even the best of graduate students live in such places and may have wondered what had become of his Princeton-educated son. It haunts me to imagine that he counted my circumstances as his failure. It is agonizing that he can't see how and with whom I live now.

During all the years my dad had these symptoms, he was not treated until within a year or so of his death. Partly this was because my dad was extremely capable and accomplished. For example, he finished second in his law school class at the University of Georgia—in fact, he finished a close second to his best friend at the time, a friend with whom he later lost touch. As another example of my dad's ability, he blazed trails in the field of business software during the early 1970s, at a time when few people had even heard the term "software." He was a talented person, able to function even when symptomatic. That was one reason he was not treated until near the end of his life. Another reason had less to do with my dad and more to do with the state of mood disorder science at the time. Treatments, the treatment climate, and the societal view of mood disorders between the 1950s and 1980s were not such as to encourage accessing care. When my dad finally did access care in 1989, he received reasonable treatments (e.g., an SSRI medicine and a mood stabilizer). The problem was not really the type of treatments, but rather, their timing. By that point his mood disorder had taken a forty-year toll, and his treatment came too late.

I mentioned earlier that my dad sustained a lot of physical injuries, some of which occurred in boating accidents. In one such boating incident, he sustained a minor injury, yet his life and the lives of others in the boat (me and our dog Jupiter) may have been threatened more than in the other instances. My dad loved to fish, and he liked for me to go with him. At times I liked to go, but conditions could get extreme for a young boy—leaving before dawn in a relatively small boat in rough surf, going out a mile or two, staying all day in the sun, and coming back at dusk, often empty-handed. In the most memorable instance, as we were fishing as usual, huge waves suddenly rose, seemingly out of nowhere. I guess our boat was about twenty-five feet long; from crest to base, these waves were bigger, because our boat would not clear a crest until a moment or two after it cleared a base. My dad was struggling with the steering wheel to keep our boat at a ninety-degree angle to these waves; if we got sideways, we'd be in real trouble. As the boat mounted a wave, our dog Jupiter would slide helplessly to the back of the boat, along with a lot of fishing poles and tackle and such. The same process occurred in reverse as we slid down the back of the wave. My dad was winning the struggle of keeping the boat at the right angle when the steering wheel broke off and shattered in his hands. He had to steer with the base of the steering wheel, which he gripped like he was trying to choke it. Within a few minutes, we were in calmer waters, and I pointed out to my dad that the steering wheel had cut one of his hands pretty badly; I'm sure that he had not noticed until then.

This story displays the kind of stoicism and toughness of mind and body my dad possessed. As I will explain later in the book, past experience with bodily injuries may be important in later suicide risk. My dad was calm in the face of pain; he hardly batted an eye as he steered our boat through a very dangerous situation, clutching the stub of the steering wheel with a bleeding hand.

There is also a touch of recklessness implicit in the story. I don't recall my dad ever checking weather reports before we went out. Spending fifteen-hour days in a small boat on the open ocean is not something that I would attempt with Malachi or Zekey. My dad was not a generally reckless character; he was not impulsive, not prone to substance abuse, not prone to fits of anger. But there was recklessness of a sort, and various kinds of recklessness may predispose people to suicide precisely because it leaves them open to injury and danger. Repeated exposure to injury and danger, in turn, makes people fearless about a lot of things, including serious self-injury.

Despite my dad's substantial history of injury and a definite stoicism and fearlessness, when it came to producing his own death, he seemingly needed to work up to the act. He died by piercing his heart, but first, he worked up to that by cutting other areas of his body. This fact about my dad's suicide—still painful to write about after many years—is, I think, important. In one way or another, everyone who dies by suicide has to work up to the act, certainly over the long-term (through getting used to pain) and sometimes over the short-term, by trying out the means of death in a milder, non-lethal way.

A day or two after my dad's funeral, my Uncle Jim and I went to retrieve some of my dad's belongings and papers from the Atlanta morgue. The attendant was a true idiot and seemed irritable about just what it was we were doing there. My Uncle Jim was a very gentle soul, but his reaction to the attendant was a perfect blend of force and rage. The attendant was transformed—he would have tried a back flip then and there if asked.

Among my dad's things that we picked up at the morgue was his watch—a gift from my mother, a 1970s waterproof Rolex. My dad wore it always on his left wrist, with the face of the watch on the inside of his wrist. When asked why he wore it like that, he'd say, "So I can see what time it is without spilling my coffee." I still have the watch, and it is evident that he wore it everywhere, given how scratched it is. I tried it on a while after he died, but it was too small.

Recently, my wife wanted her wedding ring updated. I planned a special ceremony to present it to her exactly as I did the first time, but this time around with Malachi and Zekey as our witnesses. When I picked up my wife's updated ring, I had the thought that the jeweler could repair the face and enlarge the band of my dad's watch for me. So many of my experiences and memories subsequent to my dad's death are tinged like this, sometimes in a deeply painful way (for example, he will never meet my wife or sons) and sometimes, like the episode at the jeweler's, with a kind of wistfulness that stitches his life and even his death into the lives of my family and me.

There is such a well of sadness in me even to this day. But it's become more general now—less about my dad and more about how heartsick I am that tomorrow around eighty families in the United States will lose a loved one to suicide, just like my family did. Improvements in science and clinical work can save lives and reduce the number of bereaved families.

I share with survivors the pain of losing a loved one to suicide. But I share with clinicians the challenges of treating suicidal behavior, and I share with scientists the daunting task of unraveling suicide's mysteries. I want to acknowledge this shared legacy and future, use them to pose various pressing questions about suicide, and employ them as context for my explanation of why people die by suicide.

WHAT WE KNOW

AND

DON'T KNOW

ABOUT SUICIDE

1

The last compelling theory of suicide appeared approximately fifteen years ago. The number of other prominent and coherent theories in the decades or even centuries before that can be tallied on one hand. This is a strange state of affairs for a phenomenon that kills millions.

A new theory is needed that builds on existing models and provides a deeper account of suicidal behavior to explain more suicide-related phenomena. This is a very tall order, because the extent and diversity of facts related to suicide are intimidating and baffling. For example, suicide is far more common in men than in women . . . except in China. In the United States, there has been a recent increase in suicide among African-Americans—specifically, young black men. And yet, the demographic group at highest risk is older white men. Female anorexics, prostitutes, athletes, and physicians all have elevated suicide rates. A theory that can account for these diverse facts would be persuasive.

Such a theory would not only advance scientific knowledge, but deepen the understanding of suicidal behavior among clinicians who need to assess risk, intervene in crises, and design treatment and prevention protocols. It would also help those who have lost a loved one to suicide, who suffer much misunderstanding.

In this chapter, I describe some of my own clinical work and the supervision of others' clinical work with suicidal patients. In the clinical literature, suicide is often described as an "urgent," "vexing," or "pressing" issue, one that preoccupies clinicians. Suicide *is* an urgent issue—it kills people—but urgency need not entail panic. Suicide can be understood in ways that resolutely point to clear clinical decisions . . . given, that is, a full explanatory model. My and others' clinical experiences with suicidal patients will highlight how a comprehensive account of suicide would have reduced confusion and panic and facilitated clinical progress.

This chapter also touches on some of my scientific work on suicide. My research group is one of many that have produced new and important findings regarding suicide. The chapter will include some basic scientific findings on suicide produced by my and other research groups—facts that any compelling account of suicide must explain.

I also summarize existing models of suicide in this chapter—theoretical accounts that have been developed to explain some of these facts. One of the best ways to evaluate a theoretical model is the number of facts it can explain, and some of these models are more successful than others, as we shall see. My hope is that this book's explanation of suicide will save people some of the misunderstandings my family and I went through, will refine clinicians' approach to treating suicidal behavior, and will set a scientific agenda for the study of suicide. In the process, some interesting questions will be raised and addressed. For example, should family members tell the truth about the cause of death when a loved one has died by suicide? What constitutes a proper definition of suicide itself? How are we to understand the deaths of those who jumped from the World Trade Center towers' upper floors on September 11, of the September 11 terrorists, and of those in mass suicides in cults? What protects most women from suicide, and yet, why do some very different subgroups of women—such as prostitutes and physicians—share similarly high suicide rates? Why are older, white men the demographic group in the United States most vulnerable to suicide? Why do suicide rates decrease in the United States during times of national crisis and decrease in a particular city when the city's professional sports team is making a championship run? What are the constituent parts of the genuine desire for death? These and other questions will be raised and addressed throughout the book.

Notes from the Clinic

My first job after getting my doctorate was as an assistant professor of psychiatry at the University of Texas Medical Branch at Galveston. What a blessing this job was in many ways. I saw many psychotherapy patients and worked with skilled psychiatrists who taught me a lot about the biological bases of mental disorders. Biology appears to play some role in why people die by suicide, a fact I will address later in this book. But they also taught me something more—an attitude about suicide risk in patients that was neither dismissive nor alarmist. The alarmist position is perhaps the easiest to understand—this is the idea that whenever someone mentions suicide, it is a life-threatening situation and alarms should be sounded. This idea occurs in settings in which staff see relatively few people with serious mood disorders. In settings where serious mood disorders are common, people understand that suicidality is just part of the disorder; the majority of people who experience mood disorders will have ideas about suicide, and the vast majority will neither attempt suicide nor die by suicide. If 911 were called in each of these cases, a "cry wolf" scenario would quickly develop. Alarmists are making a mistake in conditional probability. Given the existence of a suicidal thought or behavior, they mistakenly estimate the probability of death or serious injury by suicide to be higher than it is.

Although alarmists make a mistake, it is not hard to see why they do. When people have ideas about suicide, it is quite true that risk is elevated compared to people who do not have suicidal ideas. Moreover, suicide is irreversible, and everything possible should be done to prevent it. Alarmists overreact, but they are doing so in the safe direction; "better safe than sorry," they might say.

The alarmist problem is easy to notice in training clinics. Most of the pages I receive on my beeper are from therapists at the training clinic I direct who are worried that they should do more for a patient with suicidal symptoms. When I return the call, I ask a series of questions to see if the therapist is meeting the standard of care. In our clinic, meeting the standard of care is routine. And so I will then say, "Well, you've done everything I would've done; I wonder, what else is it that you think you're supposed to do?" The answer is often, "I'm not sure, I just have this feeling that there's something else I should do." Then I'll say, "Well, there's not; but don't lose that feeling, because it will ensure that you regularly do what's best for patients; also, though, don't let that feeling get out of hand, because it can burn you out, plus, ultimately these choices are not up to us, they're up to patients." Make no mistake, the standard of care is important—at times even life-saving—and therapists are expected to meet it rigorously, including involuntary hospitalization of the patient if needed. But beyond that, responsibility for life choices resides with patients. Therapists who see this are likely to enjoy their work more, to not be distracted by one patient when dealing with another, and, importantly, to enjoy their nonwork time as well.

The alarmist attitude is understandable but, especially if exaggerated, mistaken. Those who take a dismissive approach make a mistake in the opposite direction. They become blasé about suicidal behavior, often attributing it to manipulation or gesturing on the part of the potentially suicidal person. This problem is acute when it comes to the often misunderstood borderline personality disorder, which is characterized by a long-standing pattern of out-of-control emotions, interpersonal storminess, feelings of emptiness, and impulsive behaviors, including impulses toward self-injury. Some clinicians take a dismissive attitude toward patients with this disorder because they believe that these patients merely "gesture" suicide. In other words, they engage in suicidal behaviors, such as cutting themselves, but do not really intend to kill themselves; instead, they only intend to provoke or manipulate others. I wish this were true, but it is not—approximately 10 percent of patients with this disorder end up dying from their suicidal gestures (comparable to the rate for patients with mood disorders). The following quotation illustrates this misunderstanding:

> The borderline patient is a therapist's nightmare . . . because borderlines never really get better. The best you can do is help them coast, without getting sucked into their pathology . . . They're the chronically depressed, the determinedly addictive, the compulsively divorced, living from one emotional disaster to the next. Bed hoppers, stomach pumpers, freeway jumpers, and sad-eyed bench-sitters with arms stitched up like footballs and psychic wounds that can never be sutured . . . Borderlines go from therapist to therapist, hoping to find a magic bullet for the crushing feelings of emptiness.[1]

This characterization is demonstrably false. Patients with borderline personality disorder *do* get better. A persuasive study found that 34.5 percent of a sample of borderline patients met the criteria for remission at two years, 49.4 percent at four years, 68.6 percent at six years, and 73.5 percent over the entire follow-up. Only around 6 percent of those who remitted then experienced a recurrence.[2]

The dismissive attitude is dangerous for another reason. A main thesis of this book is that those who die by suicide work up to the act.

They do this in various ways—for instance, previous suicide attempts—and all of these various ways have the effect of insulating people from danger signals. They get used to the pain and fear associated with self-harm, and thus gradually lose natural inhibitions against it. Clinicians' dismissive attitudes have the potential to model a blasé attitude about self-harm. If clinicians blithely get used to suicidal behavior, their patients may vicariously do so as well.

The psychiatrists at my first job balanced the alarmist and dismissive positions very well. They clearly understood the danger and horror; in fact, most of them had had a patient who had died by suicide. They knew the standards of care for suicide risk assessment and the treatment of suicidal behavior, and they followed them faithfully. But they understood the limits of their interventions, they understood people's ultimate autonomy, including their freedom to occasion their own death if they really were committed to doing so. My impression was that these psychiatrists did their job well during the day, and slept well at night.

Consider for example the case of Gayle (a false name). In retrospect, I understand Gayle's situation clearly, but when I was seeing her, I was uneasy. She was the sort of patient who seemed potentially self-destructive. Indeed, she often fantasized about death by suicide, envisioning a particularly graphic means—severing her hand with a machete and bleeding to death (people have died in just this way, incidentally). She even owned a machete. This would be enough to concern any clinician, and I was no exception. I recommended that Gayle be hospitalized, so that she would remain safe while treatments for her substantial depression were started.

She refused hospitalization and also refused antidepressant medicines; she would agree only to psychotherapy. An initial question, then, was whether I should hospitalize her involuntarily. I had the sense that this would not be best, but I was having trouble putting my finger on exactly why she did not require hospitalization. After consultation with colleagues, I was reminded of some mildly reassuring facts. Gayle was around forty-five years old and had never attempted suicide. She had had plenty of time to have tried it, and yet had not. This is no guarantee. There are people who at age forty-five or even sixty-five attempt suicide for the first time and die. Still, the fact that she had not had previous experience with suicidal behavior was mildly reassuring. Her gender was another mildly reassuring factor—women are a lot less likely to die by suicide than are men. Also somewhat reassuring were her connections to life. There were things that she was proud of regarding her professional life, and more important, she was deeply connected to her young son. She spontaneously mentioned these things as I questioned her about suicide potential.

Gayle was also the rare person who clearly met criteria for a major depressive episode but who had an absence of depressed mood. In a study of young adults my colleagues and I conducted, this pattern was found to occur in only about 5 percent of those who were in a depressive episode. Recent work has shown lack of depressed mood to be a positive prognostic indicator among depressed people; that is, they tend to get better quicker and to have good outcomes.[3]

Throughout this book, I will argue that the acquired ability to enact lethal self-injury is crucial in serious suicidal behavior. People are not born with the developed capacity to seriously injure themselves (although they are born with factors, including certain genes, that may facilitate the future development of this capacity). In fact, if anything, they are born with the opposite—the knee-jerk tendency to avoid pain, injury, and death. That is, people have strong tendencies toward self-preservation; evolution has seen to that. Through an array of means described later, some people develop the ability to beat back this pressing urge toward self-preservation. Once they do, according to the theory laid out in this book, they are at high risk for suicide, but only if certain other conditions apply—namely that they feel real disconnection from others and that they feel ineffective to the point of seeing themselves as a burden on others. These factors, like the acquired ability to enact lethal self-injury, are covered in detail in later chapters of the book.

I now understand clearly why Gayle made me feel uneasy, but also why she was not at particularly high risk for suicide. She had acquired the ability to enact lethal self-injury. A main way that people develop this capacity is through previous suicidal behavior. As noted already, Gayle had not engaged in such behavior. What I believe led to her developing this capacity was a long history of severe substance abuse, which included many painful and provocative experiences (another way to gradually beat back the instinct to survive). Her substance abuse had ended; she had been clean for around eight years when I saw her. But her earlier experiences had left various residues.

This ability in Gayle was manifested by her having a clear and detailed suicide plan, but especially in her sense of calm and her lack of fear about the plan. These were the things that made me want to hospitalize Gayle. Nevertheless she was not at particularly high risk for suicide, and the reason involves two other factors that I believe are required for serious suicidal behavior—thwarted belongingness and perceived burdensomeness. Gayle had a fairly well-developed circle of friends and was very connected to her son. There was no evidence that she felt fundamentally disconnected from others, and plenty of evidence that her sense of belonging was very much intact. Similarly, Gayle was a particularly capable woman; for instance, even when depressed, she was the office's top performer in her professional line of work. There was no evidence that she felt ineffective, certainly not to the point that she believed she burdened others.

Her sense of belonging and effectiveness buffered her, but it is important to note that this could have changed rapidly. People cannot develop the ability to lethally injure themselves quickly; the experiences that are required take time and repetition. By contrast, people can quickly develop views that they do not belong or that they are particularly ineffective. Thus, in a case like Gayle's, suicide risk can quickly escalate. Repeated risk assessment is thus necessary in Gayle's case (and is a safe clinical practice anyway).

The case of Sharon (a false name) is interesting by way of contrast. When questioned about suicide risk, Sharon articulated no plan at all. When pressed a little on the question, she made statements like, "I can't imagine actually trying suicide, it's just that I have the sense that I'd be better off dead." Like Gayle, Sharon had never attempted suicide in the past, but unlike Gayle, she had no history of repeated painful and provocative experiences through which she might have acquired the ability to enact lethal self-injury. She thus did not have the setting condition for serious suicidal behavior, even though, as it turns out, she did have the other factors important in the current theory. That is, she felt she was a burden on others and felt disconnected from them. These feelings, combined with statements like, "I'd be better off dead" and with symptoms like sleep difficulty, clearly indicated a mood disorder, but her risk for suicide was slight. The thought never occurred to me that she should be hospitalized. Indeed, though she clearly had a mood disorder, it was of relatively moderate severity, and she remitted with less than two months of psychotherapy and stayed remitted for at least two years thereafter, which was the last time I contacted her.

The cases of Gayle and Sharon, especially when viewed through the lens of this book's theory on suicide, are informative regarding suicide risk assessment. Generally speaking, someone like Gayle is at chronically elevated risk, at least to some degree, because the capacity for serious self-injury already is in place. All that is needed for Gayle to engage in serious suicidal behavior if she chooses is a quick change in her feelings of connection and effectiveness. Accordingly, routine assessment of risk status is required with someone like Gayle. By contrast, someone like Sharon is unlikely to engage in serious self-harm because she has not beaten down the instinct to live. Even if

Sharon feels disconnected from others and ineffective, she lacks the capacity to translate the desire for death into action. These points will be expanded on in a later chapter on clinical implications.

Notes from Scientific Research

The science about suicide is not especially well developed and has certainly not permeated the public consciousness. I was reminded of this the other day at my sons' soccer game. There were five or so full-field games going on—approximately 150 people out on the fields. Off in the distance, lightning struck, and the field administrators decided to cancel the games. There was some grumbling about this decision of course, but everyone understood the rationale—lightning can be lethal.

But just how lethal is lightning? In other words, how many people die from lightning strikes? In fact, from 1980 to 1995, there were approximately eighty deaths per year from lightning strikes in the United States. During this same time period, there were more than eighty deaths *per day* from suicide.

Why do people scramble to prevent death by lightning strike but don't scramble in the same way to prevent death by suicide? The latter is approximately 365 times more common than the former. One could invoke bias or stigma against mental health problems, but I think a more mundane answer is available. It is fairly easy to understand how and why people die by lightning strike, and prevention is straightforward too—you just get out from under the weather. By contrast, it is not at all easy for people to understand how and why people die by suicide, and prevention is not clear-cut at all. To make the prevention of suicide more like the prevention of lightning strikes, people need a clearer understanding of how and why people die by suicide. This book is intended to provide such an understanding.

The example of lightning strikes does not really illustrate bias against suicide; rather, it simply indicates that lightning is a well-characterized phenomenon and its prevention is straightforward. But in other examples, bias and stigma are detectable. In Tad Friend's 2003 *New Yorker* article on suicide at the Golden Gate Bridge, he points out that a main reason for community resistance to a suicide barrier fence (which would clearly save lives) is aesthetics. For the past twenty-five years, however, a large section of the bridge has been festooned with an eight-foot-tall cyclone fence directly above a site where tourists can walk below. The fence's purpose is to prevent people dropping things—including, to take a real example, bowling balls—on other tourists below. Friend cites the bridge's former chief engineer as saying that the fence is needed because "It's a public-safety issue." True enough, it *is* a public safety issue, but not one that has ever killed anyone, bowling balls notwithstanding. By contrast, around thirty people die by suicide each year by jumping from the bridge. The acceptability of a debris fence coupled with the unacceptability of a suicide barrier seems misguided and unfair.

To digress a bit, the stigma and taboo of suicide are topics that warrant their own book. The stigma, pervasive and enduring, can be found even in the seventh circle of Dante's *Inferno*. As A. Alvarez[4] summarizes, "In the seventh circle, below the burning heretics and the murderers stewing in their river of hot blood, is a dark pathless wood where the souls of suicides grow for eternity in the shape of warped poisonous thorns . . . At the Day of Judgment, when bodies and souls are reunited, the bodies of suicides will hang from the branches of the [thorns], since divine justice will not bestow again on their owners the bodies they have willfully thrown away." According to Dante, my dad is, as I write this, *below* the murderers, and will hang from thorns for eternity—stigma indeed.

To return to the Golden Gate Bridge, aesthetics does not really provide a convincing explanation for the lack of a suicide barrier, but what about cost? As Friend points out, cost did not prevent the recent construction of a barrier between the bridge's walkway and traffic, designed to separate bicyclists from traffic. This barrier cost 5 million dollars, and yet no bicyclist has ever been killed on the bridge. Five million dollars and zero deaths for bicyclists; zero dollars and over a thousand deaths by suicide: it is difficult to avoid the conclusion of stigma and bias.

Regarding knowledge about suicide and its prevention, much remains to be learned and to be done. Some facts are established, but even for these, fitting the facts into a coherent overarching theory has proven elusive. This book provides the outlines of one such theory. Any compelling explanation of suicide should shed at least some light on various established facts, including prevalence of suicide; the associations of suicide with age, gender, race, neurobiological indices, mental disorders, and substance abuse; impulsivity; and childhood adversity, as well as issues like treatment and prevention efforts and the clustering and "contagion" of suicide. Each of these topics is defined here and accounted for later, at least in part, by the theory proposed in this book.

Definition

One might imagine that defining suicide is relatively easy. Indeed, the dictionary definition could not be clearer—"the act of killing oneself intentionally." This definition seems to apply to my dad and many others who will be mentioned throughout the book, like the poets Hart Crane and Weldon Kees and the musician Kurt Cobain. But what about people on the upper floors of the World Trade Center who jumped to their deaths on September 11, 2001? At least fifty people died in this way, and the actual number is probably closer to 200. Did they die by suicide? According to the dictionary definition, they did, but according to the New York medical examiner and intuitively to many of us, they did not. All September 11 deaths at the World Trade Center were classified as homicides. What about the

September 11 terrorists, whose actions, in addition to all of their horrible consequences, caused the terrorists' own deaths? Did they die by suicide? Again, according to dictionary definitions, they did. But the terrorists themselves would more likely have characterized their deaths as martyrdom or casualties of holy war than as suicide.

Difficulties in defining suicide arise in other situations. Did Marilyn Monroe die by suicide, or was she killed? Virtually all the evidence points to suicide, but the idea of homicide resurfaces, often for spurious reasons.

How about people who die alone in single-car motor vehicle accidents who are later found to have been intoxicated at the time of death? We cannot know with certainty whether these deaths were intentional or accidental. One basis on which to make the designation might involve the facts of the accident, such as the angle at which the car was driven into a tree or the pattern of skid marks. Someone who brakes or swerves at the last instant could be viewed as simply having fallen asleep at the wheel. This is certainly possible, but it is also possible that someone intended suicide and changed his or her mind too late. This appears to happen relatively frequently, as seen in cases of those who jump from high places, survive, and report that they regretted their decision in midair.

There are still other ambiguities regarding the definition of suicidal behavior. One of my adolescent patients took a regular sewing needle, inserted it in the side of her wrist a millimeter or two, and immediately told her mother she had attempted suicide. This scenario is of clinical concern (and of course was of great concern to the mother), but does this qualify as a real suicide attempt? Is it of the same quality as more serious attempts, such as what my patient "Gayle" had in mind (severing her hand and bleeding to death)?

I am aware of no current theory that adequately handles all of these definitional problems, but in this book I will at least address each one.

Prevalence

Though rates vary somewhat from year to year, approximately 30,000 people in the United States and more than half a million people worldwide die by suicide each year. A useful common metric for death rate is deaths per 100,000 in the population. The rate of death by suicide has been between 10 per 100,000 and 15 per 100,000 for decades. In 2001, suicide was the eleventh leading cause of death overall in the United States.

On the one hand, 30,000 U.S. deaths per year—one every eighteen minutes or so—is a lot. On the other hand, relatively speaking, suicide is a rare cause of death. For example, given that a person has died, the chance that the cause was heart disease or cancer is 52 percent. The chance that the cause of death was suicide is a little over 1 percent.

Suicide is thus a relatively rare form of death, and any compelling theory should be able to account for this fact. Many theories of suicide run aground on the simple shores of prevalence rates—for example, they propose a cause that is very common, yet do not fully explain why relatively few die by suicide. The theory to be developed in this book has something to say about the relative rarity of death by suicide.

Gender

Men are approximately four times more likely than women to die by suicide; women are approximately three times as likely as men to attempt suicide. This pattern of male lethality is partly related to a tendency toward violent behavior more common in men than women. Women's attempts are more frequent but less violent. Two of three male suicide victims in the United States die by firearm, as compared to one of three for women—the most common cause of death by suicide in women is overdose or poisoning. With one key exception, men are more likely to die by suicide than women in every country of the world.

The exception is China, where roughly as many women as men die by suicide. A persuasive account of death by suicide will need to explain the overall pattern of male lethality and address the interesting exception of China.

Suicide "Contagion" and Mass Suicide in Cults

From time to time, completed suicides cluster in space and time. For example, in a high school of approximately 1,500 students, two students died by suicide within four days. During an eighteen-day span that included the two completed suicides, seven other students attempted suicide. Occasionally a spate of deaths by suicide will occur following a well-publicized suicide, especially if media coverage in any way glorifies it. What is the mechanism underlying suicide clusters?

In 1999, I proposed an explanation that involves the concept of assortative relating, which means that people form relationships nonrandomly—they assort based on shared interests, characteristics, even shared problems, such as substance abuse. I believe that suicide clusters are, in a sense, pre-arranged, in that vulnerable people assortatively relate and then are simultaneously impinged upon by some serious stressor, which activates the suicide potential of each member of the potential cluster.[5] I provide some empirical support for this view in a study of college roommates, some of whom related assortatively in that they *chose* to room together, others of whom related randomly, in that they were paired with one another by the university housing agency. If my explanation of suicide clusters holds water, the suicide potentials of roommates who chose to room together should be more similar than the suicide potentials of those who were randomly assigned to one another. This was in fact the finding.[6]

The Internet provides another, sometimes more pernicious way in which people can assortatively relate. Consider, for example, the "pro-suicide" website alt.suicide.holiday (or ASH), where suicide is construed favorably. Visitors to the site are instructed on the best methods for suicide. As many as twenty-four completed suicides have been connected to the site. Other web forums have been documented to encourage self-destructive behavior too. On January 12, 2003, a twenty-one-year-old man died in his bedroom after ingesting huge amounts of prescription drugs, marijuana, and alcohol. It was later determined that many people had witnessed the death through the man's webcam, and that several of the onlookers had typed things like, "Eat more!" as the man ingested obviously dangerous numbers of pills. The man and the onlookers were part of an ongoing chat room that regularly discussed substance use. Excessive substance use brought these people together (assortatively related them), and in this case, self-destructive behavior was explicitly encouraged from within the group. Indeed, experimental studies have evaluated the connection between group norms and self-aggression. These studies use a self-aggression paradigm (self-administered shock during a task disguised as a reaction-time game, with self-aggression defined by the intensity of shock chosen). In this research, high levels of self-administered shock occurred when group norms were manipulated to encourage self-aggression.

In his 2003 *New Yorker* article, Tad Friend documents the death of a fourteen-year-old girl who left her high school by taxi, rode to the Golden Gate Bridge, and jumped to her death. The girl's mother later discovered that she had been visiting a website that offered advice about completing suicide and showed graphic autopsy photos. The site discourages methods like poison, drug overdose, and wrist cutting, since less than 15 percent of people who attempt by these methods die. By contrast, the site recommends jumping from a high place because "jumps from higher than . . . 250 feet over water are almost always fatal.".

Suicides occasionally do cluster in space and time; concepts like assortative relating and group norms may partially explain them. These concepts are starkly illustrated in some of the most horrific suicide clusters, those occurring in cults. In Jonestown, where 914 people died, the majority died from drinking a grape-flavored drink laced with cyanide and sedatives at the behest of leader Jim Jones. In the Heaven's Gate event, which caused the deaths of thirty-nine people (two additional cult members died by suicide in the months following), people died by ingesting high doses of phenobarbital mixed with vodka at the behest of leader Marshall Applewhite.

Mass suicide in cults raises difficult definitional issues—are these really examples of suicide or are they examples of mass homicide perpetrated by delusional and psychopathic people like Jones and Applewhite? A compelling theory of suicide should be able to address this question, as well as other difficult questions. A complete theory would also have something to say about the array of other well-established facts about suicide, only some of which were touched on above. The influence of age, mental disorders, and other factors on suicide all need to be incorporated. In later sections of the book, I will describe such a theory. This book's theory of suicide accomplishes something new: It is not only consistent with but illuminates the wide array of well-documented facts on suicide. But first, I will summarize existing theories.

Existing Theories of Suicide

The theory put forth in this book places me in competition with numerous other theorists, past and present. In one sense, that is the nature of science and scholarship. In another sense, however, I am much more a collaborator than a competitor with other theorists. This is also the nature of science and scholarship. Although we pay tribute to the achievements of past theorists, we must also point out ways in which their work needs to be expanded and modified to provide a more comprehensive and accurate explanation of why people die by suicide. The remainder of this chapter focuses on the highlights of some of the more compelling theories of why people die by suicide.

In the preface to his book *Man Against Himself*, Karl Menninger[7] wrote, "to have a theory, even a false one, is better than to attribute events to pure chance. 'Chance' explanations leave us in the dark; a theory will lead to confirmation or rejection." Although there have been persuasive and careful theories, compared to other areas of science, even compared to other areas of psychopathology research, theorizing on suicide has been somewhat slow. The dominant theories can be counted on one hand (not necessarily using all the fingers). The last major theoretical statement appeared in 1990, and a century-old theory still has a lot of influence.

That theory was put forth by the French sociologist Emile Durkheim in his 1897 book *Le Suicide*. The theory emphasizes collective social forces much more than individual factors. In Durkheim's theory, the common denominator in all suicides is disturbed regulation of the individual by society. He was concerned with two kinds of regulation: social integration and moral regulation.

Regarding social regulation, a curvilinear, U-shaped relationship between individuals' degree of integration in society and that society's suicide rates is hypothesized; too much or too little integration are both bad things, according to Durkheim. Low integration—something that in later chapters of this book will be referred to as low belongingness—leads to an increase in a type of suicide that

Durkheim labeled "egoistic." His idea was that we need something that transcends us, and he felt that the only thing that is transcendent enough is human society. When it breaks down, people feel purposeless and become desperate, and suicide rates go up.

Too much integration, according to Durkheim, is also associated with more suicide, but of a different type, namely "altruistic" suicides. Excessive societal integration leads people to lose themselves and to commit to a larger goal. Self-sacrifice is a defining aspect of this kind of suicide; self-sacrifice bears some similarities to the concept of perceived burdensomeness, which will be emphasized in my account of why people die by suicide. In Durkheim's view, when individuals are so integrated into a social group that individuality fades, they become willing to sacrifice themselves to the group's interests.

Regarding moral regulation, "anomic" suicide is caused by sudden changes in the social position of an individual, mainly as a result of economic upheavals. The idea is that any abrupt change in the regulatory function of society or its institutions on people's behavior is likely to increase suicide rates. Because society loses its scale, people's ambitions are unleashed but cannot all be satisfied, leaving a lot of unhappy people.

Durkheim contrasted anomic suicide to "fatalistic" suicide, which occurs among those with overregulated, unrewarding lives, such as slaves. Of the four types of suicide discussed by Durkheim, fatalistic suicide receives the least attention, perhaps because he viewed it as relatively rare.

One of Durkheim's goals was to study social forces, often to the exclusion of other factors, of which he was at times dismissive. He did not deny, however, that individual conditions like mental disorders are relevant to suicide. But he did claim that most such factors are insufficiently general to affect the suicide rate of whole societies, and thus should not be emphasized by sociologists. It is notable that these days many sociologists study individual factors as well as social forces.

It is remarkable, too, that a theorist who could be dismissive of the role of genes and of mental disorders in suicide is still influential, because there is absolutely no doubt that genes and mental disorders—and much else at times marginalized by Durkheim—are involved in suicidal behavior. Why, then, is he still influential? He was the first to attempt a fully empirical sociology, and he was the first to attempt a systematic, comprehensive, coherent, and testable theory of suicide. Second, he was right about some things. As I show in Chapter 3, he anticipated my model's emphasis on social disconnection as a major source for the desire for suicide. Through his emphasis on altruistic suicide, he also anticipated my theory's inclusion of perceived burdensomeness as a key precursor to serious suicidal behavior, though we differ on the details. Third, Durkheim had little competition for decades. The first half of the twentieth century was dominated by psychoanalysis, and to be blunt, it is difficult to think of a lasting contribution to the understanding of suicide from this perspective. It is easy, however, to think of many examples in which psychoanalytic theories have been obstacles to understanding. For example, the most well-known view of suicide from a psychoanalytic perspective is that suicide is hate or aggression turned inward. In defending this view, Harry Stack Sullivan[8] noted examples in which suicides were carried out in a hateful or spiteful way toward others. It certainly is the case that some suicides are arranged spitefully, but the majority are not. My dad, for example, died away from the house in a manner such that he was likely to be discovered by police personnel. I think he believed that this would be easier on us, and I think he was right. It is hard to detect the spite here. Hostility or aggressiveness is a common part of the background of those who die by suicide, but as I will demonstrate in Chapter 2, there is a way to understand this that is more plausible and consistent with scientific evidence than "hostility turned inward."

As another example, Menninger (1936) was persuaded that masturbation has an important connection to suicide. He stated, "It has been observed that suicidal attempts sometimes follow the interruption of an individual's habitual auto-erotic activities . . . the mechanisms by which the suicide is precipitated are the same: the masturbation occasions a heavy burden of guilt, because in the unconscious mind it always represents an aggression against someone. This guilt demands punishment and as long as the auto-erotic practices are continued, the punishment is bound up in the satisfaction, since masturbation is imagined by many to be a grave danger to health, and to one's life both in this world and the hereafter."[9] Menninger continues by postulating that when masturbation is interrupted, the needed punishment is no longer "bound up in the satisfaction," and suicide results as a form of self-punishment. On this view, suicide is a "violent form of sexual preoccupation."[10] Later in the same book, Menninger claims that nail-biting is similar to masturbation.[11]

These examples show that Durkheim had little real competition as a theorist for decades. Incidentally, I do not blame Menninger, Sullivan, and others for their misperceptions—had I been working in the 1930s I would have seen the world through a similar lens. I feel much less charitably, however, toward those who perpetuated these mistakes into the following decades and less charitably still to the few who promulgate these theories today.

Viable theories of suicide other than Durkheim's began to emerge in the latter half of the twentieth century. One of the most prominent theorists is Edwin Shneidman. Shneidman was influenced by Henry Murray, who focused on the nature of psychological needs and the consequences of having those needs thwarted. Shneidman's views on suicide can be described as centering on thwarted psychological needs—a general approach that I borrow from in the development of my model of suicidal behavior.

Shneidman[12] wrote, "In almost every case, suicide is caused by pain, a certain kind of pain—*psychological pain*, which I call *psychache*. Furthermore, this psychache stems from thwarted or distorted psychological needs." For Shneidman, psychache—defined as general psychological and emotional pain that reaches intolerable intensity—is a proximal cause of suicide. That is, whatever earlier risk factors are at play, they operate through increasing psychache, which in turn predisposes to suicidality.

Incidentally, in his enormous *Anatomy of Melancholy,* first published in 1621, Robert Burton invoked a similar concept. Speaking of suicidal individuals, he said, "These unhappy men are born to misery, past all hope of recovery, incurably sick; the longer they live, the worse they are, and death alone must ease them." Burton also implied a stable, perhaps biological cause to suicide—an excess of "black bile"—and at another place in the *Anatomy,* Burton labels black bile as suicide's "shoeing horn."

In addition to psychache, Shneidman[13] identified lethality as a key ingredient of serious suicidality. Lethality is clearly related to the concept emphasized in this book of the acquired ability to enact lethal self-injury. An emphasis on psychache, too, is compatible with my approach; perceived burdensomeness combined with failed belongingness constitutes psychache.

"Psychache about what in particular?" we might ask. The answer, taken from Shneidman's 1996 *The Suicidal Mind*[14] and adapted from Murray's work in the 1930s, is a list of thwarted needs: abasement, achievement, affiliation, aggression, autonomy, counteraction, defendance, deference, dominance, exhibition, harm avoidance, inviolacy, nurturance, order, play, rejection, sentience, shame-avoidance, succorance, and understanding.

I believe that Shneidman's answer is too general, because most of us identify with one or more of these thwarted needs from time to time. What *in particular,* we are then led to wonder, are people feeling psychache about? I believe the answer to this question is perceived burdensomeness and failed belongingness.

Of all the people who experience psychache, we might then ask, why do only a minority die by suicide? Shneidman[15] is aware of this issue, and captures it very well when he states, "What my research has taught me is that only a small minority of cases of excessive psychological pain result in suicide, but every case of suicide stems from excessive psychache." This suggests that psychache is necessary but not sufficient for suicide. There must be an additional factor, therefore, that differentiates those with psychache who die by suicide from those with psychache who do not.

The additional factor, according to Shneidman, is lethality. What constitutes lethality and how it develops are subjects I address in Chapter 2.

My theory does not replace concepts like psychache with brand new concepts—psychache is rather viewed as a generalized form of perceived burdensomeness and failed belongingness. My theory strives to improve upon, not replace, Shneidman's and others' definitions and inter-relations, and to articulate when they are most likely to result in serious suicidal behavior. The model I present is thus intended to provide an account of suicide that incorporates the strengths of major existing models, but goes beyond them to develop a framework that is at the same time conceptually more precise and epistemically broader, explaining more suicide-related facts.

My work rests on the shoulders of theorists like Shneidman and Aaron T. Beck. Beck and colleagues' cognitive perspective on suicidality emphasizes the role of hopelessness.[16] Hopelessness for Beck plays the role of psychache for Shneidman.

Impressive data support the view that hopelessness is involved in suicidality. For example, Beck and colleagues[17] studied a group of 207 patients hospitalized for suicidal ideation. Over the course of the next decade, fourteen patients died by suicide. Of several variables assessed, only hopelessness predicted eventual death by suicide. In this study, hopelessness was measured using a twenty-item scale with possible scores ranging from zero to twenty; a score of ten or more on the hopelessness scale correctly identified 91 percent of those who later died by suicide. Beck and colleagues[18] extended their work to a group of 1,958 psychotherapy outpatients, seventeen of whom eventually died by suicide. High scores on the hopelessness scale again predicted later death by suicide, correctly identifying sixteen of the seventeen who later died by suicide. Those with high hopelessness scores were eleven times more likely to die by suicide as compared to patients with lower hopelessness scores.

However, an emphasis on hopelessness cannot tell the whole story (an issue that Beck and colleagues understand well). What in particular are suicidal people hopeless about? If hopelessness is key, why then do relatively few hopeless people die by suicide? In my view, the reply to the first question is burdensomeness and failed belongingness, and the reply to the second is that hopelessness is not sufficient; hopelessness about belongingness and burdensomeness is required, together with the acquired capability for serious self-harm.

An emphasis on hopelessness places negative thoughts and styles of thinking front and center in explaining risk for suicide. From a similar perspective, Beck[19] has also argued that previous suicidal experience sensitizes suicide-related thoughts and behaviors such that they later become more accessible and active. The more accessible and active the thoughts and behaviors become, the more easily they are triggered, and the more severe are the subsequent suicidal episodes.[20] In one sense, this account shares similarities to the current model in that both perspectives propose psychological mechanisms underlying an escalating course of suicidal behavior over time. The difference between the models has to do with the nature of the proposed psychological mechanisms—the mechanism in Beck's view is cognitive sensitization—that is, with repetition, suicide-related thoughts and behaviors become favored—whereas the mechanisms in my view involve habituation, or getting used to the fear and pain involved in self-injury. This in turn leads to an acquired ability for serious suicidality, which, when combined with burdensomeness and disconnection, produces high risk for suicide. These mechanisms are not mutually exclusive and thus may operate jointly, incidentally. For example, thoughts of burdensomeness and failed belongingness may very well become sensitized in just the way Beck described.

My friend and colleague Roy Baumeister[21] proposes an escape theory of suicidal behavior that describes a sequence of steps leading up to serious suicidal behavior. First, an individual experiences a negative and severe discrepancy between expectations and actual events. For example, a businessperson may have imagined that a deal was going to be extremely profitable, but it costs the business dearly. He blames himself rather than chalking up the failure to bad luck or to vacillations in the market. An aversive state of high self-awareness develops, which produces negative affect. The businessperson becomes preoccupied by and often dwells on his personal inadequacies, which leads to feelings of distress, sadness, and worry. He attempts to escape from negative affect, as well as from the aversive self-awareness and the discrepancy between expectation and outcome. This is accomplished, according to Baumeister's theory, by retreating into a numb state of "cognitive deconstruction." In this state, meaningful thought about the self, including painful self-awareness and failed standards, is replaced by a lower-level awareness of concrete sensations and movements, and of immediate, proximal goals and tasks. The businessperson no longer thinks of the failed venture and its implications for the future; rather, he focuses on the concrete task of driving to the liquor store or watching television. An important consequence of the state of cognitive deconstruction is reduced inhibitions, which contribute to lack of impulse control in general and lack of impulse control for suicidal behavior in particular. The business-person drinks a bottle of liquor and contemplates suicide.

Shneidman[22] agrees that cognitive deconstruction is an important sign of impending lethality, stating that "the most dangerous word in all of suicidology is the four-letter word *only*." When people are in the lower-level state of focusing on the concrete, their ability to see alternatives is compromised. When suicide is seen as the *only* option, that for Shneidman indicates increasing lethality and for Baumeister is a sign that a state of cognitive deconstruction has developed.

There are compatibilities between Baumeister's account and the one developed in this book. For example, perceived burdensomeness and failed belongingness can be seen as the results of disappointed expectations; expectations that are internally attributed and thus as-sociated with severe states of negative affect. The state of cognitive deconstruction is not a part of the current model, but one could imagine that perceived burdensomeness and failed belongingness are painful enough to produce such a condition. To the degree that cog-nitive deconstruction, perhaps facilitated by perception of burden-someness and failed belongingness, produces disinhibition, it could lead to repeated provocative experiences (including self-harm) and thus could produce the processes emphasized here that lead up to the acquired ability to enact lethal self-injury.

Marsha Linehan[23] has theorized that biological deficits, exposure to trauma, and the failure to acquire adaptive ways of tolerating and handling negative emotion all contribute to suicidal behavior. Self-injury, according to her view, is an attempt to regulate emotions—an attempt that becomes necessary because more usual emotion regula-tion mechanisms have broken down or never developed adequately. Emotion dysregulation is a core problem in suicidal behavior, ac-cording to this viewpoint. Parameters of emotional dysregulation would include rapid onset, high intensity, and slow recovery, especially regarding negative emotional states. These irregularities are proposed to lead to efforts to moderate the intense and painful feelings, often through deliberate self-harm.

Based on this theoretical work, Linehan has developed a psychotherapy for suicidal behavior and for borderline personality disorder. The treatment is called Dialectical Behavior Therapy or DBT; it includes an array of techniques geared toward changing self-destructive ways of regulating emotion (cutting, for example) to more constructive ways of regulating emotion (seeking counsel and support from a trusted friend, for example). Linehan and colleagues have conducted impressive studies supporting the treatment's effectiveness.

Emotional dysregulation can be viewed as a prime source leading to the acquired capability to enact lethal self-injury. Those who are dysregulated are likely to face an array of provocative situations (e.g., physical altercations), many of them caused, at least in part, by dysregulation itself. Moreover, the interpersonal strains associated with emotional dysregulation are likely to contribute to feelings of disconnection and ineffectiveness. The current framework and Linehan's model are thus quite compatible; she has identified processes that can be viewed as relatively distal in the causal chain leading up to suicidal behavior; the processes, in turn, may lay the groundwork for the relatively more proximal factors emphasized here.

Though the theories of Durkheim, Shneidman, Beck, Baumeister, and Linehan are the most prominent and influential explanations of suicidal behavior, there are others that are of some interest. For example, some have contended that economic theory can explain some suicides. Changes in suicide rates vary detectably with changes in the economy such that downturns are associated with higher rates, upturns with lower rates. However, this kind of theorizing essentially reduces to sociological and psychological questions of why economic changes affect individuals in this way; the theorists summarized in this chapter all have answers, as do I, which I describe in the chapters that follow.

A more interesting and very provocative view was described by Charles Duhigg in *Slate Magazine* on October 29, 2003. Duhigg summarized the work of Dave Marcotte, a professor of public policy at the University of Maryland, who analyzed the economic consequences of attempted suicide. Marcotte's premise is that those thinking of suicide face not two, but three alternatives—to not attempt, to attempt but survive, and to attempt and die. Marcotte was particularly interested in those who attempt but survive, because this could be an economically costly action (injury, medical bills, possibly permanent disability) but conceivably carries benefits too (increased access to help and increased social support). Marcotte's results indicated that those who attempt suicide and survive subsequently see an increase in income of around 20 percent as compared to those who consider but do not attempt suicide. Among those who engage in near-lethal attempts, the subsequent increase in income was over 35 percent.

How can this be? As Duhigg points out, attempted suicide is associated with increased access to medical care and familial social support. He states, "Doubters may ask why the depressed don't seek out resources earlier. But studies have demonstrated that psychological and familial resources become "cheaper" after a suicide attempt: It is difficult to find free medical care when you are sad, but once you try to kill yourself, it's forced on you."

The danger of viewpoints like this should be pointed out. Any analysis that encourages suicidal behavior in any way—particularly in ways that romanticize or glorify it, or make it seem easy and normative—has potential negative consequences for public health. Still, an understanding of factors that promote suicidal behavior can steer the way to interventions that prevent it. In this regard, a straightforward conclusion of Marcotte's economic analysis of attempted suicide is that increased access to mental health care should lower the rate of attempted suicide. Good mental health care will treat conditions that lead to suicidal behavior but also, according to Marcotte's analysis, will remove the inducement of increased care that currently is associated with suicidal behavior.

Though this is not a serious model of suicide, and there are those who would question whether it is a serious model of anything, a certain set within the academic humanities—the deconstructionists, influenced by people like Jacques Derrida and Jacques Lacan—might question whether all the pain and hopelessness associated with suicide exist at all. Derrida is famous for the claim that *"il n'y a pas de hors-texte"* (there is nothing outside the text), and further, what is inside the text is, according to deconstructionists, but a heartless concatenation of arbitrary linguistic codes. What is left for the deconstructionist, then, is a constant questioning of the very existence of reality and meaning—including the reality of emotional pain. Try telling that to a suicidal person. In fact, David Kirby, an eminent poet and Florida State University English professor, may have tried this as a graduate student. He reports, "There was a bar . . . that served twenty-cent highballs on Wednesday nights; penny-wise grad students would moisten their clay there, shoulder to shoulder with the more routine customers. Once I explained to a morose regular that life *was* worth living, that even though his wife had left him and his kids had turned out to be disappointments and he'd just been laid off from his job, none of that mattered because the human mind was, so, uh, mental."[24] The regular appeared not to have been consoled, and interestingly, at least as far as I can tell, Kirby did not grow up to be a deconstructionist.

In the time it takes to read this chapter, one or two people in the United States have died by suicide, and many more have died worldwide. Just now, family members, police, or paramedics are discovering their bodies. Their loved ones are embarking on an intensely painful journey that involves not only sudden loss, but the potential for misunderstanding and confusion. I know about this journey from every possible angle—I lived it myself; I have seen it in patients and others; and I have studied it scientifically. I've told my sons why they don't have a grandfather, and I've told professional audiences why and how serotonin-system genes may be involved in suicide.

People who have lost a loved one to suicide often bond together in support groups—in fact, this is a healthy form of assortative relating (in contrast to pernicious forms discussed earlier in this chapter). These groups do a world of good for people. In some of these circles, there occasionally arises a feeling that people who have not lost a loved one to suicide could not possibly understand it. I sympathize with this view, mainly because of the confusion and misunderstandings that can complicate death by suicide, but ultimately, I don't share this sentiment. Given the right framework, anyone can understand—indeed, everyone needs to understand if real progress on suicide is to occur. By the same token, there is a feeling in some scientific circles that nonscientists cannot possibly understand suicide in any fundamental way because it is so complex, with factors ranging from the molecular to the cultural levels. Here too, I sympathize but disagree. A full account of suicide will no doubt be complex, but a main point of science is to render the complex accessible.

THE ABILITY
TO ENACT
LETHAL SELF-INJURY
IS ACQUIRED

2

Existing theories of suicide illuminate some important facts and concepts, but they also leave key questions unanswered. If emotional pain, hopelessness, emotional dysregulation, or any variable is crucial in suicide, how then to explain the fact that most people with any one of these variables do not die by or even attempt suicide? How do we make sense of the anecdotal and clinical evidence suggesting that there are people who genuinely desire suicide but do not feel able to carry through with it? What are the ingredients for the genuine desire for suicide?

The ability to enact lethal self-injury is acquired through particular kinds of experience that I will describe in this chapter (genetics and neurobiology are also important). Though the fact has been neglected by theorists and researchers, those who repeatedly attempt suicide emphasize how very difficult it is. On reflection, this is as it should be—of course it is difficult to overcome the most basic instinct of all; namely, self-preservation. How do people do it? This chapter will show that it is no easy matter, and that it is impossible to do without previous experiences that allay the fear of self-injury, inure people from the pain of self-injury, and build knowledge that facilitates self-injury.

According to the overall explanation of suicide presented in this book, the acquired capability to engage in serious self-injury is but one precursor to attempted suicide or death by suicide. There are many people who, through an array of provocative experiences, have become fearless, pain-tolerant, and knowledgeable about dangerous behaviors, and yet who have no desire whatsoever to hurt themselves. Those who do have the desire, coupled with the ability, are viewed as at high risk for serious suicidal behavior. Chapter 3 explores the constituents of the genuine desire for death. Drawing on diverse literatures, the case is made that people desire death when two fundamental needs are frustrated to the point of extinction; namely, the need to belong with or connect to others, and the need to feel effective with or to influence others. When both these needs are snuffed out, suicide becomes attractive but not accessible without the ability for self-harm.

Working Up to the Act of Suicide

On February 1, 2003, the space shuttle *Columbia* disintegrated as it flew over the western United States, finally showering down over East Texas and Louisiana in thousands of pieces. All seven crew members were killed. The cause was a dense, dry, brownish-orange piece of foam weighing about 1.7 pounds, 19 inches long and 11 inches wide. The foam, traveling 545 miles per hour, hit *Columbia*'s left wing, causing what investigators now know was a significant breach.

Foam strikes had happened before. For example, *Atlantis* was hit in 1988, causing such damage that an astronaut said "the belly looked as if it had been blasted with shotgun fire." William Langewiesche, in the November 2003 issue of *Atlantic Monthly*, wrote, "Over the years foam strikes had come to be seen within NASA as . . . a problem so familiar that even the most serious episodes seemed unthreatening and mundane."[1] One of the members of the panel investigating the accident said, "The excitement that only exists when there is danger was kind of gone—even though the danger was not gone." Foam strikes were routinely designated by NASA officials as "in-flight anomalies," but even this weak designation was removed in October 2002, just months before *Columbia*'s doomed mission. Key NASA administrators decided against getting in-flight satellite images of *Columbia*'s left wing, in part because their sense of danger about foam strikes had eroded over the years due to repeated experience with them.

What does this have to do with suicide? A key point of this book is that when people get used to dangerous behavior—when they lose the excitement that only exists when there is danger—the groundwork for catastrophe is laid down. Just as NASA administrators became inured to a very real danger, so too, I will argue, potentially suicidal people lose the danger signals and alarm bells that should accompany self-injury. When self-injury and other dangerous experiences become unthreatening and mundane—when people work up to the act of death by suicide by getting used to its threat and danger—that is when we might lose them.

This is a novel approach to understanding suicidal behavior, but the same idea appears to have occurred to Voltaire almost three hundred years ago. Voltaire was thinking about the death by suicide of the Roman orator Cato, and he wrote something that I've come to see as revelatory: "It seems rather absurd to say that Cato slew himself through weakness. None but a strong man can surmount the most powerful instinct of nature." The simple but compelling idea here is that the first step to death by suicide is to grapple with the results of eons of evolution, to grapple with one of nature's strongest forces—self-preservation.

This viewpoint also appears in the writings of Arthur Schopenhauer. Schopenhauer points out that the fear of death, rather than the love of life, encourages people to continue. He believed that burdened people would think seriously of suicide, were this a purely negative act. But suicide involves the destruction of the body, and Schopenhauer believed most are incapable of this. The eminent suicidologist Edwin Shneidman wrote, "Each day contains the threat of failure and assaults by others, but it is the threat of *self*-destruction that we are most afraid to touch."[2]

Shneidman's words were illustrated by the controversial and disturbing case of Florida death row inmate John Blackwelder. On May 26, 2004, Blackwelder was executed for the murder of Raymond Wigley, Blackwelder's fellow inmate. At the time of the murder, Blackwelder was serving a life sentence without the possibility of parole for a series of convictions for sex crimes. Blackwelder claimed that he strangled Wigley, pleaded guilty to first-degree murder, and waived all appeals, all because he wanted to die by suicide but could not bring himself to do so. According to Blackwelder (a suspect source, it should be acknowledged), killing someone else (and committing a series of sex crimes) was not beyond him, but suicide was.

It may be that few people *want* to die by suicide, but also, and perhaps more important, that even fewer people *can*. Self-injury, especially when severe, has the potential to be painful and fear-inducing. Who can tolerate such high levels of pain, fear, and the like? The view taken here is that those who have gotten used to the negative aspects of suicide, and additionally, who have acquired competence and even courage specifically regarding suicide, are the only ones capable of the act—anyone else is unable to complete suicide, even if they want to.

Karl Menninger noticed this fact in passing; he said, "One sees people who want to die but cannot take the step against themselves . . . like King Saul and Brutus [who] beseech[ed] their armor bearers to slay them."[3] Menninger provides another example, a great poet of

Italy "who longed for death in exquisite rhymes ever since he was a boy and was the first to fly in abject terror from cholera-stricken Naples."[4]

Robert Lowell said that "if there were some little switch in the arm which one could press in order to die immediately and without pain, then everyone would sooner or later commit suicide."[5] Lowell is probably mistaken—he neglects how scary death is to most people, but his remark does imply that without such a "little switch," suicide is difficult to do.

Alfred Alvarez also pointed out that in some warrior societies that worship gods of violence and uphold ideals related to bravery, suicide was viewed positively. For the Vikings, for example, the Feast of the Heroes never ended in Valhalla. "Only those who had died violently could enter and partake of the banquet. The greatest honor and the surest qualification was death in battle; next best was suicide."[6]

Even in the United States in the twentieth century, some accorded those who died by suicide a measure of respect. In a poem entitled "By the Road to the Contagious Hospital," William Carlos Williams wrote, "The perfect type of the man of action is the suicide." Poetry like this falsely romanticizes or glorifies suicide, but as good poetry tends to, the lines contain an important truth: suicide does require an extreme and difficult form of action.

I happen to view suicide as anything but glorious or romantic. Recall that my dad died by suicide. We have to grapple with the balance between not glorifying suicide on the one hand, and on the other hand, pointing out a process that is akin to courage and that is implicated in suicide. How does one get used to and become competent and courageous regarding suicide? In a word, practice. People who have hurt themselves before (especially intentionally but also accidentally), who know how to work a gun, who have investigated the toxic and lethal properties of an overdose drug, who have practiced tying nooses, and who can look someone in the eye and show resolve about following through with suicide, are viewed here as at substantial risk for suicide.

I can cite abundant anecdotal evidence that practice and increasing fearlessness amplifies suicidal behavior. The life and death of the musician Kurt Cobain illustrates the key role that newly acquired capabilities can play in self-destructive behavior. Cobain was temperamentally fearful—afraid of needles, afraid of heights, and afraid of guns. Through repeated exposure and practice, a person initially afraid of needles, heights, and guns later became a daily self-injecting drug user, someone who climbed and dangled from thirty-foot scaffolding during concerts (at which times, incidentally, he would yell, "I'm going to kill myself!"), and someone who enjoyed shooting guns. Regarding guns, Cobain initially felt that they were barbaric and wanted nothing to do with them; later he agreed to go with his friend to shoot guns but would not get out of the car; on later excursions, he got out of the car but would not touch the guns; and on still later trips, he agreed to let his friend show him how to aim and fire.[7] Cobain died by self-inflicted gunshot wound in 1994 at the age of twenty-seven.

Another compelling example appeared on the Public Radio International show *This American Life*. The narrator read from a diary entry regarding some of his own experiences with suicidal behavior: "I wonder why all the ways I've tried to kill myself haven't worked. I mean, I tried hanging; I used to have a noose tied to my closet pole. I'd go in there and slip the thing over my head and let my weight go, but every time I started to lose consciousness, I'd just stand up. I tried to take pills; I took 20 Advil one afternoon, but that just made me sleepy. And all the times I tried to cut my wrist, I could never cut deep enough. *That's the thing, your body tries to keep you alive no matter what you do*" (italics added). Later diary entries described how the narrator doused himself with gasoline and set himself on fire; he survived, badly burned.[8] Jim Knipfel, in his memoir *Quitting the Nairobi Trio*, wrote of his past suicide attempts: "It was clear that it was cowardice that had kept me from going all the way before. I had never succeeded because I didn't have the nerve . . . No matter how hard I tried, nothing worked. I threw myself down a flight of stairs, drank bleach, cut my wrists, stepped in front of buses, all to no avail."[9] These examples illustrate Voltaire's "most powerful instinct of nature" as well as the progression that allows people to do extreme things in attempting to overcome it.

Richard Heckler noted a similar example. "I was trying to slash my wrists. It was really difficult, because I hadn't previously realized that it was so hard to cut your own flesh. It's tough stuff and I ended up beating on my wrist with a knife for a long time to get it to go numb. It hurt so much to cut."[10]

Shneidman's case example of Beatrice implies much the same thing. Beatrice wrote, "I know now that slitting my wrists was not as poetic nor as easy as I imagined. Due to blood clotting and fainting, it is actually difficult to die from such wounds. The evening dragged on with me busy reopening the stubborn veins that insisted upon clotting up. I was patient and persistent, and cut away at myself for over an hour. The battle with my body to die was unexpected, and after waging a good fight, I passed out."[11]

Incidentally, Beatrice's statement deserves emphasis. It is easy to find instances in the media or on the Internet in which suicide is romanticized and glorified. Glorification can be dangerous, because others may be emboldened to try suicide. Still, a kind of courage is implicated in suicidality, and this fact must be faced for a full understanding of suicidal behavior to develop. Indeed, an interesting conceptual consideration involves the definitions of courage and fearlessness, and their relation to suicidal behavior. The psychologist Stanley J. Rachman[12] defined losing fear in the face of a true threat as fearlessness, whereas he defined courage as an approach behavior (to the threat), even in the context of fear. Those who develop the capacity for serious suicidal behavior might become more fearless (if fear actually decreases), or they might become more courageous (if fear persists but they are better able to tolerate it), or both.

The idea of grappling with the self-preservation instinct can also be seen in examples of people who initiated serious suicidal behavior and then instantly regretted it. Some people who have jumped from high places and survived report that they very much regretted the act in midair. For instance, as previously noted, a *New Yorker* article in 2003 by Tad Friend quotes a man who had jumped off the Golden Gate Bridge and survived: "I instantly realized that everything in my life that I'd thought was unfixable was totally fixable—except for having just jumped." Another Golden Gate Bridge survivor, quoted in the same article, said, "My first thought was What the hell did I just do? I don't want to die."

Shneidman addressed this topic, stating, "I believe that people who are actually committing suicide are ambivalent about life and death at the very moment they are committing it. They wish to die *and* they simultaneously wish to be rescued."[13] I would state it somewhat differently. People who die by suicide not only desire it but also have developed the capacity to enact lethal self-injury; nevertheless, even in people who have developed this capacity to the extreme, they retain some fear of suicide because it flies in the face of the extremely powerful push for self-preservation. This fear produces the wish to be rescued.

Other examples illustrate this point. A man who jumped into the water leading up to Niagara Falls in 2003 said that he changed his mind the instant he hit the water. "At that point," he said, "I wished I had not done it. But I guess I knew it was way too late for that." He survived the plunge over the falls, and now feels he has a new lease on life. Menninger wrote, "Every hospital intern has labored in the emergency ward with would-be suicides, who beg him to save their lives."[14] Harry Stack Sullivan described people who had ingested bichloride of mercury: "One is horribly ill. If one survives the first days of hellish agony, there comes a period of relative convalescence—during which all of the patients I have seen were most repentant and strongly desirous of living."[15] Unfortunately for these patients, another phase of several days of agony then resumes, usually ending in death. The fear of death by suicide is so powerful that it returns even in people who have suppressed it enough to imbibe bichloride of mercury, to jump off the Golden Gate Bridge, or to go over Niagara Falls.

Suicide is undoubtedly a fearsome thing, and people on the verge can be brought back for this reason, as demonstrated by these newspaper clippings noted by Menninger: "1) In Fort Lee, N.J., O. P. wrote two farewell notes, climbed up on a railing of a bridge, ready to jump 250 feet to death. As he teetered, Policeman C. K. shouted, 'Get down or I'll shoot.' Down got O. P. 2) In Denver, T. S. burst out laughing when a $1 pistol he had bought to kill himself exploded and sent a bullet bouncing off his chest. Calmed by police, T. S. announced he would try to go on living."[16]

The life and death of the poet Weldon Kees also illustrate the evolving competence and fearlessness involved in serious suicidal behavior. Several days before his death, Kees mentioned to a friend that he had been contemplating a jump to his death from the Golden Gate Bridge. In fact, Kees continued, he had gotten so far as to put his foot on the rail, but could not bring himself to put his foot over the edge of the rail. Soon after this conversation, Kees disappeared; the California Highway Patrol found his car in a parking lot near the bridge, keys still in the ignition.[17] Kees's body was never recovered, which is common with those who jump from the Golden Gate Bridge.

Kees worked up to the act of death by suicide. He took at least one preparatory trip to the bridge (the one he mentioned to his friend).

Odds are that there were other such trips. Through these visits, Kees habituated to the fear that initially kept him from even putting his foot over the rail. Jon Hilkevitch wrote in the July 4, 2004 edition of the *Chicago Tribune* of the death a thirteen-year-old girl who was struck by a train. Her death was ruled a suicide, in part because her friends stated that they had pulled the girl from the same tracks months earlier.

Menninger reported on the death by suicide of a former state executioner. The newspaper article describing the death said, "The iron nerve which enabled [the executioner] calmly to send 141 men to their deaths in the electric chair during his career . . . stayed with him to the last."[18] I think this newspaper report gets it right, more so than Menninger, who attributed the suicide to the man's guilt over the executions. An explanation emphasizing guilt—like those emphasizing psychache or hopelessness—does not explain the very low rates of suicide among people who have the putative causal factor (whether guilt, emotional pain, or hopelessness). By contrast, an explanation emphasizing the acquired capability to enact self-injury fits the executioner, who had ample time to habituate to pain and death (especially since he was working in the 1920s and 1930s). Why don't all executioners die by suicide, then? For the same reason all racecar drivers don't. They can stare down death. They could enact it, but the vast majority do not want to.

The death of another poet, Hart Crane, also illustrates the extended process by which people work up to the act of death by suicide. Crane died at age thirty-two by jumping off a cruise ship into the Atlantic Ocean.[19] He was on his way back to the United States from Mexico, where he had spent a year or so. From approximately age sixteen until his death, Crane attempted suicide at least six times. One of these attempts involved Crane being physically restrained moments before jumping off a tall building, and another involved him being physically prevented from jumping off the cruise ship the day before his death. Crane had had the opportunity to get used to the idea of jumping to his death.

He had also had the opportunity to habituate to pain and provocation in general. People work up to the extreme act of death by suicide through various means. The clearest involves previous suicidal behavior. But other means are possible too—any activity that allows people to get used to pain and provocation can serve to reduce fear of injury in general and self-injury in particular. Crane had plenty of opportunities to habituate to pain and provocation. He could not control his drinking, and frequently had drunken episodes that involved physical fights or the destruction of property. He spent time in jail in three different countries. Crane also had perhaps hundreds of anonymous sexual experiences, picking up sailors at New York's docks. Anonymous sex might qualify as a provocative experience if some of the experiences turned violent, which seems likely given his history of alcohol use and drunken violent behavior.

Crane's life and death are clear examples of some of the themes of this book. For instance, many people who die by suicide appear to engage in short-term practice—I noted for example that my dad cut his wrists before the lethal wound to his heart. By contrast, through years of frequent provocative and painful experiences, people like Crane do not need short-term practice; they just go. And in fact, witnesses described Crane as "vaulting" over the rail of the ship. Crane's lifetime of pain and provocation left him with no hesitation about death by suicide.

Another fact about Crane is important, and it is that he characterized a relationship that intensified near the end of his life as "something of a reason for living." The relationship was with the wife of a friend—their marriage had neared its end, and in the wake of it, and in the wake of Crane's many troubles, a deep relationship emerged. Crane was gay, and it is not clear whether or not this relationship was sexual, though it was intense enough that Crane entertained ideas of marriage. In the days before his death, there were serious disruptions in this relationship. Crane had developed the capacity for self-injury already, and used it once his one remaining close relationship appeared to be falling apart.

I have pointed to two of the three key components of completed suicide regarding Crane's death—acquired ability to enact lethal self-injury (the focus of this chapter) and thwarted belongingness (a focus of the next chapter). The third component—a deep sense of incompetence or ineffectiveness (also a focus of the next chapter)— can be detected as well. In the days before his death, he said to many people that he felt "utterly disgraced," in part by his drunken behavior on the ship, but also by his long history of such behavior.

The death by suicide of the actor Spalding Gray in early 2004 is still another illustration of some of these principles. Gray was last seen on January 10 in New York City and was reported missing on January 11. There were reports that a Staten Island Ferry worker believed he saw Gray coming off the ferry on the night of January 9. This left Gray's wife and brother with the fear that the January 9 ferry ride was a "dry run" to prepare for the next day's suicide. Their fears were confirmed when Gray's body was found in the East River two months later, on March 7.

Gray had attempted suicide multiple times since a 2001 car accident in which he was badly injured. In September 2003, Gray left a phone message for his wife saying goodbye and indicating his plan to jump from the Staten Island Ferry. His wife called police, who radioed the ferry; ferry workers found a dejected Gray and escorted him off the boat.

His lethal attempt was different. Before Gray was found, his wife stated that if her husband's disappearance involved suicide, it had a different character than previous attempts. His past attempts had always involved a note telling her what he would do, where he would be, and so forth. For his lethal attempt, there was no note; he just suddenly disappeared.

There are other aspects of Gray's death that are instructive. As was mentioned, he was badly injured in a car accident approximately three years before his death; he sustained a severely broken hip as well as head injuries. The experience of having been injured—having to endure the pain; facing the fear of bodily damage—may have inured Gray to the pain and provocation of self-injury. Just as Hart Crane habituated to pain and provocation through an array of provocative experiences, including previous suicidal behavior, Gray's injuries, combined with his subsequent suicide attempts, may have left him prepared to fully face down death on his final attempt.

Gray's wife reported that his depression, which had been severe and treatment-resistant following his car accident, seemed to have been lifting in the days and weeks prior to his death. A well-known piece of clinical lore cautions that there is a window of heightened suicide risk as people emerge from depression, perhaps because they have the energy and cognitive clarity to act on long-standing suicidal ideas. There are anecdotal reports that appear to support this possibility. For example, Alvarez noted that the poet Sylvia Plath experienced increased energy and artistic productivity during the period before her suicide.[20] This possibility was also noted—memorably— by the psychologist Paul Meehl in his famous paper "Why I Do Not Attend Case Conferences," in which he describes upbraiding a student. Meehl, incredulous, asks the student if he has never heard that a psychotically depressed patient is more likely to kill himself when his depression is lifting. The student says no.

"Well you have heard of it now," says Meehl. "You better read a couple of old books, and maybe next time you will be able to save somebody's life."[21]

The diminution of fear through repeated self-injury is, according to my account, necessary for serious suicidal behavior to occur. Shneidman described the case of Ariel,[22] a young woman with previous suicidal behavior (e.g., an overdose) who went on to attempt to burn herself to death. Her plan was to fill a gallon jug with gasoline, douse the inside of her parked car and herself with the gasoline, and then strike a match. She wrote, "I remember kind of shaking when I was getting the jug because I think I was a bit afraid." Fear thus surfaced even in Ariel, a woman who was clearly resolved to die by suicide. Ariel did strike the match, and was terribly burned. She survived, but a few years later, died from natural causes.

To be competent at and courageous about anything, one must have experience with it—the more experience, the more competence and the more courage. The implications of continued experience with provocative or painful stimuli, such as self-harm, are far-reaching.

First, with repeated exposure, one habituates—the "taboo" and prohibited quality of suicidal behavior diminishes, and so may the fear and pain associated with self-harm. Second, and relatedly, opponent processes may be involved. Briefly, opponent process theory[23] predicts that, with repetition, the effects of a provocative stimulus diminish, and the opposite effect, or opponent process, becomes amplified and strengthened. For example, with repeated use, the euphoric effects of heroin (the "a" process) weaken, and the aversive effects of withdrawal (the opponent process) increase; similarly, with repetition, the fear-inducing effects of skydiving (the "a" process) diminish, and the exhilarating effects of the opponent process are amplified. Skydivers become more competent and more courageous with skydiving practice and experience increasing reinforcement (e.g., exhilaration).

So may suicidal people become more competent and courageous with repeated practice at suicidal behavior, and may even experience increasing reinforcement. Indeed, as will be expanded on later, many patients report that self-harm has calming and pain-relieving effects—they self-injure because it distracts them from even deeper emotional pain, or because it makes them feel alive, or because it brings their inner world back into harmony with the world at large.

What is the evidence that, through practice and the attendant accrual of competence and courage regarding suicide, people "work up" to the ability to enact lethal self-injury and may even find suicidal behavior increasingly rewarding? The several anecdotal examples described in this chapter are consistent with this view, but anecdotal evidence, by itself, is not particularly persuasive. If the view espoused here is true, what facts should be empirically demonstrable? In the following sections, several lines of research are described that, considered together, suggest that this viewpoint has merit.

Multiple Suicide Attempts

Alvarez wrote, "It is estimated that a person who has once been to the brink is perhaps three times more likely to go there again than someone who has not. Suicide is like diving off a high board: the first time is the worst."[24] Indeed, if past experience with suicidality facilitates future suicidality, such that it becomes more serious and more lethal, people with multiple past suicide attempts should be demonstrably different from others, even including those with one past suicide attempt. My colleagues and I compared 134 current suicide ideators, 128 people who had recently made their first suicide attempt, and 68 people who had recently attempted suicide for at least the second time (i.e., multiple attempters). We compared the three groups on an array of symptom and personality indices. It should be noted that patients in all three groups were in crisis—they had either recently attempted suicide or ideated about it to the point that a mental health professional became concerned—and so the three groups did not differ in terms of why they were included in the study. All were suicidal in one way or another. A unique feature of this study was the comparison of multiple attempters to one-time attempters. The three groups did not differ with regard to age, so any differences among them were not likely age-related.

And there were differences among them. As compared to those

with suicidal ideas and those with one attempt, multiple attempters experienced more intense suicidal symptoms, such as desire to die, plans to attempt, resolve to die, intensity and duration of suicidal ideation, and so forth. This was the case on both self-report and clinician-rated scales of suicidality, which is important because the two data sources do not always agree (when they do, confidence in the results is higher). There were also differences on some personality variables, such as hostility. Even though all participants were in a suicidal crisis, multiple attempters stood out from others in terms of the severity of their suicidality as well as some features of their personality.[25]

They had more past practice at suicide, and thus had moved further along the trajectory toward serious suicidal behavior than the others. Their position on this trajectory is indicated by the severity of their current suicidal symptoms. Other research groups, too, have affirmed this pattern of findings.[26]

What does the association between past suicide attempts and current suicidality mean? For example, it is possible that repeated suicidal behavior occurs simply because of an ongoing, chronic mood disorder. To rule out explanations like these, studies need to first document that an association between past and current suicidality exists, but also document that it persists when variables like chronic mental disorders are accounted for.

In fact, several studies have shown that past suicidal behavior confers risk for later suicidality, including death by suicide, *taking into account other key variables* like mood disorders, for example. One study compared those who died by suicide to living controls. Suicides and controls were matched for presence and severity of mental disorders (also for gender and age), so any differences between the groups were not likely to be attributable to one group having more psychopathology than the other group. One of the main variables that distinguished those who died by suicide from living controls was a significant past history of deliberate self-harm.[27] In a similar study, past attempts comprised a significant predictor of later death by suicide, even taking into account several other powerful predictors, such as presence of mood disorders.[28] In these studies, multiple attempt status conferred risk to death by suicide, even beyond the effects of other powerful predictors, a finding quite consistent with the current conceptualization that people may "work up" to death by suicide through repeated episodes of deliberate self-harm (as well as through other means, noted later).

Similarly, Boardman and colleagues compared those who died by suicide to controls who had died from other causes; cases and controls were matched for age and sex. Among the variables that distinguished deaths by suicide from other deaths was a past history of deliberate self-harm as well as a history of past criminal charges or contact with the police. Those who died by suicide had more significant histories of past self-harm and more police contact.[29] The finding on criminality and legal contact is interesting; deliberate self-harm is the clearest means to habituate to self-injury, but not the only way. As will be expanded on later, other provocative experiences, including those associated with police contact (e.g., assault; injury from recklessness or substance abuse), may serve as well.

A study following 529 mood-disordered patients over fourteen years found a similar pattern. Thirty-six participants died by suicide and 120 attempted suicide during the study. Among the variables that differentiated those who died by or attempted suicide from those who had no suicide attempt were history of previous attempts, impulsivity, and substance abuse.[30] As with the previous finding on police contact, this result on substance abuse and impulsive behavior as precursors to suicidality is consistent with the view that an array of provocative experiences lays the groundwork for future self-injury. Another finding from this study was intriguing: Assertiveness was found to be a predictor of later suicidality among these mood-disordered patients. This finding on assertiveness as a predictor of suicidality squares with the current view that serious suicidality requires the accrual of a kind of courage or strength.

My colleagues and I have recently conducted two studies that support the conclusion that past suicidal behavior is related to future suicidal behavior in a fundamental and important way. We tried to take the same approach as some past investigators in that we assessed the relation of past suicidal behavior to later suicidality, again *accounting for other key predictors*. That is, we wanted to show that past and future suicidal behavior were related directly, as opposed to being associated simply because they are both related to a third thing, like a chronic mood disorder or personality disorder (this is known as "the third variable problem" in some research circles). The title of our paper included the phrase "the kitchen sink," denoting our attempt to include as many "third variables" as we could think of. This paper included four different studies. A representative list of third variables would include: The demographic variables of age, marital status, and ethnicity; family history of suicide, depression, bipolar disorder, and alcohol abuse; personal history of legal trouble as an adult and as a juvenile; current and past diagnoses of depression and bipolar disorder; and scores on indices of depression, hopelessness, problem-solving difficulties, borderline personality symptoms, drug dependence symptoms, alcohol dependence symptoms, and negative life events. Each of these variables has a resilient association with suicidal symptoms, and to account for all of them simultaneously would make it difficult for the association between past and future suicidality to remain.

Nevertheless, across all four studies, the relation of past to future suicidality persisted, even when this impressive list of suicide-related variables was statistically accounted for. Essentially, this rules out the possibility that repeated suicidal behavior simply occurs because of an ongoing mental disorder. Rather, according to my view, it occurs because one instance of suicidal behavior lays the groundwork for later instances, and it does so specifically through the accrual of fearlessness and competence.

In this "kitchen sink" study, we also tried to determine if any other variable besides past suicidality displayed this resilient relation to current suicidality. To do this, we conducted comparison analyses in which, for example, we examined the association between current diagnosis of major depression and current suicidal symptoms, and then examined this same association accounting for the list of other key variables, now including past suicidality. In no case did any other variable besides past suicidality display a resilient relation to current suicidality. The bottom line was that there is something special about the relation of past to future suicidality—it is hard to explain it away. And I believe that something special has to do with the escalating trajectory of lethality fuelled by habituation and opponent processes.

Incidentally, another aspect of this paper was that the four studies involved diverse participants: young adults in the United States with clinical levels of suicidality, U.S. undergraduates, mood-disordered Brazilian outpatients, and an older adult psychiatric inpatient sample from the United States. Conclusions from the study are strengthened by the convergence of results across multiple and diverse samples.[31]

Another of our studies involved a similar approach, but focused especially on childhood physical and sexual abuse. The framework developed in this book is that repeated painful experience may lay down the ability to enact future lethal self-injury; childhood physical and sexual abuse may constitute pathways by which this occurs. Again, the most direct pathway from past provocative experience to current suicidality is past self-injury. Less direct ways to habituate to pain and provocation and thus to potentially acquire the capability for serious self-injury include involvement in violence, either as perpetrator or victim. It is in this last connection that childhood sexual and physical abuse may serve as a means to habituate to pain and injury and thus to facilitate later self-injury.

Childhood physical abuse and certain forms of childhood sexual abuse may be more closely linked to acquisition of lethality than other forms of abuse (i.e., neglect or verbal abuse) because they are, on average, more physically painful than the other forms of abuse. Painful forms of childhood sexual abuse are more associated with suicidality than less painful forms.[32] On the other hand, as will be made clear in the next chapter, the desire for death is also very important in serious suicidal behavior. I believe that the desire for death stems from feeling a burden on loved ones and others, and feeling disconnected and alienated from others. To the degree that any form of abuse facilitates either lethality (through habituation to pain and provocation) or desire for death (through increased feelings of burdensomeness or disconnection), it should, according to the model, constitute a risk for later suicidal behavior. Childhood physical and sexual abuse may particularly confer risk because they are both painful and imply burdensomeness and disconnection.

Our study analyzed data collected in the National Comorbidity Survey, which was a large project on the occurrence of mental disorders and associated variables in U.S. adults. As part of the survey, data were collected on childhood experiences of various forms of abuse and on suicidal behavior. Our analyses showed that some forms of abuse were more linked to subsequent suicidality than were other forms; specifically, the effects for childhood physical abuse and sexual abuse on later suicidal behavior were relatively pronounced and similar to one another, and exceeded effects for molestation and verbal abuse. Other researchers have reported similar findings. For example, in a representative study, researchers interviewed over 3,000 female adolescent twins and found that childhood physical abuse was one of the factors most associated with a suicide attempt history.[33]

A link between abuse and suicidality is consistent with many possible explanations. For example, genetically transmitted personality traits (like impulsivity) or disorders (like personality disorders) could simultaneously explain a parent's abusive behavior and a child's subsequent suicidal behavior, with no need to invoke a contributory link between abuse and suicidality. However, judicious choice of which other variables to account for can, at least to a degree, rule out many explanations. For example, an association between abuse and suicidality accounting for a parent's impulsivity or personality disorder would, to a degree, rule out the explanation that both parental abuse and child suicidality are a result of shared impulsivity or personality symptoms.

In fact, that is exactly the approach we took. Specifically, we statistically accounted for such variables as the respondent's mental disorders, the respondent's parents' mental disorders, and family-of-origin variables like divorce and poverty. Even after accounting for all of these variables, there was an association between childhood sexual and physical abuse and later suicidality. Viewed within this book's framework, the reason for this association is that abuse habituates people to pain and provocation and thus lowers their resistance to self-injury; abuse also sends messages regarding low self-worth and alienation from others, which, as will be argued in Chapter 3, can facilitate the desire for death.

The studies on those who attempt suicide multiple times and on the vigorous association between past and future suicidality (even accounting for "kitchen sink" variables) are consistent with the view that people habituate to self-injury and thereby gain the ability to enact increasingly severe suicidal behaviors. As a complement to these studies, it would be persuasive if it could be shown that the more people attempt suicide, the more dangerous and the more intent on dying they become. In fact, increasing lethality and intent in those with past suicidal behavior have been documented in several studies.

For example, in one study, fifty adults were interviewed the morning following a self-harm incident. Some of the patients had harmed themselves numerous times before; for some patients this was their first self-harm incident. These researchers compared those whose self-injury was their first to those who had harmed themselves before. Those who had engaged in repeated self-injury reported that their current episode of self-harm was more aggressive and potentially more lethal than first-time self-injury patients; moreover, patients in the repeat group showed more intent to die than did the first-time group.[34] A similar study assessed 500 patients after an episode of self-injury. Just after the incident, the patients completed a measure evaluating their intent to die during the self-harm incident. The patients were then followed for five years. Those patients with high scores on the baseline intent-to-die measurement were the most likely to die by suicide during the five-year follow-up interval.[35] Studies like this square with the view that some people get on an escalating trajectory toward serious suicidal behavior, and that past self-injury, as well as other painful and provocative experiences, can accelerate movement along this trajectory.

Paul H. Soloff and colleagues conducted a similar study assessing the effect of previous suicidal behavior on the extent of medical damage from a person's most serious suicide attempt. These researchers examined patients with major depression alone, borderline personality disorder alone, or both disorders. In this study, the number of previous suicide attempts was a strong predictor of the extent of medical damage resulting from the most serious lifetime suicide attempt.[36] This is consistent with the view that experience with suicidality—or other provocative and painful experiences—is necessary before people can inflict serious physical damage on themselves. Overall, this pattern of findings suggests that escalating severity of suicidality is furthered by earlier episodes of self-injury.

In summary, those who attempt suicide multiple times experience more severe suicidal symptoms, including more medically damaging self-injury and higher rates of eventual death by suicide. Many of the reviewed studies documented an association between past and subsequent suicidal behavior, even accounting for other powerful variables like presence of mental disorders generally or mood disorders in particular. It is therefore unlikely that this association can be fully explained with reference to aspects of mental disorders like hopelessness, mental pain, and impaired coping. Rather, there appears to be a meaningful and fundamental relation between past and future suicidality, and according to the present view, this relationship involves habituation and opponent processes. Multiple suicide attempts are viewed here as the most important (but not the only) way that, through habituation and opponent processes, people acquire the ability to enact lethal self-injury.

Pain, Injury, and Suicide

As has been mentioned previously, past self-injury is the most powerful and dangerous way to acquire lethality. According to the present theory, however, it is not the only means. There should be high rates of suicidality in people who have repeatedly experienced and thus habituated to injury and pain, even if not through self-harm per se.

If an association of this sort were clear, it would support the theory, but only somewhat. Other explanations may also adequately describe the relation between repeated exposure to pain and suicidality. Studies relevant to my theory of lethality will be reviewed first, and then studies that address some competing explanations will be noted too. Partly because of the abundance of competing explanations, this material is among the most speculative included in this chapter.

The famous philosopher of science Sir Karl Popper wrote in his 1959 *Logic of Scientific Discovery,* "We usually accord to the first corroborating instances far greater importance than to later ones: once a theory is well corroborated, further instances raise its degree of corroboration only very little. This rule however does not hold good if these new instances are very different from the earlier ones, that is if they corroborate the theory in a new field of application."[37] My theory of suicidal behavior has, so far, been consistent with emerging facts. For example, because those who regularly tattoo or pierce themselves have numerous chances to habituate to pain, I would predict an association between tattooing and piercing and suicidal behavior. In a study comparing people who died by suicide to people who died in accidents (matched for gender, race, and age), those who died by suicide were more likely to have tattoos.[38] There are many possible reasons for an association between tattooing and completed suicide (for example, both tattooing and suicide may be associated with substance abuse). It is an intriguing if speculative interpretation, however, that eventual suicide victims have obtained courage regarding suicide partly via painful and provocative experiences such as tattooing.

Menninger mentioned another possible way to habituate to pain and provocative experiences, namely, compulsive submission to multiple surgeries.[39] And, in fact, women who engage in repeated self-injury have more surgeries than controls.[40] Patients with Body Dysmorphic Disorder (a condition characterized by obsessions with one's imagined ugliness) have both high rates of surgery (usually cosmetic surgery to correct imagined defects) and high rates of suicidality.[41]

On June 14, 2004, the Associated Press filed a report entitled, "Doctors Remove Rods From Man's Stomach." On a bet from his drinking buddies, Huynh Ngoc Son, twenty-two, swallowed three metal construction rods, each around seven inches long. About a month later, Son went to the hospital complaining of serious stomach pains, and doctors quickly saw the problem in X-rays of his stomach. Surgeons removed the rods, and apparently Son is doing well, with no permanent damage to his stomach. It is experiences like these that lay down the ability to enact lethal self-injury. Should Son develop the desire for suicide, he would likely be at high risk, because he has developed the ability to do extreme things to his body.

David Reimer, described in John Colapinto's 2000 book *As Nature Made Him: The Boy Who Was Raised as a Girl,* died by suicide at the age of thirty-eight. Reimer, born a boy, was badly injured as a baby in a botched circumcision. He was raised as a girl thereafter, including estrogen treatments that induced breast growth, though this identity clearly did not suit him. Bravely, he insisted that he revert to his true identity in adolescence, and this meant numerous painful surgeries. As Colapinto states, David "underwent a double mastectomy, an intensely painful procedure that left him in agony for weeks afterward."[42] Later, he underwent a procedure to construct a penis from muscles and skin from the inside of his thighs; during the following year, he was hospitalized eighteen times for blockages and infections associated with this procedure. Soon after this, he attempted suicide twice within one week, both times involving an overdose of his mother's antidepressant medicines. A second procedure to improve the earlier surgery to create a penis was a twelve-stage operation that took three surgeons thirteen hours to perform. Apart from these painful experiences, Reimer's most satisfying job was in a slaughterhouse. These and many other painful and provocative experiences may have facilitated Reimer's later suicide.

Based on the perspective proposed here, one would predict that those prone to suicide have witnessed, experienced, or engaged in more violence than others, because violence exposure would be one way to habituate—either directly or vicariously—to pain and provocation. Research has borne out this prediction. A representative study compared fifty persons attempting suicide with fifty nonsuicidal psychiatric patients and with fifty nonpsychiatric control patients attending a heart clinic (here, as in so many of these studies, groups were matched for age, sex, and social class). Suicidal patients had experienced an array of violent episodes to a significantly higher degree than either control group.[43] Conner and colleagues surveyed next-of-kin and other respondents close to people who had died in the last year (by suicide and by other means). Respondents indicated that those who had died by suicide more frequently threatened and attempted violence in the last year, as compared to accident victim controls.[44] A lifetime history of aggression differentiates adolescent suicide victims from matched controls, even after accounting for differences in mental disorders between suicides and controls.[45]

Other factors too point to an association of experience with violence and suicidality. Prison inmates are at increased risk for suicide compared to community dwellers, and inmates completing suicide are more likely to be incarcerated for manslaughter or murder as compared to other prisoners.[46] In these instances, as violence exposure (as indexed by incarceration or manslaughter/murder convictions) increases, so does suicidality, perhaps because violence exposure lowers barriers to injury in general, self-injury in particular.

Of course, if the perspective presented here has merit, then those who have habituated to pain and provocation through such means as serious drug abuse and prostitution should have demonstrably high suicide rates. Heroin users are fourteen times more likely than peers to die from suicide, and the prevalence of attempted suicide is also orders of magnitude greater than that of community samples. Of course, several other perspectives might predict this association—for example, maybe it is just that heroin overdoses are misclassified as suicides. However, heroin overdoses per se appear to play a relatively small role in suicide among this group.[47]

Regarding prostitution, a qualitative analysis of the narratives of twenty-nine street youth involved in prostitution revealed that 76 percent of them had made at least one suicide attempt.[48] The authors of the study concluded that the experience of trading sex was heavily implicated in the youths' suicidality. In another study, homeless youth involved in prostitution were compared to homeless youth not involved in prostitution; those involved in prostitution had more suicide attempts than others.[49]

Of course, several psychiatric syndromes are at least partly defined by behaviors that would be viewed here as incurring pain and provocation and thus potentially engaging habituation and opponent processes—to name two examples, borderline personality disorder (which involves serious behavioral impulsivity, including self-injurious behavior), and anorexia nervosa (which involves self-starvation). The relevance of these and other disorders will be explored in a later chapter, but for now, I'll note that borderline personality disorder and anorexia nervosa are among the most lethal of all psychiatric disorders, with the usual mechanism of death being suicide.[50]

Daredevils—those who are thrill-seekers—are often injured, and may be more prone to self-injury. Menninger believed that this connection is explained by a death wish on the part of daredevils.[51] I have a different explanation—daredevils habituate to injury, including self-injury, and thereby acquire the ability to enact lethal self-injury. As to why daredevils are daredevils in the first place, I think that personality traits like impulsivity, to be addressed in a later chapter, are a more convincing explanation than a death wish.

Thus far, I have focused on those who have engaged in or observed injury, pain, or violence and who are in some way under-privileged or victimized. Though these studies are generally consistent with the view that those engaging in or observing provocative behaviors experience more suicidality, it might be more convincing still if research indicated that engaging in or observing provocative behaviors conferred higher risk to suicidality even in high-privilege groups. This may be especially persuasive for the additional reason that high-privilege groups may enjoy more protection from suicide than others (e.g., through greater access to social and material resources and to mental health care); any increased risk in a high-privilege group is thus not explained by lack of these protective factors.

Physicians are of interest in this regard. Through their training and practice, physicians frequently observe the consequences of pain, violence, and injury, and they gain specialized knowledge about lethal agents, dosing, methods of death, and so forth—that is, they develop considerable competence and capability regarding suicide. In this connection, Menninger observed regarding suicidal behavior, "We physicians, familiar from our daily experiences with these unlovely sights, often forget that for most persons these barriers imposed by taboos are quite high."[52] A review of published original studies concluded that physicians in general have an elevated risk for suicide compared either to the general population or to other professionals.[53]

This is true for female and male physicians alike, but it is possible that the discrepancy between female physicians and other women regarding this issue exceeds the discrepancy between male physicians and other men regarding this issue. This differential discrepancy may be mirrored in suicide rates. Suicide rates are particularly pronounced in female physicians—that is, as compared to other women (either in the general population or in other professional groups), female physicians have quite elevated rates of suicide, on the order of 3 to 5 times higher than other women. Rates are 1.5 to 3 times higher for male physicians as compared to other men.[54] Because men in general have more opportunities than women in general to experience pain and provocation (e.g., through contact sports), it may be more difficult for male physicians to outpace other men regarding experiencing pain and provocation (thus there is a smaller discrepancy between suicide rates in male physicians versus other men). By contrast, the average female physician easily outpaces the average woman with regard to experiencing pain and provocation (thus, according to the present view, there is a large discrepancy between suicide rates in female physicians versus other women). It is also possible that female physicians' relatively high suicide rates involve gender-specific pressures at work.

An alternative explanation to the association between suicidality and provocative and difficult experiences is that people who undergo such difficulties become demoralized and hopeless, and because of this, more prone to suicidality. This possibility is important to consider (and is actually consistent with other parts of my model on feeling a burden on others and feeling that one does not belong, discussed later), but there are aspects of the findings summarized above that do not square very well with this alternative explanation. For example, Grassi and colleagues assessed suicidal ideation in injecting drug users, 81 of whom were HIV positive, 62 of whom were positive for hepatitis C and HIV negative, and 152 of whom were negative for both HIV and hepatitis C. Suicidality scores were elevated in the sample as a whole, but there were no differences among the three groups in suicidality.[55] If demoralization were the key mechanism, one might expect the infected groups to display more suicidality; by contrast, if a key mechanism is the provocative experience of repeated self-injection of illicit drugs (which all participants in this study had experienced), one might expect equal suicidality across the noninfected and infected groups (this was in fact the finding). Also, given issues of status and privilege, the findings on physicians may not be explicable through demoralization, although issues related to burnout and job stress may be involved.

A second alternative explanation is that impulsivity—the tendency to act without thinking—underlies and explains any relation between painful or provocative experiences and suicidality; after all, impulsive people are, on average, more likely than others to experience various provocations and more likely than others to engage in suicidal behavior. Indeed, it will be argued in a later chapter that an impulsive personality style is conducive to the acquisition of the ability to enact lethal self-injury mainly because of the tendency of impulsive people to experience various provocations. To address the possibility that impulsivity explains the relation between provocative experiences and suicidality, studies are needed that account for impulsivity in examining the relation between provocations and suicidal symptoms. Few studies have explicitly taken this approach; nevertheless, some extant findings are relevant. For example, studies have shown that previous experience with suicidality predicts future suicidality, even accounting for various indicators of impulsivity.[56] Indeed, the "kitchen sink" study mentioned earlier documented a relation between past and future suicidality, even when borderline personality symptoms—closely related to impulsivity—were statistically accounted for. There are also clear cases of people with impulsive personality features whose suicidal behavior was carefully planned over days or weeks—Kurt Cobain's suicide was of this sort.[57] In these cases, a *direct* influence of impulsivity on suicidal behavior is hard to conceive; by contrast, the current proposal that impulsivity *indirectly* relates to suicidality via the accrual of the capacity for lethal self-injury is compatible with the phenomenon of planned suicides in impulsive people. Finally, it is hard to imagine that physicians are more impulsive than the general population, yet, as documented above, they have somewhat higher suicide rates as compared to the general population. A view centered on impulsivity does not constitute a satisfying explanation for elevated rates of suicide among physicians.

The model proposed here would predict that those who have faced repeated violence, pain, or injury would, on average, experience higher suicide risk (without necessarily having been suicidal before), because their painful and provocative experiences will have engaged, at least to a degree, the same habituation and opponent processes engaged by self-injury. Studies on topics ranging from tattooing, to violence, to self-injected drug abuse, to suicide rates among physicians can all be interpreted as consistent with the model.

Pain Tolerance

If prior suicide attempts habituate people to provocation and pain, it might be expected that their pain tolerance exceeds that of others. That habituation to pain is implicated in suicidality is illustrated starkly by some of the anecdotal evidence, described earlier. But is there empirical evidence on this?

Israel Orbach and colleagues have reported that suicidal people can tolerate extreme temperatures applied to the skin better than other patients.[58] This is termed a "thermal pain threshold," and suicidal patients tend to have higher thermal pain thresholds and higher general pain tolerance as compared to controls. Additionally, in response to electric shock, suicidal participants showed higher tolerance for pain and appraised the pain as less intense than psychiatric control groups. Similarly, in another study, suicidal patients endured more pain as compared to accident victims who had similar levels of injuries.[59] Suicidal inpatients show the highest thresholds for another index of pain threshold, tolerance of pressure applied to the skin, as compared to nonsuicidal inpatients and controls.[60] Even among preschool children, some of whom had suicidal ideas and behaviors, the suicidal children show significantly less pain and crying after injury than does a psychiatric control group.[61]

Suicidal inpatients are not as physiologically reactive to a movie on suicide as compared to controls.[62] This would be consistent with the idea that suicidal patients have gotten used to suicidal stimuli and thus do not react to them as much as do nonsuicidal patients. Remarkably, a large proportion of people with borderline personality disorder who self-injure report no pain on self-injury, even in response to considerable physical injury (e.g., deep cuts), and their self-reports of no pain are supported by psychophysiological measures.[63] Here again, it appears that with repeated experience, people get used to self-injury, even to the point that it is not painful.

My colleagues and I found a similar result among adolescent psychiatric inpatients, many of whom had significant histories of suicide attempts.[64] Many also regularly self-injured (usually by cutting on their arms or legs), not in an attempt to die, but rather, in an attempt to feel better when they were emotionally distressed. We asked these youths about the amount of pain they felt on self-injury. Almost half reported that they felt no pain, even when fairly serious damage resulted—another demonstration that people appear to get used to even medically damaging injury. Others reported that they did feel pain on self-injury. Very interesting in the present context, those who felt no pain on self-injury reported an average of almost four lifetime suicide attempts (self-injury when intent was death), whereas those who did feel pain on self-injury reported a lower number of lifetime suicide attempts (around two, on average). My interpretation of these data is that those with more lifetime suicide attempts have habituated more than others to the pain of self-injury, so much so that self-injury no longer causes them pain, even though they are engaging in self-injury that would be quite painful to most people.

Though not on suicidality, J. R. Seguin and colleagues showed that boys with a history of physical aggression were less sensitive to pain (as measured by a finger pressure device) as compared to less aggressive boys.[65] Studies of this sort raise the possibility that pain sensitivity is suppressed by past self-injury as well as by engaging in other provocative behaviors (like aggression). According to the model developed here, decreased pain sensitivity—whether gained through self-injury or other provocative experiences like aggression—may remove a barrier to serious suicidal behavior.

There are people who have neurological conditions that render them unable to experience pain. This is a serious condition, often involving repeated injury and even death due to the person's lack of awareness of serious injury. This is a rare condition so that data on suicidal behavior among such patients are unavailable. Even if they were available, their interpretation would be clouded by the fact that these patients often die at early ages as a result of their condition. Nevertheless, the very existence of the syndrome and the problems it causes illustrate the value of at least some pain sensitivity, and the dangers that emerge as people lose pain sensitivity.

It should be noted that this literature on pain sensitivity and suicidality is relatively small, and that there is a lack of longitudinal studies showing that pain tolerance is related to later suicidality. Overall, however, it appears that those who attempt suicide, relatively speaking, become buffered from physical pain and some other pro-vocative stimuli, consistent with the current view that the trajectory toward serious suicidality is characterized by increased ability to en-dure pain and provocation.

Implications for Accrued Lethality

The nature of suicidal symptoms may change as experience with pre-vious suicidal behavior accrues. That is, serious suicidal symptoms (as compared to less severe suicidal symptoms) may become more and more prominent with repeated suicidal experience. This begs a key question—what represents "severe" versus "less severe" suicidal symptoms?

Like others before us,[66] my colleagues and I showed that all sui-cidal symptoms are not the same and can be categorized into two do-mains, which, while of course correlated, are discernible, and which we named "resolved plans and preparations" and "suicidal desire and ideation."[67]

The "resolved plans and preparations" category was made up of the following symptoms: a sense of courage to make an attempt; a sense of competence to make an attempt; availability of means to and opportunity for attempt; specificity of plan for attempt; prepara-tions for attempt; duration of suicidal ideation; and intensity of sui-cidal ideation. It is worth noticing that this category explicitly in-cludes indicators emphasizing courage and competence regarding suicide, which, according to the view proposed here, are reflective of the acquired ability to enact lethal self-injury.

The "suicidal desire and ideation" category was comprised of the following symptoms: reasons for living; wish to die; frequency of ideation; wish not to live; passive attempt; desire for attempt; and talk of death/suicide. This factor does not include content related to courage, competence, and the like, but rather, emphasizes thwarted desire to live and reasons for death. In the next chapter, it will be argued that thwarted desire to live can be understood in terms of feeling a burden on and disconnected from others. Thwarted desire to live is of course important in suicidality, but in an important sense, it is less clinically worrisome than the "resolved plans" category.

Although the presence of symptoms corresponding to either category is of clinical concern, the symptoms of "resolved plans and preparations" are, relatively speaking, of more concern than the symptoms of "suicidal desire and ideation." And crucial to the prediction that serious suicidal symptoms should become more and more prominent with repeated suicidal experience, "resolved plans and preparations" was significantly more related than "suicidal desire and ideation" to status as a multiple suicide attempter.[68]

A subsequent study reached similar conclusions regarding attempt status as well as eventual death by completed suicide. Specifically, my colleagues and I studied several hundred current suicide ideators, who were evaluated regarding their "worst-point" suicidal crisis, and then who were followed for many years.[69] The "worst-point" was defined as a past suicidal crisis that was the most severe in the respondent's life. In this study, as in the earlier reports, the distinction between "resolved plans and preparations" (which includes courage and competence regarding suicide) and "desire for death" (the less serious dimension) was emphasized, in that respondents rated their "resolved plans" and their "desire for death" with regard to their worst-point crisis.

According to the model proposed in this book, people who have experienced severe episodes of suicidality in the past (particularly if the episode involved loss of fear and other "resolved plans and preparations" phenomena) may be most at risk for severe suicidality in the future, and possibly even death by suicide. Our results conformed to this view: The "worst-point resolved plans and preparations" symptoms were the strongest predictor of suicide attempts during the follow-up period, and the *only* significant predictor of eventual death by suicide in the sample; the "suicidal desire and ideation" symptoms were not associated with later death by suicide. Consistent with these findings, a separate eighteen-year follow-up study found that *planfulness* regarding episodes of deliberate self-harm represented a significant risk factor for later completed suicide.[70] Planfulness requires competence, which in my model is a key aspect of the acquired capability for lethal self-injury.

That fearlessness and accrued courage and competence regarding suicide—key indicators of the "resolved plans and preparations" factor—are implicated in severe suicidality is a central assertion of the present theory. In this connection, it is of interest to recall the fourteen-year prospective study of several hundred mood-disordered patients mentioned earlier.[71] Assertiveness was found to be a predictor of severe suicidality during the fourteen-year follow-up period. My model is perhaps the only theory of suicide that is compatible with a relation between assertiveness and suicidality.

My colleagues and I analyzed notes written by those who died by suicide as well as those who attempted and survived[72] using a software program called Linguistic Inquiry and Word Count (LIWC).[73] The program divides text into its components—for example, tendency to use action verbs, words denoting negative emotion, and so on. Among the clearest variables that differentiated notes by those who died by suicide from notes by those who attempted suicide and survived were indices related to assertiveness, specifically anger combined with confidence. The combination of anger and confidence bears some similarity to the combination of courage and resolution of ambivalence regarding suicide.

Another aspect of the "resolved plans and preparations" category should be noted. In addition to indicators related to courage and competence regarding suicide, the factor also involved intense, vivid, and long-lasting ideation about one's death by suicide. People who experience this say that they can see their death by suicide very clearly in their mind's eye—it is as if they are watching a clear and vivid video of their own death by suicide. In this context, it is an interesting possibility that courage and competence regarding suicide may develop mentally as well as behaviorally. That is, vivid and long-lasting preoccupation regarding one's suicide may represent a form of mental practice. To the extent that one rehearses for suicide, whether actually or mentally, suicide potential is increased. The concept of mental rehearsal may be helpful in understanding those who die by suicide on their first attempt—studies have found rates of first-attempt completed suicide as high as 50 percent.[74] Mental practice may facilitate suicide completion among those attempting it for the first time.

Shneidman's case example of Beatrice illustrates this aspect of mental practice. She says, "For the next two years . . . every night, before fading off to sleep, I imagined committing suicide. I became obsessed with death. I rehearsed my own funeral over and over, adding careful details each time."[75] Beatrice later planned her suicide for three months, and tried to die by self-cutting; she survived.

In 1992 and 1993, musician Kurt Cobain obsessively watched a videotape of the suicide of R. Budd Dwyer, a Pennsylvania state official who died at a live press conference (that Dwyer himself had called) by putting a gun in his mouth and firing.[76] This may have represented a form of mental practice for Cobain's 1994 death by a similar method.

David Reimer, mentioned earlier and described in the book *As Nature Made Him: The Boy Who Was Raised as a Girl,* said that in eighth grade, when he was living as a girl, he "kept visualizing a rope thrown over a beam."[77] He would have continued experience with suicidality as well as numerous other provocative experiences, and at age thirty-eight, died by suicide.

A study of over 3,000 patients at risk for suicide, thirty-eight of whom subsequently died by suicide, provides some indirect evidence regarding mental practice.[78] Of the factors that predicted death by suicide, an important one was "contemplation of hanging or jumping." Through mental rehearsal of violent death by suicide, these patients may have acquired more of the ability to enact lethal self-injury.

Also relevant here is the concept of aborted suicide attempts, defined as an event in which an individual comes close to attempting suicide but does not do so and thus sustains no injury. Barber and colleagues interviewed 135 psychiatric inpatients, and over half reported at least one aborted suicide attempt.[79] Intent-to-die ratings for aborted suicide attempts were similar to those for actual suicide attempts, indicating that aborted attempts can have severe qualities—qualities that could potentially produce habituation and practice effects. Moreover, patients who reported aborted attempts were nearly twice as likely to have made an actual suicide attempt as patients with no aborted attempts. Practice regarding suicide may occur in the absence of actual suicidal behavior, either through mental rehearsal or through aborted suicide attempts.

One additional reason to worry about the accrual of courage about suicide relates to the concept of cognitive sensitization. Cognitive sensitization occurs when one undergoes a provocative experience, and subsequently, images and thoughts about that experience become more accessible and easily triggered. As applied to suicidality, as suicidal experience accumulates, suicide-related cognitions and behaviors may become more accessible and active.[80] The more accessible and active these thoughts and behaviors become, the more easily they are triggered (e.g., even in the absence of negative events), and the more severe are the subsequent suicidal episodes. My colleagues and I have documented that, in fact, as episodes of suicidality increase, their relation to external triggers decreases, and their severity increases.[81]

Vicarious Habituation: The Example of Guns in the Home
As the example of aborted suicide attempts shows, there are multiple ways that people may habituate to dangerous stimuli. One way is through habituating to danger by observing someone else do so, or by repeatedly being exposed to cues associated with danger. The example of Kurt Cobain's obsessively watching a videotaped suicide was mentioned earlier, as was his gradually increasing interest in guns. Guns in the home are an issue in this regard.

First, let me disclose that I am not a huge fan of guns—I don't own one myself—but neither do I have strong feelings against gun ownership. Regardless of one's viewpoint on this topic, there appears to be an undeniable association between the presence of guns in a home and suicides occurring in that home. For example, a study across twenty-one countries documented this association very clearly.[82] In twelve countries, another study found that the percentage of households with guns was strongly associated with the overall mortality rate from guns in children aged 0–15 years, including death by suicide.[83] An association does not prove a causal connection between presence of guns and suicide, but the association is consistent with the possibility that having guns around acquaints people—renders them fearless—about a potentially lethal stimulus.

Brent and colleagues did an interesting study on whether families with a depressed adolescent follow recommendations to remove guns from the house. Of families advised to remove firearms from their homes, 26.9 percent did so. Interestingly, the decision to keep a gun, even when advised not to, was associated with the father's psychopathology as well as marital dissatisfaction.[84]

Repetition May Reinforce Suicidal Behavior

The singer Pink, who has numerous body piercings and tattoos, said in the December 2003 issue of *Jane* magazine, "I took out my tongue ring when I was 21 and regretted it a week later. I like putting holes in my body. It's addictive, it's pain to know you're alive."[85] The evidence summarized so far suggests that habituation and practice effects may be implicated in the escalating trajectory toward serious suicidality. In addition to habituation and practice, the theory put forth here suggests that repeated suicidality may engage opponent processes, such that not only do people habituate to self-injury, they also come to experience it as increasingly rewarding, similar to the way Pink reported that "putting holes" in her body is addictive.

Many people appear to share Pink's perspective. There is clear and consistent evidence that a primary motive for self-injury is relief, and that people find self-injury rewarding, at least in the immediate period following the incident. This may seem hard to imagine, but recall the example of skydiving. In a way, flinging yourself out of an airplane makes no more sense than cutting the side of your arm— indeed skydiving deaths occur every year. Why do people do this, then? The first time they skydive, they feel some of the thrill and exhilaration of it, and a large dose of the fear of it. But as they keep doing it, encouraged by the thrill and exhilaration, the primary process of fear fades, and the opponent process of exhilaration strengthens.

So it goes with self-injury. As people continue to do it, the primary process of pain fades, and the opponent process amplifies. What is the opponent process? As noted earlier, according to patients who self-harm, it is relief because it distracts from even deeper emotional pain, or because it makes them feel alive, or because it brings their inner world back into harmony with the world at large.

Several studies support this idea.[86] These findings appear to implicate what is called negative reinforcement (i.e., the self-injury is reinforcing because it stops or reduces noxious experiences). However, positive reinforcement (i.e., the self-injury is reinforcing because it induces positive feelings) may be operative as well—for example, in a study of female psychiatric inpatients with borderline personality disorder (a main feature of which is repeated self-harm), patients rated various dimensions of their self-injury experiences. Results revealed significant mood elevation as a consequence of self-injury among these patients.[87] Many patients report that although negative reinforcement (i.e., relief) is a primary motive for self-injury,[88] other motives exist, including positive reinforcers such as fascination with the injury and reaffirming the ability to feel[89]—or, in Pink's words, "pain to know you're alive."

To my knowledge, however, only one study has directly evaluated whether the rewarding properties of self-injury increase with repetition. Participants who frequently engaged in self-injury were compared to those who infrequently did so, with regard to responses to a self-mutilation imagery task. In response to the imagery task, those in the frequent self-injury group reported more relief and more reductions in anxiety and sadness as compared to the infrequent group.[90] As people continue to engage in self-injury (or undergo other provocative experiences), they change. Self-injury loses its painful and fear-inducing properties and may even begin to gain rewarding properties. As this occurs, the main barrier to suicide erodes.

The Psychological Merging of Death and Life

To this point, the argument has been made that those prone to serious suicidal behavior have reached that status through a process of exposure to self-injury and other provocative experiences. As this process unfolds, fear of death and pain on self-injury decreases. As reviewed above, certain scientific facts seem to support this view.

Little has been said so far about how potentially suicidal people view death (except that they come not to fear it). When someone is far along the trajectory toward suicide, when they have acquired the ability to enact lethal self-injury, what is their view of death? Though there are very few scientific data on this point, anecdotal and case summary data suggest that people who are near death by suicide view death in a very peculiar way—namely, that death is somehow life-giving.

For most people, the notion that death is life-giving or nurturing is not only irrational but very disturbing. Suicidal people appear to see it differently, however. For example, in Shneidman's case study of Ariel, she stated, "We were in this old cemetery, and what was interesting and unique about this cemetery is that it is very old and the crosses are wooden and they were rotting away and they were waving in the breeze and they were just—just gorgeous really, just really fine . . . and the daisies were blooming and the grasses were growing tall on the graves and the breeze was blowing and I was just so impressed by the earthiness of it and life, of this part of death." Ariel goes on to describe her impression in the cemetery that death's completion of the circle of life is "graceful" and "gracious."[91] For Ariel, life and death have begun to merge, such that there is beauty, grace, and indeed life in death.

On this same point of merging death and beauty, Sylvia Plath (who died by suicide) described a poem she wrote called "Death & Co." "This poem is about the double . . . nature of death—the marmoreal coldness of Blake's death mask, say, hand in glove with the fearful softness of worms, water and other katabolists."[92] Notice not only the reference to softness but the intimacy implied by "hand in glove" and indeed by the title "Death & Co.," implying a togetherness in death. Lines from Plath's poem "Edge" convey some of these same qualities:

> The woman is perfected.
> Her dead
> Body wears the smile of accomplishment . . .
> Her bare
> Feet seem to be saying:
> We have come so far; it is over.

In his book on suicidal experiences, the psychologist Richard A. Heckler included this example: "The window looked out over the river and it was a beautiful scene. The moon was full and I was feeling this real peacefulness. I said to myself, 'It's a beautiful night to die' . . . it's like when you go to weddings, you take pictures to remember everything that happened. Well, I was taking mental pictures to remember this [referring to death by suicide]."[93]

In his 2004 book *My Life Is a Weapon*, Christoph Reuter described suicide attacks by Iranians in the Iran-Iraq War as follows: "Many of the deaths were celebrated . . . with the macabre-seeming designation of death as a wedding celebration."[94] A traditional Iranian wedding table with mirrors and candles was placed above their graves. Though it is questionable whether suicide attackers represent true suicides—a question that is addressed in a later chapter—it is noteworthy that in this example, as in others, self-sacrifice merges themes of death and vitality.

Jon Hilkevitch reported in the July 4, 2004 edition of the *Chicago Tribune* on death by suicide—in this case, that of a sixteen-year-old boy. The boy was struck by a train. A police officer who examined the boy's computer found lyrics from Led Zeppelin's song "In My Time of Dying": "In my time of dying, want nobody to mourn. All I want for you to do is take my body home. Well, well, well, so I can die easy. Well, well, well, so I can die easy." Here, as in previous examples, death is merged with positive things like ease and homecoming.

Kurt Cobain, the lead singer of the rock band Nirvana, died by suicide in April of 1994; the band's last album, *In Utero*, was released a few months before, in September of 1993, and it is clear that suicide was on his mind as he worked on the album. Lyrics from this album illustrate the merging of death with themes of nurturance and life, sometimes in stark and disturbing ways.

In the song "Milk It," the lyrics include the phrase "I am my own parasite," which, on reflection, is a very succinct and even sublime way to combine urges toward death and life. In the same song, the lyrics continue, "I won my own pet virus, I get to pet and name her, Her milk is my shit, My shit is her milk." Though not necessarily pleasant reading, Cobain clearly had a penchant for disturbing imagery in which themes of nurturance are merged with themes of disease and waste. A similar example appears in the song "Heart Shaped Box," in which Cobain refers to an "umbilical noose."

This fusing of death and life themes and urges may be at play in the selection of suicide methods and locations. In Tad Friend's 2003 *New Yorker* article, he stated, "several people have crossed the Bay Bridge to jump from the Golden Gate; there is no record of anyone traversing the Golden Gate to leap from its unlovely sister bridge. Dr. Richard Seiden, a professor emeritus at the University of California at Berkeley's School of Public Health and the leading researcher on suicide at the bridge, has written that studies reveal 'a commonly held attitude that romanticizes suicide from the Golden Gate Bridge in such terms as aesthetically pleasing and beautiful, while regarding a Bay Bridge suicide as tacky.'" Why does it matter that one's location of death be beautiful? One possibility is the merging of needs for nurturance and death that occurs in the suicidal mind.

The same *New Yorker* article described the suicide of a fourteen-year-old girl who bought a book on suicide methods as a way to prepare for her fatal jump from the Golden Gate Bridge. The book stated, "The Golden Gate Bridge is to suicides what Niagara Falls is to honeymooners." Here again, the invocation of the imagery of love and life in explaining choice of location for death is striking.

In that same article, Friend wrote, "At a 1977 rally on the Golden Gate supporting the building of an anti-suicide barrier above the railing, a minister, speaking to six hundred of his followers, tried to explain the bridge's power. Matchless in its Art Deco splendor, the Golden Gate is also unrivalled as a symbol: it is a threshold that presides over the end of the continent and a gangway to the void beyond. Just being there, the minister said, his words growing increasingly incoherent, left him in a rather suicidal mood. The Golden Gate, he said, is 'a symbol of human ingenuity, technological genius, but social failure.'" The minister's words emphasize the awe-inspiring aspects of the bridge; the minister's growing incoherence and reference to social failures and feeling suicidal were foreshadowing for a horrible event a year or so later. The minister was Jim Jones, who died by suicide along with over 900 followers at Jonestown, Guyana—an incident that will be explored in more detail in a later chapter.

One wonders if similar processes are at play regarding suicide in natural locations that are beautiful or awe-inspiring. Alain de Botton, in his book *Status Anxiety,* notes that the vastness of places like the Grand Canyon is soothing to us because it represents infinite space, in which differences in things like status, effectiveness, and belongingness seem trivial. He says, "Whatever differences exist among people, they are as nothing next to the differences between the most powerful humans and the great deserts, high mountains, glaciers and oceans of the world. There are natural phenomena so enormous as to make the variations between any two people seem mockingly tiny."[95] The vastness of natural phenomena can be both awe-inspiring and soothing, qualities that could appeal to someone thinking of death as somehow life-giving. In June of 2004, a man who was touring the Grand Canyon in a helicopter removed his seatbelt and jumped to his death, 4,000 feet to the canyon floor. Just before that, I received a call from a reporter who was pressing me to explain a similar death, this time that of a man whose death was originally seen as a skydiving accident, but on investigation seemed an intentional suicide. The man had apparently cut the lines of his own parachute hours before skydiving. The only explanation that makes sense to me—but that I still view as tentative and speculative—is that in the minds of people who are far along the trajectory toward suicide, death is not only not ugly, but has become beautiful and sustaining, so much so that places like the open sky or the Grand Canyon seem a fitting context for suicide.

A detail about Spalding Gray's death by suicide may involve the merging of themes of death and comfort as well. Police said Gray was last seen at around 6:30 P.M. on the evening of his disappearance, and was last heard from at around 9 P.M. that same evening when he called his home and spoke with his six-year-old son, saying he loved him and was on his way home. Perhaps Gray was simply lying to his son about returning home, so as to protect him, at least for a little while longer. But for a very thoughtful writer like Gray, who understood what his son would go through (because Gray himself lost his mother to suicide), one wonders whether Gray was trying to leave a message of reassurance, something along the lines of, "It's okay now, don't worry about me, I'm home"—and whether he actually believed this message himself.

In my opinion, the most disturbing suicide of all was also a murder. It occurred in Germany in March 2001—the case of the cannibal Armin Meiwes. Meiwes, forty-one, a computer expert, met forty-three-year-old Bernd-Jurgen Brandes in early 2001 after Meiwes advertised for "young, well-built men to slaughter" on websites emphasizing sexual masochism, cannabilism, and the like. Brandes willingly accompanied Meiwes to the latter's home, where Miewes killed Brandes with his consent. Meiwes recorded the gruesome two-hour episode on video, and he cannibalized Brandes's body over the ensuing months.

The video documented several highly graphic and grotesque events, but also documented two important points—Brandes seemed to be coherent and nonpsychotic, and also seemed to give genuine and full consent for his killing. These points were key in Meiwes's trial; there is no law against cannibalism in Germany, leaving prosecutors only the options of a murder charge or a kind of manslaughter charge akin to what in the United States would be termed assisted suicide. A murder conviction seemed unlikely because Brandes seemed sane and repeatedly asked to be killed. Meiwes was convicted of the other charge and sentenced to 8.5 years in jail with the possibility of parole.

How to understand Brandes's baffling death? Little is known about Brandes; it would be of interest to know, for example, whether he had ever attempted suicide. It is clear that he was extremely masochistic and fantasized often and intensely about being killed and eaten—perhaps a form of mental practice for this highly unusual method of suicide. Extreme masochism does not seem to provide a full explanation of Brandes's death, however; there are numerous people who are extremely masochistic, yet I am aware of none who have died in the way that Brandes died. I believe that Brandes's highly unique state of mind shared similarities with suicidal people who fuse imagery and feeling about death and life. For him, his death affirmed his desires and met his deepest wish; for us, his death was deeply horrific. The discrepancy between his view and ours indicates the difference between those who have moved far along the trajectory toward serious suicidal behavior compared to the rest of us. It is possible that the process that led Cobain to write phrases like "umbilical noose" and "I am my own parasite" was horribly amplified in Brandes, such that he progressed from thought to unthinkable action.

For the majority, death is a fearsome prospect. When this fear erodes, behavioral and psychological changes can occur. Behaviorally, people who have habituated to the fear of death are capable of extreme forms of self-injury. Psychologically, they may come to view death as alluring, even sustaining. This can only happen, I believe, when people have habituated to death and the like to an extreme degree, so that they are no longer repulsed by death, but attracted to it, not just as a way to negate pain and suffering, but as a positive and even beautiful thing. That most of us have trouble wrapping our minds around this concept shows the distance necessary to travel— both behaviorally and psychologically—before one has developed the capacity for serious suicidal behavior.

The current model proposes that the acquired ability to enact lethal self-injury is a necessary precursor to serious suicidality, especially to completed suicide. This acquired ability involves fearlessness about confronting pain, injury, and indeed death; the reinforcing qualities of repeated self-injury may also be involved. How does one acquire this ability to "surmount the most powerful instinct of nature?" The answer, according to the theory proposed here, is through repeated experience with painful or provocative stimuli, especially (but not limited to) deliberate self-harm. As this occurs, people are able to engage in more and more seriously injurious behavior, and may come to view death and related things in peculiarly positive ways.

Just because someone has, through various means, acquired the capacity for severe self-injury does not mean that they desire it. Racecar drivers, to take one example, must habituate to conditions that would be harrowing to most people, and thus develop the ability to stare down fear and pain. But they are unlikely to be at high risk for suicide, because the acquired ability to enact lethal self-injury is but one part of the story. Serious suicidal behavior requires both the desire for suicide and the acquired ability to carry it through. The examples of Hart Crane and Spalding Gray illustrate both sides of this deadly equation—both men had developed the capacity for lethal self-injury (through past suicide attempts and other provocative experiences), and both men struggled to belong and to feel effective.

My account argues that desire for suicide occurs when basic needs for effectiveness and connectedness are thwarted. Shneidman stated, "A basic rule for us to keep in mind is this: We can reduce the lethality if we lessen the anguish."[96] I believe this is close but not quite right. Lethality is a stable quality, built up over time with numerous painful and provocative experiences—it doesn't come and go, at least not very much. By contrast, anguish—viewed here as perceived burdensomeness and thwarted belongingness—does come and go. The basic rule then is this: We can lessen the chance that people will enact their lethality if we lessen their anguish. The next chapter examines the specific nature of this anguish.

THE

DESIRE FOR DEATH

3

I phoned my mother recently, and among the updates about her grandchildren and the family, she said, "Do you remember my friends Kevin and Julie?" I said I did. "Do you remember their son Steve? He was just a year younger than you." I said I thought I might, vaguely. "Well, they just had awful, *awful* news on Steve. He hanged himself last week, just after his girlfriend left for work." I asked the usual questions about Steve's state of mind before his death ("happy as far as anyone knew," my mom said) and his circumstances (happy with his girlfriend though struggling to find a career, according to my mom).

There was a painful subtext to the conversation—my dad, her husband, died by suicide too, years ago. We didn't really need to speak the subtext; it was clear already, and it amounted to a one-word question—"Why?" Why did my dad do that? Why did Steve do that?

Later that night I searched for Steve's name on the Internet, and found his obituary as well as a kind of virtual guest book where people could express condolences and memories. There was no mention of work or career anywhere, though there was this: "Steve was recently re-baptized as a Christian and was a member of Springview Church, and he had found great joy in his renewed faith."

Great joy in faith, and yet dead by suicide in his thirties? My dad was also very religious and involved in his church, yet dead by suicide in his fifties.

The desire for life—life-sustaining desire—can't be about faith and religion only, or else Steve and my dad would be alive. What is it about, then? Career success does not really constitute a satisfying answer either. For one thing, plenty of people who do not have particularly satisfying careers never consider suicide; for another, a lot of people who die by suicide appear to have had successful careers. Six weeks before my dad's death, he made a very large amount of money in a stock deal. A child of the 1930s, my dad had worked toward a deal like that most of his life. He might have said that that *was* his life's desire, along with his faith and family; his death six weeks later shows that somehow he was mistaken.

How was he mistaken, though? Many prominent psychologists and others have considered psychological needs as a way to understand human motivation and human nature. Several lists of needs exist, and a premise associated with them is that people are highly motivated to meet these needs. When they do, the theory goes, well-being and health are achieved. Of course, the flipside to this is that frustrated needs can lead to an array of problems.

Perhaps the most famous work on this topic is that of Henry Murray,[1] who identified twenty such needs, including autonomy, nurturance, play, understanding, dominance, and achievement, among others. Shneidman, heavily influenced by Murray, highlights these needs as well, postulating that the thwarting of them leads to psychache and thus to suicidality.[2] These theorists might have guessed that though my dad belonged to a church and had career success, something was still missing—some of his fundamental needs were still not being met.

But which needs? Exactly how many are there, and are some more important than others? Models including as many as twenty needs pose a problem for a model of suicide based on needs. Given that there are so many needs and thus so many people with one or more thwarted needs, how to understand that very, very few of these people attempt suicide, and fewer still die by suicide?

Murray was aware of this problem. He wrote, "In many cases the succorance drive is subsidiary to the *need for affiliation* (a basic tendency, whose aim is to establish and maintain friendly relationships with others)."[3] I am intrigued that Murray believed the need for affiliation was a superordinate need, because as I have noted already and will expand on in this chapter, I do too, and more to the point, I believe that the thwarting of this need is a main component of the desire for death.

Shneidman, writing specifically of suicide, stated, "For practical purposes, most suicides tend to fall into one of five clusters of psychological needs. They reflect different kinds of psychological pain."[4] The five are thwarted love, ruptured relationships, assaulted self-image, fractured control, and excessive anger related to frustrated needs for dominance.

My solution to this problem is to assert two bedrock needs, the fulfillment of which satisfies most others and can compensate for frustration of other needs. The thwarting of both of these needs constitutes the desire for death. Shneidman's five failed needs are important, but they are collapsible into the two major categories of thwarted belongingness (i.e., thwarted love, ruptured relationships) and perceived burdensomeness (assaulted self-image, fractured control, anger related to frustrated dominance).

Regarding the first bedrock need, belongingness, the need to belong involves a "combination of frequent interaction plus persistent caring."[5] Thus, there are two components of a fully satisfied need to belong: interactions with others and a feeling of being cared about. In order to meet the need to belong, the interactions an individual has must be frequent and positive. Interactions within a stable relationship will more fully satisfy the need to belong than interactions with a changing cast of relationship partners (i.e., higher levels of stability). The need to belong will be only partially met if an individual feels cared about but does not have face-to-face interactions with the relationship partner (i.e., greater proximity). The model of suicidal behavior developed here asserts that an unmet need to belong is a contributor to suicidal desire: suicidal individuals may experience interactions that do not satisfy their need to belong (e.g., relationships that are unpleasant, unstable, infrequent, or without proximity) or may not feel connected to others and cared about.

I would argue that the other bedrock need is effectiveness or a sense of competence. When this need is thwarted, when one perceives oneself as ineffective, it is painful indeed. To perceive oneself as so ineffective that loved ones are threatened and burdened is even worse, so much so that the desire for death could be generated. The perspective taken here proposes that feelings of ineffectiveness contribute to the desire for suicide, and moreover, that feeling ineffective to the degree that others are burdened is among the strongest sources of all for the desire for suicide.

Those who view themselves as a burden on others have a negative self-image, feel out of control of their lives, and possess a range of negative emotions stemming from the sense that their incapacity spills over to affect others besides themselves.

Thwarted Effectiveness: The Sense that One Is a Burden

If you let yourself down, the experience is not pleasant, but it is contained—it affects just you. If you let your group down, you experience all the negative aspects of letting yourself down (because you are part of the group), but you also experience the sense that your ineffectiveness is not contained, that it negatively affects others.

To take a relatively trivial example, I returned to playing soccer recently, after a layoff of a couple of weeks because of injury and travel commitments. I didn't play very well. I was tentative because I was a little concerned about re-injury, and I was not energetic, because I was out of shape after the layoff. I was disappointed in myself and had the sense that my teammates felt that way about me too. Not pleasant.

So why didn't I just quit? And why didn't my teammates want me to quit? The main reason, I think, is that my teammates and I remember that I have a track record of holding my own, of contributing to the team. Relatedly, everyone understands or at least hopes that my injury-related tentativeness and my layoff-induced lack of stamina are remediable—I can recover from both with time and training.

But what if I judged that my failings were not remediable, that I was a burden to my team and would be permanently? And what if I thought my teammates felt the same way? Under such conditions, I might very well quit the team. In this scenario, I have perceived myself to be a burden on others and, lacking the remedy of time and training, am left with quitting the team as my only solution.

I believe this example, though trivial, is analogous to the non-trivial, life-and-death psychological processes of people seriously contemplating suicide. They perceive themselves to be ineffective or incompetent, but it's not just that. They also perceive that their ineffectiveness affects others, too. Finally, they perceive that this ineffectiveness that negatively affects everyone is stable and permanent, forcing a choice between continued perceptions of burdening others and escalating feelings of shame, on the one hand, or death on the other hand.

When I refer to "perceived burdensomeness," I would like to emphasize the term *perceived*. People who are contemplating suicide *perceive* themselves a burden, and *perceive* that this state is permanent and stable, with death as a solution to the problem. It is very important to point out that their perceptions are mistaken. Indeed, that their perceptions are mistaken is the basis for the psychotherapeutic treatment of suicidal symptoms. Any perception, mistaken or not, can influence behavior. My contention is that perceived burdensomeness, though mistaken, influences suicidal behavior.

The idea that how others see us and how we see ourselves is a life-or-death matter is not hard to fathom. For example, duels to the death were a common feature of society in Europe from the Renaissance to the First World War. Duelling claimed the lives of hundreds of thousands of Europeans. Often, the disputes leading up to duels were very petty (e.g., a duel in 1678 in Paris occurred because one man said another's apartment was tasteless; another duel was over ownership of an Angora cat).[6] The causes may have been petty, but the duels themselves were serious, not only in the obvious sense of the possibility of death, but also regarding *standing* in one's own and others' eyes. In some societies, to have won a duel was to establish oneself as a man. To have fled one was a dishonor worse than death.

But surely we have left to the past such things as duels? Apparently not. R. E. Nisbett, D. Cohen, and colleagues have conducted fascinating research on cultures of honor. In the United States, "the South and West have developed 'cultures of honor,' in which insults and threats to reputation, self, home, or family are taken quite seriously and are often met with violence."[7] These researchers have documented that the U.S. South and West do in fact have more of certain forms of violence (e.g., murder in reaction to a threat) than other areas of the United States. People in these regions who perceive themselves as dishonored may be especially prone to suicide. Is suicide more common in culture-of-honor states?

Interestingly, excluding Alaska (which is ranked sixth, and which has a distinct cultural heritage), all fifteen of the states with the highest suicide rates are culture-of-honor states—specifically, New Mexico, Montana, Nevada, Wyoming, Colorado, West Virginia, Idaho,

Oklahoma, Oregon, Arizona, Arkansas, Florida, Utah, South Dakota, and Delaware. The association of suicide rates with culture-of-honor states is even higher than the association of murder with "culture of honor" states—eleven of fifteen culture-of-honor states are in the top fifteen with regard to murder rates; the four non-South and non-West exceptions in the top fifteen are Illinois, Indiana, Michigan, and Missouri.

Our sense of effectiveness—the view that we are not burdens but rather contributors—can be sustaining. By contrast, feeling ineffective and helpless can be life-draining. "Learned helplessness" experiments on animals illustrate this point. In these experiments, some animals learn helplessness by being exposed to noxious stimuli (e.g., shock) from which they cannot escape; other animals are also exposed to the aversive stimuli but have the ability to escape and thus do not develop helplessness. It appears that helplessness suppressed animals' will to live, as evidenced by passivity and appetite suppression, for example.[8] In fact, Seligman made this connection in his description of rats who had not learned helplessness and swam for days to avoid drowning, as compared to those who had learned helplessness and drowned almost immediately.[9] Also germane to the will to live, self-efficacy—the opposite of perceived burdensomeness—was a significant predictor of survival in a study of patients with chronic obstructive pulmonary disease.[10] Relatedly, it has also been found that people with positive perceptions of aging, measured as much as twenty-three years earlier, lived an average of 7.5 years longer than those with less positive self-perceptions of aging, even accounting for variables like age, gender, socioeconomic status, loneliness, and functional health.[11] Feeling effective, like a contributor instead of a burden, can be life-saving.

The specific role of perceived burdensomeness in suicidal behavior is clear in some cultures. There have been reports that among the

Yuit Eskimos of St. Lawrence Island, for example, those who become too sick, infirm, or old may threaten the group's survival; in the past, the explicit and socially sanctioned solution to this problem was ritual suicide. Reportedly, the ritual was graphic, often involving the family members' participation in the shooting or hanging of the victim.[12] There is some question as to the veracity of this specific example, but the general pattern has been noted many times in Eskimo cultures.[13] Arguably, this represents an example of anecdotal evidence being quite persuasive—cultures have sanctioned ritual suicide specifically in response to burdensomeness. Another example is ancient Ceos, where the law obliged all inhabitants over sixty years of age to die by drinking hemlock to make room for the next generation (a law that apparently was enforced only in times of famine).[14]

Similarly, among the ancient Scythians, it was a great honor to die by suicide when one was too old to continue in and contribute to their nomadic lifestyle. Quintus Curtius, who described the Scythians, said: "Among them exists a sort of wild and bestial men to whom they give the name of sages. The anticipation of the time of death is a glory in their eyes, and they have themselves burned alive as soon as age or sickness begins to trouble them."[15]

In 2004, as reported on the news website Ananova.com, an elderly Malaysian couple died by suicide by jumping from the fifteenth floor of their apartment building specifically because they did not want to be a burden on their family. Their suicide note read, "If we had waited for our death due to sickness, we would have caused much inconvenience to all of you." Ritual murder of widows among the Lusi people in New Guinea has been described as essentially suicidal: "A Lusi widow would rather die than be dependent on her children; Lusi widowers are not viewed as a burden on their kin and are not ritually killed by their kin."[16]

Examples like this illustrate that perceived burdensomeness could play a role in suicidal behavior and also shows the link, mentioned in Chapter 1, between perceived burdensomeness and Durkheim's concept of altruistic suicide. For Durkheim, altruistic suicides occur when people are so integrated into social groups that individuality fades, and they become willing to sacrifice themselves to the group's interests. My account also emphasizes self-sacrifice in context of the perception that others will benefit, but I do not think this usually occurs when people are especially connected to a group—in fact quite the contrary, as will be expanded on in the next section on failed belongingness.

Returning for now to the concept of perceived burdensomeness, some material from suicide notes also illustrates its potential role in suicidal behavior. A seventy-year-old man wrote "Survival of the fittest. Adios—unfit."[17] The closing line from musician Kurt Cobain's suicide note (addressed to his wife Courtney regarding their daughter Frances) provides anecdotal evidence that perceived burdensomeness is implicated in suicide: "Please keep going Courtney for Frances for her life which will be so much happier without me." A suicide note left by a teenage girl who died by electrocution read, "I have just been a very bad person, but now you are all rid of me."

Shneidman summarized several other examples from suicide notes: "Life is unmanageable. I'm like a helpless 12 year old" (from a 74-year-old widowed woman who died by self-cutting); "The failures and frustrations overwhelm me" (from a 49-year-old married man who died by self-inflicted gunshot wound).[18]

Perhaps the clearest example cited by Shneidman is from a woman's suicide notes to her ex-husband and her daughters. To her ex-husband, she writes, "[the girls] need two happy people, not a sick, mixed-up mother. There will be a little money to help with the extras—it had better go that way than for more pills and more doctor bills." To her daughters, she writes, "Try to forgive me for what

I've done—your father would be so much better for you. It will be harder for you for awhile—but so much easier in the long run—I'm getting you all mixed up."[19]

Another example: "I started to list the people who wouldn't mind if I wasn't around. I clearly wasn't a good wife for my ex-husband. He wouldn't miss me. And I never felt that comfortable in my role as a mom—didn't feel like I was a good mom necessarily . . . It's like I'll be a burden off their backs. Clearly their lives will be enhanced because I'm not around. At that point, I honestly felt I was doing them a favor."[20]

Alvarez quoted a man who had spent most of his life in mental institutions: "If I commit suicide, it will not be to destroy myself but to put myself back together again. Suicide will be for me only one means of violently reconquering myself . . . By suicide I reintroduce my design in nature, I shall for the first time give things the shape of my will."[21] A paraphrasing of his words would be that "I feel so ineffective that I focus on one sure way I can have dramatic effect, namely my own death by suicide." The man's words can also be seen as another example of the blending of life and death that I believe occurs in at least some instances of serious suicidal behavior. In Chapter 2, I described Shneidman's example of Ariel, who viewed things in the cemetery as "graceful" and "gracious." The blending seemed to be of death by suicide with beauty and caring. In this man's example, by contrast, the blending seems to be of death by suicide with a lively sense of taking charge and imposing will. One type seems to involve seeing suicide as a means to belong or be cared for; the other type as a means to feel effective—these types correspond to the bedrock issues of thwarted belongingness and perceived burdensomeness.

Research studies also show a connection between feeling ineffective or being a burden on the one hand, and feeling suicidal on the other. In the sections below, this work is summarized, starting with research on the general connection between depressive symptoms (one of which is suicidality) and experiences of ineffectiveness, especially in social domains.

Social Skills and Depression

There is little doubt that depression and suicidality are associated with social skills problems.[22] People with depression consistently evaluate their own social skills more negatively than do nondepressed people[23]—this result applies to depressed children as well as depressed adults.[24]

Given the pessimistic outlook associated with depression and suicidality, it is not too surprising that depressed people evaluate their social skills negatively. But is there an objective basis for their negative evaluations; that is, do others also rate their social skills negatively? In fact, when observers or conversational partners rate depressed people's social skills, a common finding is that depressed people's skills are rated as lower than those of nondepressed controls.[25]

A related line of research has examined the communication behaviors of depressed versus nondepressed people. For example, as compared to nondepressed people, depressed people speak more slowly, and with less volume and voice modulation; depressed people have longer pauses in their speech patterns, and take longer to respond when someone else addresses them.[26] Voice modulation and rate account for the animated and appealing qualities of speech; because depressed and suicidal people's speech often lacks these qualities, they are often negatively perceived by others.

In addition to the quality of speech, the content of speech in depression has been evaluated. In studies of married couples with a depressed member, themes involving dysphoric feelings and negative self-evaluation were likely to emerge in their conversations.[27] It has been found that depressed people may be at their most expressive with their spouses when they are discussing negative issues.[28] There is some evidence that negativity in social interactions is particularly likely to emerge between depressed people and intimate relationship partners (as opposed to strangers or nonintimate acquaintances). For example, in a study of depressed and nondepressed students discussing "events of the day" with either a friend or a stranger, researchers reported that depressed students tended to withhold negative verbal content when talking with strangers but were more likely to disclose negative topics when talking with a friend.[29] Other work has found that depressed people are more likely than nondepressed people to make unsolicited negative self-disclosures.[30] This problem may be particularly acute in relationships between depressed people and intimate others. Depressed and suicidal people, then, are likely to instill negative views of themselves in others, perhaps especially those close to them.

This research shows that depressive symptoms (a key one of which is suicidality) are associated with feelings of social ineffectiveness, and that these may manifest particularly in close relationships. These findings are roughly consistent with the view espoused here, that an extreme form of ineffectiveness, perceived burdensomeness, is implicated in suicidality, but it would be more satisfying if studies focused specifically on perceived burdensomeness and suicidality. In the next section, several such studies are summarized.

Perceived Burdensomeness Contributes to Suicidality

To my knowledge, five studies have been framed as direct tests of the possibility that perceived burdensomeness is involved in serious suicidal behavior; all five affirm the connection. One study was conducted to test DeCatanzaro's model of self-preservation and self-destruction.[31] Arguing from a sociobiological or evolutionary standpoint, this model posits that staying alive actually may reduce inclusive fitness for an individual if the individual is low in reproductive potential and if the individual's continuing to live poses such a burden to close kin that it costs them opportunities for reproduction. One upshot of this view is that suicidal behavior may have been selected for in the course of evolution—a controversial point to which I return later.

To test this model, Brown and colleagues conducted a questionnaire study of college students and found the predicted correlation between feeling a burden on kin and suicidality. Burdensomeness stood out as a unique and specific predictor of suicide-related symptoms even when other variables, such as the individual's reproductive potential, were accounted for.[32]

My students and I also conducted empirical tests of the association between perceived burdensomeness and suicidal behavior. We trained raters to evaluate actual suicide notes regarding the following dimensions: perceived burdensomeness, hopelessness, and generalized emotional pain. The raters read each note and then made three separate ratings on a 1-to-5 scale of the amount of perceived burdensomeness, hopelessness, and generalized emotional pain conveyed by the note.

Unknown to the raters, half of the notes were from people who died by suicide, and half were from people who attempted suicide and survived. The goal of the study was to compare perceived burdensomeness versus Shneidman's emphasis on emotional pain versus Beck's emphasis on hopelessness. In statistical analyses, the notes from those who died by suicide contained more perceived burdensomeness than notes from attempters; no effects were found regarding hopelessness and emotional pain. This study's relatively stringent comparison of notes from those who died by suicide to notes from those who attempted and survived (which distinction was unknown to raters), with perceived burdensomeness emerging as the only unique predictor of death by suicide, added to our confidence in the results.[33]

Moreover, a second study from this same paper on a separate collection of notes took a similar approach, except that all notes were from those who died by suicide, and perceived burdensomeness, hopelessness, and generalized emotional pain were used as predictors of lethality of suicide method (e.g., self-inflicted gunshot wound was viewed as relatively more lethal than overdose). Here again, perceived burdensomeness was a significant predictor of lethality, whereas hopelessness and generalized emotional pain were not. The convergence of the two studies made the findings more persuasive.

A survey on reproductive behavior, quality of family contacts, and suicidal ideation on several hundred community participants as well as on five high-suicide-risk groups (e.g., general psychiatric patients and incarcerated psychiatric patients) found that perceived burdensomeness toward family and social isolation were especially correlated with suicidal ideation.[34] It is important to note that these two variables correspond to two of the three main aspects of the present model, burdensomeness and lack of belonging.

My students and I recently completed a study on perceived burdensomeness and suicidality among 343 adult outpatients of the Florida State University Psychology Clinic. Areas of diagnosis for these patients were represented in the following proportions: 39 percent mood disorder, 14.6 percent anxiety disorder, 6 percent substance use disorder, 12.2 percent personality disorder, 9 percent adjustment disorder, and 18 percent other disorders.

We hypothesized that perceived burdensomeness would directly relate to both past number of suicide attempts and an index of current suicidal symptoms, and furthermore, that this relationship would exist even when accounting for known risk factors such as personality disorder status, depressive symptoms, and hopelessness. This is similar to the "kitchen sink" approach in our paper described in the last chapter. We also wanted to see if there was a special connection between perceived burdensomeness and suicidality. So, for purposes of comparison, the associations of hopelessness to suicide indices (controlling for personality disorder status, depressive symptoms, and perceived burdensomeness) were examined. Our reasoning was that if perceived burdensomeness is important in suicidality, its associations to suicidality should be as rigorous as those regarding the documented risk factor of hopelessness.

Here, as in other studies, the connection of perceived burdensomeness to suicidality was supported. Specifically, there was an association between measures of perceived burdensomeness and suicidality, and this association persisted even when a host of other variables was accounted for (specifically, age, gender, hopelessness, depressive symptoms, and personality disorder status). Furthermore, the link between perceived burdensomeness and suicidality was at least as strong as that between hopelessness and suicidality.

Other Research on Burdensomeness and Suicidality
Although not direct tests of the burdensomeness view of suicidality, several other studies have reported results consistent with this perspective. For example, in a study on genuine suicide attempts vs. nonsuicidal self-injury, genuine attempts were defined as those with lethal intent and bodily injury; nonsuicidal injury involved things like superficial cuts made without the intent to die. The researchers reported that genuine suicide attempts were often characterized by a desire to make others better off, whereas nonsuicidal self-injury was often characterized by desires to express anger or punish oneself.[35] "Making others better off" is similar in concept to perceived burdensomeness. In this study, as in those reviewed earlier, an index related to perceived burdensomeness was associated with relatively severe suicidal behavior. Persuasive aspects of the study were that suicide attempters were compared to a compelling control group (those engaging in nonsuicidal self-injury), and that effects of burdensomeness were compared to effects of other relevant dimensions,

such as anger expression and self-punishment, with burdensomeness emerging as among the most important.

One might imagine that feelings of burdensomeness might be particularly acute among depressed, terminally ill people. In fact, Filiberti and colleagues studied vulnerability factors for suicide in five terminal cancer patients who died by suicide while they were cared for at home by palliative care teams.[36] Of all the various possible factors identified, being a burden on others was judged to be one of the two most important. Interestingly, the other was fear of the loss of general competence, which, according to the current model, is a related but weaker form of perceived burdensomeness. In a study mentioned earlier on 3,005 psychiatric patients at risk for suicide, of whom thirty-eight died by suicide within two months of evaluation, nine clear risk factors were identified, among which were feelings of being a burden on others.[37]

O'Reilly and colleagues reached similar conclusions. They studied psychiatrists' reports on their patients' suicides, and of the three variables seen as frequently present in the month preceding suicide, one was "feeling a burden on others." The two others, incidentally, were related to thwarted belongingness—social withdrawal and turning down help from others.[38]

If burdensomeness were involved in suicidality, one might expect that suicidal patients' self-views would be especially discrepant from how they view other people. In a telling study, researchers compared self-views as well as views of other people among suicidal patients and psychiatric and nonpsychiatric controls. Not surprisingly, the suicidal patients endorsed more negative self-views than the other two groups, similar to the research reviewed earlier in which depressed people evaluated their social skills negatively. Notably, the suicidal patients rated other people more favorably than did the other two groups.[39] The conclusion is that suicidal people view themselves in quite negative terms, and this is particularly true when their self-views are compared to their views of other people. This marked discrepancy in suicidal people between self-ratings and views of others could instill a sense of burdensomeness—the idea that "I'm bad but I'm especially bad when compared to others, who are good."

A roughly similar dynamic emerged in a study of chronically ill patients. The researchers predicted that among chronically ill patients who are dependent on a caregiving spouse (but whose health status prevents their reciprocating the care), receipt of support may exacerbate feelings of burdensomeness, and thus may increase suicidality. This hypothesis was in "grave danger of refutation" (Popper, 1959), given the pervasive positive associations between social support and health. But the hypothesis survived the test—the study found a *positive* correlation between social support and suicidal ideation among physically ill participants.[40]

The concept of perceived burdensomeness is fairly easy to understand as applied to adults—the image of the failed breadwinner imagining his family will be better off without him is tragic but not hard to conceive. But what about perceived burdensomeness as applied to younger people, including children? Young people do die by suicide, and so if perceived burdensomeness plays a role in suicide in general, it should be applicable to youth too. In fact, researchers have studied burdensomeness and suicidality in youth in their work on the "expendable child."[41] These authors hypothesized that suicidal adolescents would be rated higher on a measure of expendability than would be a psychiatric control group. The expendability measure specifically included a sense of being a burden on one's family. Results conformed to predictions: Suicidal youth scored higher on the expendability measure than did a psychiatric comparison group.

Studies of youth like this one suggest that the concept of burdensomeness may affect a broad range of ages. Related to feeling a burden on one's family, suicide attempts among children have been linked to perceived inability to meet parental demands.[42] Again, the emphasis on the term *perceived* bears repeating; the facile explanation that parents are responsible for their children's death by suicide because of high demands is hardly worth considering. However, the explanation that people who *perceive* themselves as not measuring up and as being a burden are prone to suicidal behavior is more serious and is supported by numerous research studies.

The potential importance of perceived burdensomeness emerged in a study of low-income, abused African-American women. This study identified protective and risk factors that differentiated suicide attempters from those who had never made an attempt. Protective factors associated with nonattempter status included self-efficacy as well as effectiveness in obtaining material resources.[43] In the current framework, these results could be viewed as suggesting that those who feel effective in general, as well as effective in providing material resources in particular, are buffered from feeling a burden and thus at relatively low risk for suicidality.[44]

Data on suicide in the Netherlands in the early twentieth century are in accord with a role for perceived burdensomeness as well. A higher suicide rate in rural as compared to urban areas was noted and was attributed to "the peculiar conditions of the Dutch farming system under which the aged find themselves a burden,"[45] an experience not shared by older Dutch people in the cities.

One implication of the burdensomeness view is that suicides may be more common during difficult economic times; when resources are strained, the consequences of perceived burdensomeness may be more acute (for example, the socially sanctioned suicide among the Yuit Eskimos of St. Lawrence Island outlined earlier in this chapter). Other data support this view. A significant association between deprivation and the suicide rate in thirty-two London boroughs has been documented. This study is unique in contemporaneously studying closely contiguous and roughly culturally homogenous areas that nevertheless vary with regard to socioeconomic variables and suicide rate.[46] Several others have reached the conclusion that economic prosperity has a beneficial impact and economic downturns a detrimental effect on suicide rates.[47] In a study of suicide in African-American men, the risk of suicide was higher in areas where occupational and income inequalities between African-Americans and Caucasians were greater.[48] At the individual level, too, several studies have found that financial hardship constitutes a risk factor for suicide.[49]

Suicidal Behavior in an Evolutionary Context
Some believe that suicidal behavior must have conferred some benefit in the course of evolution, in part because it is common across cultures today. But how would a behavior that leads to pain, impairment, and death produce any sort of increased ability to pass on one's genes?

According to DeCatanzaro's[50] model of self-preservation and self-destruction, there are conditions under which death may produce an adaptive advantage. Specifically, death may produce an evolutionary edge for an individual who has few prospects for reproduction and who poses such a burden to close kin—who carry his or her genes—that it reduces *their* prospects for reproduction.

For any case for adaptive benefit to be made, a lot of compelling evidence would need to be marshalled (and even then, as I will point out, questions will remain). For example, if suicidal behavior is an exclusively human phenomenon not occurring in other primates and animals, then the case for evolved behavior becomes more difficult. If, by contrast, suicidal behavior is documented in primates and other animals, the case is not made, but it may become a little easier to imagine.

Is suicidal behavior an exclusively human phenomenon? Many presume it to be so. For example, the promotional material for

Shneidman's *The Suicidal Mind*[51] makes the claim that "suicide is an exclusively human response to extreme psychological pain." In *Conceptions of Modern Psychiatry,* the American psychiatrist Harry Stack Sullivan stated, "So far as we know, there is nothing remotely approaching [suicide] in the infrahuman primates or any of the lower animals. It is a distinctly human performance."[52]

The most famous possible case—lemmings dying by mass suicide in a kind of intentional population control effort—is not really a case at all. Lemmings do die en masse, but this is because they migrate en masse after they exhaust their food source—a type of slow-growing moss—and many die in the hardship and chaos of the migration.

Still, Shneidman and Sullivan may have been wrong in thinking that suicide is an exclusively human phenomenon. Perhaps the clearest examples of animal suicidal behavior involve a phenomenon dubbed "adaptive suicide" in insects and possibly in birds. For instance, researchers have studied pea aphids, which are parasitized by a specific species of wasp.[53] The wasp injects an egg into the host aphid; the young wasp matures inside the aphid, feeding upon its organs. When the wasp is ready to emerge as an adult, it chews a hole out the back of the aphid's body. Aphid populations can be devastated by parasitic wasps.

Recall that DeCatanzaro theorized that self-sacrifice carries survival value for an individual who has few prospects for reproduction and who poses such a burden to close kin—who carry his or her genes—that it reduces *their* prospects for reproduction. The parasitized pea aphid could be viewed as just such an individual—prospects for reproduction are few, because death is imminent; a potential burden is posed to close kin, because the parasite wasp will live on to infect other pea aphids. Aphids parasitized early in development, and who thus would not produce any offspring, frequently engage in a kind of "aphid suicide"—specifically, they drop from their host plant to the ground, where they are frequently preyed on by ladybugs and other natural predators.

Worker bumblebees parasitized by a specific species of fly will often abandon their nest altogether, cutting themselves off from the hive and ensuring their death. The bees' behavior can be seen as an instance of adaptive suicide because the parasitized bee's premature death kills the parasite and avoids its spread in the bee colony.[54]

A similar phenomenon may affect birds. Under famine conditions, evolutionary pressures may select for behaviors like fratricide (one member of a brood killing its sibling), infanticide (a parent killing the offspring), and suicide (by the nestling with the shortest life expectancy, which abandons the nest prematurely).[55] This kind of self-sacrifice is sort of what Durkheim had in mind (though from an entirely different perspective) when he wrote about altruistic suicide, which he defined as self-sacrifice for the good of the group. A key difference, however, is that adaptive suicide takes place not for the good of the group, but for the good of one's own genes.

Perhaps an even clearer example of self-sacrifice for the good of one's genes occurs in the Australian redback spider. Male redback spiders submit to being cannibalized by females after sex. They do so apparently because they thereby gain advantages in the competition for females: Cannibalized males copulate longer and fertilize more eggs as compared to males that survive copulation. Also, female redbacks are more likely to reject subsequent males after consuming their first mate.[56] Self-sacrifice has been selected for in the course of male redback spider evolution.

Self-injurious behavior has been documented in nonhuman primates; most studies are on rhesus monkeys. The form of their self-injury is usually self-biting—at times of distress, some monkeys will bite their arms or legs, sometimes causing injury. This body of research suggests that self-injury in nonhuman primates is a way to self-regulate at times of stress (e.g., accelerated heart rate decreases when the behavior is enacted). Animals with early stress experiences are vulnerable to the behavior, suggesting that these early experiences disrupted the development of more normal stress-regulation abilities. Self-injury as a means to regulate emotions has been documented in humans too, of course, particularly among those with borderline personality disorder.

Apart from adaptive suicide in insects, birds, and spiders, there is very little evidence of death by suicide in animals. There is at least one claim that dogs sometimes die by suicide—by drowning or by food refusal in response to being cast out of a household or remorse[57]—but this assertion would need more systematic scientific support before it is given much credence.

I said earlier that I believe suicidal people are mistaken when they view themselves as burdens. An adaptive suicide viewpoint would suggest otherwise—specifically, that suicidal behavior evolved in humans to remove actual (not just perceived) burdens from kin and thus facilitate kin's survival. In fact, when researchers interviewed the significant others of eighty-one people who had recently attempted suicide, a majority of significant others reported that their support of the patient represented a burden to them.[58]

Nevertheless, I do not much like this adaptive suicide view; my own dad died by suicide and the idea that he was an actual burden is offensive. My view is that self-sacrifice is adaptive in some animal species. It may have been adaptive under certain conditions in the course of human evolution, but we will never really know. Most important, it does not really matter now. What matters now is that perceived burdensomeness—and, to the extent that it exists, actual burdensomeness—are remediable through perception- and skill-based psychotherapies. Death is no longer adaptive, if it ever was.

A Note on Life Insurance

Perceived burdensomeness implies a kind of calculation along the lines of, "my death will be more valuable to others than my life." It is interesting to consider the issue of life insurance in this regard. The usual life insurance policy will pay for death by suicide provided that the death occurs two years or more after the initiation of the policy. If the death occurs before two years have passed, a usual practice is that premiums plus interest are returned, but the policy is not paid.

If people are considering suicide and they imagine that their death will confer benefits to loved ones, then life insurance could enter into suicidal people's thinking. A higher benefit could conceivably encourage suicide. It would be interesting to know the percentage of those who die by suicide with life insurance versus the percentage of those who die by other means with life insurance. Any comparison like this should adjust for demographics, which are very different between those who die by suicide versus those who die by other means. One way to do this would be to limit comparisons to one ethnicity and age range, say, white men over fifty. If, after such adjustments, more suicides are insured, it would suggest that life insurance possibly figured into the calculations made by suicidal people. It would only be suggestive, though, because other factors could have influenced the data. Perhaps a personality variable like lack of optimism would explain both the tendency to take out life insurance policies and a tendency toward suicidal behavior.

Perhaps not surprisingly, data on this issue are hard to come by. In the 1920s and 1930s, Metropolitan Life paid out more life insurance money per claim on suicide versus other deaths, though it was not clear that this was corrected for gender and ethnicity. The figures in 1925 were $2,283 (suicide) versus $1,867 (nonsuicide). In 1931, the respective figures were $3,580 versus $2,216.[59] These numbers are obviously quite dated, but suicide often remains the most expensive category of death for life insurance companies today.

As with the findings related to the acquired ability to enact lethal self-injury, alternative explanations exist for some of the results linking perceived burdensomeness to suicidality (e.g., the studies on increased suicide in difficult economic times are amenable to many interpretations). Relatively few studies have explicitly tested the specific role of perceived burdensomeness in suicidality. On the positive side, every study specifically examining burdensomeness and suicidality had stringent features, and each produced results supportive of the role of burdensomeness in serious suicidality. As with the findings on acquired ability to enact lethal self-injury, the results reviewed on burdensomeness were from a wide array of topic areas, samples, and methodologies. That such diverse data are at least consistent with the parsimonious construct of perceived burdensomeness inspires some confidence in its role in suicidality.

The current model asserts that to perceive oneself as so ineffective that loved ones are threatened and burdened is a source for the desire for suicide. *Perceived* burdensomeness, not actual burdensomeness, is the key variable in this account. Empirical data to date, including studies explicitly testing this assertion, are supportive. Assuming the capability for suicide, perceived burdensomeness removes one of the two key barriers to suicide. Even for a person who has acquired the capability for suicide and perceives him- or herself to be a burden, there remains one "saving grace"—belongingness. In my view, if the need to belong is satisfied, the will to live remains intact.

Thwarted Connectedness: The Sense that One Does Not Belong

William James, in *The Principles of Psychology* (1890), wrote, "No more fiendish punishment could be devised, were such a thing physically possible, than that one should be turned loose in society and remain absolutely unnoticed by all the members thereof. If no one turned around when we entered, answered when we spoke, or minded what we did, but if every person we met 'cut us dead,' and acted as if we were non-existent things, a kind of rage and impotent despair would before long well up in us, from which the cruelest bodily torture would be a relief." I think James's use of the phrase "cut us dead" is telling, as is the insight that bodily torture can, under some circumstances, be a relief.

The need to belong is a fundamental human motive. When this need is thwarted, numerous negative effects on health, adjustment, and well-being have been documented. It is interesting to note that the pain of thwarted belongingness may activate similar brain areas as physical pain. It has long been known that a brain center called the anterior cingulate cortex is important for the processing of physical pain signals. Eisenberger and colleagues[60] obtained brain scans of undergraduates as they played "cyberball." "Cyberball" is a computerized ball-tossing game. Participants believed they were playing with two other players, and during the game, the two players excluded the participant. In reality, there were no other players; participants were playing with a preset computer program.

If someone is in a brain scan machine and receives a pain stimulus, the scan will show activity in the anterior cingulate cortex. Similarly, for participants who were excluded during "cyberball" and received the psychological pain stimulus of feeling socially excluded, the brain scan detected activity in the anterior cingulate cortex. The researchers argued that evolutionary processes had recruited the physical pain system to warn us of something potentially as dangerous as physical pain—namely, social exclusion or ostracism (which is like death, figuratively and often literally, for highly social animals). The need to belong is psychologically fundamental, and may have been fundamental in conferring evolutionary benefits to our ancestors.

My view is that this need to belong is so powerful that, when satisfied, it can prevent suicide even when perceived burdensomeness and the acquired ability to enact lethal self-injury are in place. By the same token, when the need is thwarted, risk for suicide is increased. This perspective, incidentally, is similar to that of Durkheim, who proposed that suicide results, in part, from failure of social integration.

Some of the Stoic philosophers were proponents of rational suicide, but even they could not overcome the need to belong. For example, Seneca said, "Does life please you? Live on. Does it not? Go from whence you came. No vast wound is necessary; a mere puncture will secure your liberty. It is a bad thing (you say) to be under the necessity of living; but there is no necessity in the case. Thanks be to the gods, nobody can be compelled to live." But when Seneca became seriously ill and desired suicide, he could not carry through, specifically because he could not bear to think of how his father would react. His connection to his father prevented his suicide. (I believe he also underestimated the ease with which suicide is completed—his statement that "No vast wound is necessary; a mere puncture will secure your liberty" contrasts with statements in Chapter 2 about the extreme difficulty of death by suicide.) Notably, Seneca later died by suicide, but well after his father's death.

This same sentiment is often expressed in suicide risk assessments. When asked about the likelihood of suicide, many patients respond that though they have thought of suicide, their connection to a loved one makes it impossible (e.g., "I couldn't do that to so-and-so"). This is of course no guarantee that someone will not attempt suicide, but, as noted below, this clinical anecdote has some empirical support. Women with numerous children may be less prone to suicide than women with no or few children, for example.[61]

In his work *The Metaphysics of Ethics,* Immanuel Kant writes, "To dispose of one's life for some fancied end is to degrade the humanity subsisting in his person, and entrusted to him that he might uphold and preserve it." Kant misses the perspective of the truly suicidal individual, whose belongingness is so thwarted that she or he does not feel connected to humanity, and who feels that *living* life, not dying, degrades humanity.

Sylvia Plath, the poet who died by suicide at the age of thirty, wrote, "So daddy, I'm finally through. / The black telephone's off at the root, / The voices just can't worm through." I think these lines convey that thwarted belongingness is more than just loneliness; rather, it is the sense that sustaining connections are obliterated ("off at the root"). These lines also conflate belongingness and death (voices worming), which can be seen as an instance of the pattern mentioned previously, in which imminently suicidal people fuse death and life.

Shneidman's Ariel recalled that on the day of her self-immolation "I had various friends that I did know and it just seemed like they really just didn't have time for me." Just before her self-immolation, Ariel described going to her friends' house to return a borrowed toaster; she wrote, "I remember just walking in and walking through the house and by this time I was sobbing again. And not one word was said to me by these people . . . And I just walked through the house, put the toaster on the kitchen table and walked right out. And nobody touched my arm, nobody asked what's wrong, nobody even gestured, and it upset me even more that this was sort of the end."

In his 2003 *New Yorker* article on suicide at the Golden Gate Bridge, Tad Friend quoted psychiatrist Jerome Motto on the suicide that affected him most. Motto said, "I went to this guy's apartment afterward with the assistant medical examiner. The guy was in his thirties, lived alone, pretty bare apartment. He'd written a note and left it on his bureau. It said, 'I'm going to walk to the bridge. If one person smiles at me on the way, I will not jump.'"

Shneidman noted several other poignant examples of failed belongingness in suicide: "I haven't the love I want so bad there is nothing left" (from a forty-five-year-old married woman who died by overdose); "I really thought that you and little Joe were going to come back into my life but you didn't" (from a twenty-year-old married man who died by hanging); "I just cannot live without you. I might as well be dead . . . I have this empty feeling inside me that is killing me . . . When you left me I died inside" (from a thirty-one-year-old separated man who died by hanging).[62]

David Reimer, the man described in Chapter 2 who was born a boy, raised as a girl, and then changed back to a man in adolescence, felt this inability to belong. A few years before his death by suicide, he described some of his past experiences in relating to others, and said, "There's no belonging. So you're an outcast. It doesn't change."[63] When asked how he had felt as a girl watching his classmates pair off romantically, he said, "These people looked like they knew where they belonged. There was no place for me to feel comfortable with anybody or anything."[64]

On January 5, 2002, fifteen-year-old Charles Bishop stole a small single-engine plane and crashed it into the Bank of America building in Tampa, Florida. An article from the June 14, 2004 Tampa Bay Online described the final report on the boy's death (classified as a suicide). The last line of the article read, "Bishop's mother said he had no neighborhood friends, and she had not met any of his friends from school."

The empirical literature also affirms a connection between failed belongingness and feeling suicidal. In the sections below, this work is summarized, starting with research on the general connection between depressive symptoms (one of which is suicidality) and experiences of disconnection from others.

Behavioral Features of Depression Indicating Low Social Connection
Connection to others can be seen in basic behavior, like eye contact and harmony between one person's and another's facial expressions or gestures. Several studies have demonstrated that depressed people engage in less eye contact than do nondepressed people.[65] Similar findings have emerged with regard to non-verbal gestures. For example, as compared to others, depressed people may engage in less

head-nodding during conversation; head-nodding is a gesture affirming connection that communication partners find rewarding.[66] Depressed and suicidal people have trouble engaging in the subtle back-and-forth dance of nonverbal communication—they often do not return eye contact, do not display animated facial expression in reactions to others, and do not use gestures like head-nodding that others find affirming and engaging.

Research on Social Isolation, Disconnection, and Suicidal Behavior
In the last section on perceived burdensomeness, I noted that relatively few studies had empirically assessed the connection between burdensomeness and suicidality, though all studies were supportive of the link. The situation is different with regard to failed belongingness: The fact that those who die by suicide experience isolation and withdrawal before their deaths is among the clearest in all the literature on suicide.

An intriguing example involves language use by poets who died by suicide compared to nonsuicidal poets as the poets' deaths neared.[67] These researchers used the Linguistic Inquiry and Word Count (LIWC), mentioned earlier, to analyze text into its components—for example, tendency to use action verbs, words denoting negative emotion, and so on. Their results suggested escalating interpersonal disconnection in the suicidal poets but not the poets who died by other means. Specifically, as the suicidal poets' deaths approached, their use of interpersonal pronouns (e.g., "we") decreased noticeably. Similarly, Shneidman reports on a young man who had survived a self-inflicted gunshot wound and later wrote, "Those around me were as shadows, bare apparitions, but I was not actually conscious of them, only aware of myself and my plight. Death swallowed me long before I pulled the trigger. I was locked within myself."[68]

I recently conducted a study using the LIWC software to examine psychological variables associated with suicidal behavior by analyzing differences in linguistic patterns in two literary characters in William Faulkner's novel *The Sound and the Fury*. These characters, the brothers Quentin and Jason Compson, each have a section in the novel that is written from a first person, stream-of-consciousness point of view. Quentin's section is written the day before he dies by suicide. Jason's section is written approximately ten years later. Each section of the novel reveals characters' inner thoughts and cognitive processes as they are occurring. Accordingly, an analysis of psychological variables over time as written by Faulkner for Quentin and Jason seemed feasible.

I wondered whether Faulkner was skilled enough to accurately portray psychological aspects of approaching suicide, phenomena that were not well elucidated by those studying suicide at the time Faulkner was writing *The Sound and the Fury* (published in 1932). Indeed, we found that Quentin's use of social words decreased as his death by suicide approached; Jason's use of social words did not change over time.[69] Faulkner accurately portrayed relatively poorly understood, intense, and rare psychological processes—still more indication of his literary genius.

Work on nonfictional people reaches similar conclusions. In a survey on several hundred community participants, as well as on five high-suicide-risk groups (e.g., general psychiatric patients, incarcerated psychiatric patients), social isolation stood out as a correlate of suicidal ideation (perceived burdensomeness toward family was also a strong correlate).[70] Similarly, in a study of psychiatrists' reports on their patients' suicides, three variables were seen as frequently present in the month preceding suicide: feeling a burden on others; social withdrawal; and help negation.[71] Help negation (the tendency to thwart help, especially therapeutic help) has been viewed as a process of interpersonal disconnection, and as such, may represent an instance of thwarted belongingness.[72]

Conner and colleagues assessed men with alcohol dependence

who died by suicide. Among the risk factors for completed suicide were living alone and loss of a partner within the last month or two before death.[73] Similarly, a comparison of those who died by suicide and those who died by other means revealed that those who died by suicide were more likely to have been recently separated and living alone.[74] Significant others of people who had recently attempted suicide pointed to loneliness in the patients as an important factor in their suicide attempt.[75]

A study of African-American women examined reasons for the association between types of childhood maltreatment and suicidal behavior. Of various factors examined, alienation (defined as inability to establish basic trust and achieve stable and satisfying relationships) was the most robust, fully explaining the link between all forms of childhood maltreatment and later suicidal behavior.[76]

Marital Status, Parenting, and Suicidality

As the studies on social isolation might suggest, nonmarried status is a demographic risk factor for suicide. The majority of deaths by suicide among Native Americans of the Apache, Navajo, and Pueblo tribes, for instance, were of single people.[77] Statistics indicate the following suicide rates in the United States in 1999: divorced—32.7 per 100,000; widowed—19.7 per 100,000; single—17.8 per 100,000; married—10.6 per 100,000.[78] These national statistics are of course open to many interpretations, but they are consistent with the view that belongingness (as indicated by married status) is a suicide buffer, whereas thwarted belongingness (as indicated by nonmarried status) is a risk for death by suicide. This is particularly evident with regard to divorce (which confers a threefold increase in risk relative to married status). In context of the model proposed here, it is tempting to speculate that suicide rates among divorced people are particularly high because divorce can affect both basic feelings of effectiveness (e.g., feeling a failure as a spouse) and basic feelings of connectedness (losing social contact not only with a spouse, but potentially with the spouse's family, with children, and with friends previously shared with the spouse).

These statistics on marital status converge with a literature inspired by Durkheim's emphasis on failures of social integration as a source for suicide.[79] For example, a study of suicidality and family and parental functioning in over 4,000 high school students in Iceland concluded that those adolescents who were well integrated into their families thereby derived protection from suicide; the indices related to family integration (cf. belongingness) wielded stronger influence on suicidality than did indices related to how the parents were functioning.[80]

With regard to connections with children, there is evidence that having large numbers of children protects against suicide. In a study of nearly a million women in Norway, over 1,000 died by suicide during a fifteen-year follow-up. Women with six or more children had one-fifth the risk of death by suicide as compared to other women.[81] The suicide rates in Canada's provinces are associated with birth rates, such that more births correspond with fewer suicides, consistent with the possibility that ties to new children buffer against suicidality.[82] In a very persuasive study on this point on over 18,000 Danish people who died by suicide and over 370,000 matched controls, having children, especially young children, was protective against suicide, even when accounting for powerful suicide-related variables like marital status and psychiatric disorder.[83] To my knowledge, no studies like this have been conducted specifically on fathers, parenthood, and suicide.

The result on mothers, parenthood, and suicide may even extend to pregnancy. Marzuk and colleagues examined the autopsy reports for all women who died by suicide in New York City from 1990 to 1993 and compared them to overall mortality statistics in age- and race-matched women in New York during the same time period.

During the study, there were 315 women who died by suicide in New York City, six of whom were pregnant, which was one-third the number that was expected given New York City female population rates.[84] These researchers concluded that pregnancy conferred protection from suicide; I would suggest that the protective influence involved feelings of connection to the baby, as well as feeling needed by the baby and thus not a burden.

Pregnancy, by itself, is no solution to longstanding feelings of disconnection and perceived burdensomeness, however. In fact, consistent with this assertion, my colleagues and I found that initially pessimistic teenagers reported low depression while pregnant (perhaps because of the belief that connection to the baby and the baby's father would solve ongoing problems), but reported high depression postpartum (perhaps because, in addition to the usual physiological and psychological challenges of childbirth, the idea that motherhood would solve ongoing problems was not confirmed).[85]

If failed belongingness is implicated in suicidality, one might predict that twins enjoy some protection from suicide, given the belongingness inherent in twinship. If fact, there is evidence to support this prediction. Using population-based register data from Denmark, researchers found that twins have a reduced risk of suicide. The suicide rate among the more than 21,000 twins, as compared to nontwins, was 26 percent lower for men and 31 percent lower for women.[86] Some studies have found mental illness to be slightly more common among twins than among singletons. Twins' belongingness may offset the risk for suicide conferred by slightly higher rates of mental disorders.

The loss of a parent relatively early in life appears to confer risk for suicide later in life. In Eskimos in the Bering Strait region, the majority of a sample of suicide attempters had lost a parent during childhood.[87] Close to half of a sample of famous people who died by suicide experienced loss of a parent before age eighteen.[88] Researchers compared the records of patients with borderline personality disorder who had died by suicide to living control patients with borderline personality (a stringent comparison, because some proportion of the living control patients were at elevated risk for later suicide by virtue of their borderline personality disorder diagnosis). The suicide group experienced childhood losses such as death of a parent more frequently than the control group.[89] There are of course alternative explanations to the link between early separation from a parent and later suicidality in the child (especially if the parent's death was by suicide, in which case genetics would be implicated), but a diminished sense of belongingness from losing a parent is one viable viewpoint.

Immigration and Suicide

Like separations from parents, separations from a "mother country," according to a belongingness view, might be associated with heightened suicidality. The very high rate of suicide in Buenos Aires, Argentina in the late 1800s was attributed to massive immigration, with a high rate of suicide among foreign-born males.[90] In a study of nearly lethal suicide attempts by 153 people and 513 matched controls, participants were asked about changing residence over the past year. Changing residence in the past year was associated with a nearly lethal suicide attempt, as were specific dimensions related to the move, such as distance and difficulty staying in touch.[91] All of these aspects of moving are associated with a sense of disconnection.

National Tragedies and Suicide

In times of acute national crisis, people pull together, and belongingness should thus increase. According to my model, then, national crises, despite their negative aspects, should nevertheless suppress suicide rates. There are data to support this view, at least regarding three salient national tragedies in the United States. First, suicide rates in response to the assassination of President John F. Kennedy were investigated. In the twenty-nine U.S. cities included in the report, *no* suicides were reported during November 22–30, 1963. By contrast, several suicides occurred during November 22–30 of years before and after 1963.[92] Second, in the two weeks preceding the Challenger disaster in 1986, there were 1,212 suicides in the United States; in the two weeks following the disaster, there were 1,099. Third, although detailed suicide rates are not readily available for the period following the terrorist attacks of September 11, 2001, calls to 1-800-SUICIDE, a national toll-free suicide crisis hotline, plummeted from an average of around 600 calls per day to around 300 per day—an all-time low—in the days following the attacks.

An additional documented phenomenon that conforms to this pattern is decreased suicide rates during times of war.[93] Regarding war, in their classic study, Dublin and Bunzel stated, "Contrary to what might be expected, times of disorganization and chaos such as prevail during a war apparently do not increase that personal disintegration which leads to a larger number of self-inflicted deaths. It would seem that the all-engrossing, unaccustomed activities and the enlargement of interests to include more than the ordinary petty concerns of a limited circle of family and friends absorb people's entire attention and prevent them from morbid brooding over individual troubles and disappointments . . . There is no time during war to indulge in personal or imaginary worries."[94] They go on to document relatively low rates of suicide during the American Civil War and the Franco-Prussian War.

Statistical bulletins put out by Metropolitan Life Insurance Company in the 1940s also show low suicide rates during World War II. A bulletin from 1942 states, "The death rate from suicides among the policyholders of the Metropolitan Life Insurance Co. for 1942 is practically the same as for 1941 and is with one exception the lowest on record. Likewise, 1941 suicide rates in England were 15%, in Germany 30% below the 1939 level. Wartime drop in suicide rates is a general phenomenon observable even in neutral nations. The phenomenon is ascribed to economic forces and such psychological forces as forgetting one's petty difficulties and finding a new purpose in rallying to the defense of one's country."

A postwar bulletin put out in 1946 read, "The downward trend characterizing the suicide death rate in this country during the war was abruptly reversed following V-E Day." Thus, nationally absorbing incidents, whether they are tragedies or wars, tend to suppress suicide rates, probably because they pull people together. In the case of war, the pulling-together effect appears to fade as the war ends.

Does Being a Sports Fan Have Anything to Do with Suicide?
The camaraderie and sense of belongingness from being a fan of sports teams can be considerable, especially under conditions of success (as many who have lived in university towns have observed when the university wins a national championship). It is interesting to consider, then, whether teams' success affects suicide rates; from the present perspective, it might, in that increased belongingness should be associated with lower suicide rates.

Believe it or not, some studies suggest a connection between sports teams' performance and suicide rates. One study assessed the suicide rates as they related to success of professional sports teams in twenty U.S. metropolitan areas from 1971 to 1990. Results showed that the team making the playoffs and winning a championship both were related to a decline in the local suicide rate.[95] Another study examined the association between a soccer team's defeat (high-profile defeats of Nottingham Forest in 1991 and 1992) and deliberate self-poisoning. The accident and emergency records of a university hospital were examined, and results indicated an excess of deliberate self-poisoning incidents during the time frames following the defeats.[96] A third study postulated that a long run by hockey's Montreal

Canadiens in the Stanley Cup playoffs is a time when people in Quebec experience increased informal interpersonal contact, and that this would serve to suppress the suicide rate in the area. By contrast, when the Canadiens are eliminated early on, the study hypothesized that interpersonal contact (belongingness) would be relatively less, and the suicide rate might increase. One of the study's clearer results was an increase in the suicide rate in young men in Quebec when the Canadiens were eliminated from the playoffs early on.[97]

It appears that sports teams' poor performance can affect suicide rates. Can good performance do so as well? My students and I recently conducted three studies to see if sports-related "pulling together" is associated with lower suicide rates.[98] In the first study, the suicide rates in Franklin County (Columbus), Ohio, and Alachua County (Gainesville), Florida were correlated with the final national ranking of the local college football teams—the Ohio State Buckeyes and the Florida Gators, respectively. These teams are of substantial concern to the local population. Given the effect that these teams' success has on their communities, we expected that there may be an association between the teams' final national ranking (which is known by early January of a given year) and the suicide rate in that year. In fact, we found that suicide rates in both Franklin County and Alachua County were associated with national rankings of the college teams, such that better rankings were related to lower suicide rates.

In the second of our three studies, we made a prediction regarding the "Miracle on Ice," when the U.S. Olympic hockey team upset the Russians, the world's dominant hockey team at the time. This occurred on February 22, 1980. It is fair to say that the 1980 U.S. Olympic hockey team's surprising victory over the dominant USSR team captured the country's attention. In fact, twenty-two years later, the players were the final torchbearers for the Salt Lake Winter Games, and there was a 2004 movie about the team entitled *Miracle.* The victory itself was amazing, but its resonance was heightened by the geopolitical climate at the time. On February 22, 1980—the date of the "Miracle on Ice"—the Iran hostage crisis was in its 111th day, and the Soviet Union's invasion of Afghanistan was approximately thirty days old. The victory, both in and of itself and because of its symbolic qualities, clearly exerted a "pulling together" effect on people in the United States. We therefore expected that the U.S. suicide rate might be particularly low on February 22, 1980 as compared to other February 22nds before and after. In fact it was—fewer suicides occurred on the day of the "Miracle on Ice" than on any other February 22 in the 1970s and 1980s.

These first two studies, as well as the previous literature on sports phenomena and suicide, leave open the possibility that suicide rates are lower at times of success not because of pulling together, but because of a sense of increased efficacy, vicariously obtained through the team's success. The studies on national disasters are not compatible with this possibility; nevertheless, in our third study, we were able to address it directly in the domain of sports by examining the number of suicides occurring in the United States on Super Bowl Sunday, as compared to suicides occurring the Sunday before and after. Though approximately a third of the U.S. population watches the Super Bowl, the majority are not devoted fans of either of the teams in a given Super Bowl; thus the "vicarious efficacy" explanation would not be a convincing explanation for any Super Bowl effect. We predicted that suicide rates on Super Bowl Sundays would be lower than on comparison Sundays, but only from the mid-1980s on, when the Super Bowl was firmly entrenched in the national consciousness as an occasion for social gathering (not just for men, but for women too, in part because of the advertising and spectacle associated with the game—a phenomenon that took hold in the early- to mid-1980s).[99] This was precisely what we found.

Although none of these three studies alone provides conclusive evidence that sports-related "pulling together" increases belongingness and thus leads to reduced suicide rates, taken as a whole these studies provide converging evidence that is consistent with the hypothesis. This is particularly true when it is considered together with the diverse and converging lines of evidence (on twins, parents, poets, Faulkner, etc.) relating low belongingness and suicidality.

Fans of teams that have not won championships in decades may be wondering where they fit in here. A prominent example involves fans of the Chicago Cubs (though having grown up in Atlanta, I would point out that I can count major Atlanta sports championships on one finger, whereas people in Chicago have fared far better). Would I predict high suicide rates in Chicago because of the Cubs? My answer is no, and again, it has to do with belongingness. There is a kind of camaraderie inherent in the Cubs' plight, and Cubs fans have pulled together, much as people do for serious tragedies. Another interesting example, of course, is the Boston Red Sox. Like the Cubs, their fans were long-suffering . . . until the fall of 2004, that is, when the Red Sox won the World Series. When detailed suicide data are available for this period in Boston, it will be very interesting to see whether the success of the Red Sox suppressed local suicide rates.

Belonging to Death

In the previous chapter, I noted that people who are far along the trajectory toward suicide come to see death in a very peculiar light; they use terms like "beautiful" and "graceful" when describing it, and seem to fuse concepts of death, destruction, and waste, on the one hand, with life, sustenance, and nurturance, on the other hand. I believe this can only happen once someone has lost the visceral fear of death—in other words, has acquired the ability to enact lethal self-injury, as described in the last chapter. Thwarted belongingness may also be implicated. As people lose connections to others, they may start to form connections to the idea of death. Consider, for example, the quotations in Chapter 2 from Sylvia Plath's poem "Edge" and Richard Heckler's interviews with suicide survivors.[100] In such examples, there is no mention of other people; the connection is to death and its symbols.

Some people do, however, merge the need to belong with suicidality. In the September 13, 2003 issue of *Asia Times Online*, reporter Suvendrini Kakuchi wrote, "Japan, a suicide-prone country, is grappling with a new trend—a spate of Internet-related suicides linked to websites where young people, who are total strangers, can contact one another to plan their deaths." The article continues, "The latest incident was reported in May, when a 24-year-old man and two women, 23 and 20, met for the first—and last—time at a train station, got into a car together and drove to a wooded area where they asphyxiated themselves." The Japanese media reported they had accessed a suicide website, and a letter left by the man in the car revealed they had become acquainted for only one reason—"just wanted to die together, nothing else." By the logic of the model presented here, I assume that these people's need to belong was thwarted, which contributed to their desire for death. But it is a testimony to the power of the need to belong that even in suicide, some people want company.

Similarly, in Jon Hilkevitch's *Chicago Tribune* article in 2004 on recent suicides on subways and other rail lines, he wrote, "Almost always, suicide victims peer into the locomotive cab in their final moments. They stare right into the eyes of the engineer, perhaps reaching for a last human connection." An engineer said of a recent suicide, slowly shaking his head, "He looked up at me right when I hit him." The engineer continued, "I've heard other engineers say [people committing suicide] look at you. I don't know why they do it. I sure wish they wouldn't, because the picture stays with you. You try to forget about it, but you don't ever, really. It ain't easy."

How Do Burdensomeness and Thwarted Belongingness Relate to Each Other?

My model assumes that two psychological conditions are necessary to the will to live, effectiveness and connectedness. If one is intact, so is the will to live. Numerous theorists have articulated aspects of this assumption in a variety of ways. William James, with regard to those who do not feel a sense of belongingness, wrote, "to those who must confess with bitter anguish that they are perfectly isolated from the soul of the world . . . [contributing to society] may not prove such an unfruitful substitute. At least, when you have added to the property of the race, even if no one knows your name, yet it is certain that, without what you have done, some individuals must needs be acting now in a somewhat different manner. You have modified their life; you are in *real* relation with them . . . And is that such an unworthy stake to set up for our own good, really?"[101] James is claiming that effectiveness can be sustaining, even in the context of failed belongingness.

The emphasis on feeling effective and connected is reminiscent of the famous dictum that mental health involves satisfying work and love.[102] Much of the material reviewed above is consistent with the assumption that effectiveness and connectedness are the key ingredients of the will to live. In fact, a recent study is consistent with this assumption. Researchers used several scales from the Minnesota Multiphasic Personality Inventory (MMPI), administered in early adulthood, to predict later death by suicide. Numerous scales were examined, but the only two that could discriminate those who died by suicide from depressed living controls and from non-depressed living controls were related to burdensomeness and low belongingness—the scales were "self-blame" and "social introversion."[103]

Incidentally, the *Atlanta Journal-Constitution* reported that on July 7, 2004, a man threatening to jump off a bridge onto the northbound lanes of interstate I-75/I-85 (which combine in downtown Atlanta) brought all northbound interstate traffic to a halt. This was the sixth such incident from March to July 2004 in Atlanta. What is the psychological experience of someone who feels isolated and ineffective enough to threaten suicide, and then within minutes, has an audience of very concerned emergency personnel and has shut down a big part of a large city's transportation, affecting thousands of people? One wonders whether the rush experienced by having such an effect (affecting the city) and belonging (concern of a crowd of emergency personnel) allays the initial suicidal desire.

One also wonders if any of the attempted suicides in Atlanta occurred on a Monday. My guess is that they did not, because the six people in Atlanta did not seem resolved to die by suicide; Monday is the day of the week on which most people actually die by suicide.[104] There are multiple reasons why this is so, including people withdrawing from weekend substance abuse. But it is interesting to speculate that for the person wracked by feelings of burdensomeness and low belongingness, Monday may be especially difficult. The upcoming week may be perceived as a further challenge to one's effectiveness, and whatever belongingness one could manage over the weekend may be disrupted by a return to the work week.

However, some questions about the roles and interrelations of perceived burdensomeness and failed belongingness remain. For example, it could be argued that, to feel a burden on others, one must feel connected to them; thus, burdensomeness implies belongingness. This of course would pose a problem for the view proposed here that the co-occurrence of burdensomeness and *thwarted* belongingness lays the groundwork for suicidal desire. In reply, to perceive oneself as a burden on others (whether on family or society) requires only a minimal connection to them. To view oneself as a member of a family or of a society is all that is required to feel a burden on them. Therefore, only the complete absence of any ties whatsoever to others might prevent one from feeling a burden, even if one feels ineffective. An assumption of the present view is that human nature in general, and the need to belong in particular, are such that virtually no one experiences no ties whatsoever to others.

Of course, it is likely that feeling disconnected could affect feelings of effectiveness, and vice-versa. For example, low feelings of effectiveness may threaten belongingness. In a relevant study, researchers led participants to believe that their partner perceived a problem with their relationship. In response, those lower in effectiveness engaged in behaviors that reduced relationship closeness, whereas those higher in effectiveness did not. In this study, low effectiveness facilitated low belongingness.[105]

According to the model described here, serious suicidal behavior requires the desire for death. The desire for death is composed of two psychological states—perceived burdensomeness and failed belongingness. On belongingness, recall the example of the man who left a note in his apartment that said, "'I'm going to walk to the bridge. If one person smiles at me on the way, I will not jump.'" The man jumped to his death. On burdensomeness, recall the study that genuine attempts are often characterized by a desire to make others better off, whereas nonsuicidal self-injury is often characterized by desire to express anger or punish oneself. Examples like these support the direct involvement of failed belongingness and perceived burdensomeness in the desire for death. Either of these states, in isolation, is not sufficient to instill the desire for death. When these states co-occur, however, the desire for death is produced; if combined with the acquired ability to enact lethal self-injury, the desire for death can lead to a serious suicide attempt or to death by suicide.

WHAT DO WE MEAN BY SUICIDE? HOW IS IT DISTRIBUTED IN PEOPLE?

4

In the previous chapter, I asserted that those who desire suicide die by suicide only if they can. Those who can die by suicide will die only if they want to. But who can? Those who have acquired the capability to enact lethal self-injury. Who wants to? Those who perceive that they are a burden on loved ones *and* that they do not belong to a valued group or relationship. There are relatively large numbers of people who desire suicide, and large numbers of those who have developed the capacity for suicide. But there are relatively few people in the dangerous convergence zone—those who are at greatest risk for serious suicidal behavior.

The components of the model have some interesting relationships to each other. The interrelations of burdensomeness and low belongingness have been discussed, but what of the associations between acquired ability for suicide, on the one hand, and burdensomeness and low belongingness, on the other hand? In fact, there is evidence that social isolation may lead to increases in pain tolerance. Researchers have shown that the pain threshold of mice increases after thirty days of isolation.[1] Sensory deprivation increases the pain threshold in people as well.[2]

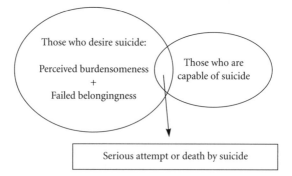

Just as isolation may lead to the ability to bear increased pain, behaviors that increase the pain threshold may lead to isolation. Provocative behaviors, like self-injury, can be off-putting. These behaviors can also lead others to perceive one as a burden. In one study, a majority of the significant others of those who had recently attempted suicide reported that their support of the patient represented a burden to them.[3] If people who engage in self-harm are ostracized and viewed as a burden because of it, their sense of belongingness may diminish and their sense of perceived burdensomeness may increase. In a number of ways, then, components of the model presented here may feed each other. Any one of the components could be viewed as an entry into a process whereby all three components, and thus high risk for serious suicidal behavior, escalate.

Any persuasive explanation of suicide should shed at least some light on the existing data, including prevalence; the clustering and "contagion" of suicide; and the associations of suicide with age, gender, race, neurobiological indices, mental disorders, substance abuse, impulsivity, and childhood adversity. The present model may also contribute to the resolution of long-standing dilemmas in the field of suicide research, treatment, and prevention, and explain some puzzling suicide-related facts. For example, what constitutes a proper definition of suicide itself? Are mild suicidal ideation and lethal suicidal behavior located at different points along the same underlying continuum, or are they categorically different phenomena? The model may help us think about what we mean by suicide.

Definitions of Suicidal Behavior

A man is discovered dead in his car, which has veered off the road and slammed into a tree. There are no skid marks and alcohol is in his system, though not at levels exceeding the legal limit. Family and friends state that he has been somewhat despondent over the disruption of a romantic relationship, but generally doing well. Is this a suicide or an accident?

A woman ingests half a bottle of pills and then immediately tells a family member what she has done. She is rushed to the hospital, where she initially recovers, and she confides that she did not mean to die. Complications arise due to the overdose, however, from which she later dies. Is this a suicide?

An adolescent pricks the side of her wrist with a pin, barely drawing blood, and then immediately tells her mother what she has done. Is this a very mild version of the same type of behavior by which people die by suicide, or is this behavior qualitatively different than more serious forms of suicidal behavior?

As these examples show, defining suicidal behavior is not always straightforward. Indeed, the definition and classification of various forms of suicidality have been a vexing and long-standing issue.[4] The questions have centered on whether suicidality represents a true continuum, ranging from mild and fleeting suicidal ideation all the way on up to death by suicide,[5] or whether some forms of suicidality are categorically different from others (e.g., a medically lethal attempt with stated intent to die as distinct from mild ideation).

A complete answer to this question requires a program of research involving a statistical technique called taxometrics.[6] This technique is complicated, but its main point is to differentiate categorical, either-or phenomena, like biological gender, from qualitative, dimensional continua (like temperature). This program of research needs to be done, but to date, awaits its steward.

Until then, another approach to solving problems like this is through theory development, and in this regard, the current model provides some perspective. In one sense, the theory identifies a cut-point along the continuum of suicidal symptoms; namely, the point at which, for a given individual, suicidal ideation or behavior further engages habituation and opponent processes. This point varies from individual to individual, depending on the degree to which the individual has previously acquired the capability for lethal self-injury. In another sense, however, the current theory suggests that any cut-point may be deceiving, because burdensomeness and failed belongingness may be on the relatively less serious side of any line (because they constitute suicidal desire, the less serious aspect of suicidality), yet they are nevertheless key contributors to serious suicidal behavior, according to the current model. Whether suicidality represents a true continuum, ranging from mild and fleeting suicidal ideation all the way on up to death by suicide, or whether categories are involved (for example, medically damaging versus ideation), is a question that future research will have to resolve.

Is Killing Oneself Always Suicide?
Another complicated issue regarding definitions involves those who clearly caused their own deaths, but who may not be classified as having died by suicide. The terrorist attacks of September 11, 2001 brought this issue into stark focus. First, there were people on the upper floors of the World Trade Center who jumped to their deaths.

At least fifty people died in this way, and the actual number is probably closer to two hundred.[7] Did they die by suicide?

According to the New York medical examiner, they did not. All September 11 deaths at the World Trade Center were classified as homicides. Had even one person survived from the upper floors from which people jumped, perhaps a case for suicidal elements could be made, but no one from those floors survived. These people presumably realized that death was imminent, and chose one form of death over another.

Moreover, if these deaths contained suicidal elements, the demographic profile of suicide, for example regarding gender, should correspond to the profile of people who jumped from the World Trade Center. Overall, three times as many men as women died in the disaster. For deaths due to jumping to conform to suicide demographics, then, the ratio of men to women who died by jumping would need to approximate twelve to one (i.e., the 3:1 ratio of male to female deaths in the disaster combined with the 4:1 preponderance of male suicides in the United States). To my knowledge, specific information on proportion of men and women who died in this way is not available; anecdotal impressions from photographs, however, suggest that, among those whose gender was identifiable, the ratio of men to women was substantially less than 12:1. Classifying these deaths as suicides therefore seems arguable at best.

Still, the case can be made that these deaths technically were suicides, and if so, the current model should have something to say about them. The situation on the upper floors of the World Trade Center forced people to make horrible probability calculations (to the degree that people under duress were even capable of such calculations)—jumping meant a quick end to suffering and certain death; not jumping meant a minuscule chance of survival at the cost of near-certain death by more painful means. Who would cling to this minuscule chance of survival? By the logic of the current model, there are two possible answers—those who wished to jump but could not because they were unable to enact lethal self-injury, and those whose desire to live was enormously strong—enough so to risk intense pain and suffering in exchange for even the smallest chance to live.

Second, there were the terrorists themselves. Did they die by suicide? As I have stated in Chapter 1, according to dictionary definitions (e.g., "the act of killing oneself intentionally"), they did. Their views appeared to have been that their self-sacrifice was for their society's greater good, which, in his classic work on suicide, Durkheim might have characterized as altruistic suicide. Here again, however, classifying these deaths as suicides seems quite arguable. The terrorists themselves would almost certainly have described their actions as those of martyrs or casualties of holy war,[8] especially since Islam views suicide as a serious sin.[9]

Still, some might characterize these deaths as suicide, and if they were, how does the current model understand them? It is clear that suicide terrorists and bombers work up to the act, going through months and sometimes years of training and preparation for the act; in this way, they are consciously and deliberately attaining the capability for lethal behavior. Moreover, they do appear to use a kind of calculation related to burdensomeness (i.e., their death is worth more to their community than their life). Their sense of belongingness, however, seemed quite high—another reason, from the perspective of the current model, to view their deaths as other than suicides, and many Muslim clerics concur that self-martyrdom and suicide are distinct.[10] Even here, however, the current view has something to contribute. It is possible that death and life merge for suicide terrorists, such that they view death as a way to belong, and to belong more fully than by anything they could do in life. In his 2004 book entitled *My Life Is a Weapon,* C. Reuter identifies belonging in the memories of family and society at large as perhaps the prime motive for suicide terrorists. As noted earlier, in at least one example—suicide attackers in the Iran-Iraq War—self-sacrifice was celebrated as a marriage of the attacker to death.

Japanese kamikaze pilots can be viewed similarly. Excerpts from the pilots' "how-to" manual have been published.[11] One excerpt read, "Just before the collision it is essential that you do not shut your eyes for a moment so as not to miss the target. Many have crashed into the targets with wide-open eyes. They will tell you what fun they had." An excerpt entitled, "You are now 30 meters from the target" read, "You will sense that your speed has suddenly and abruptly increased. You feel that the speed has increased by a few thousand-fold. It is like a long shot in a movie suddenly turning into a close-up, and the scene expands in your face." A subsequent passage entitled, "The moment of the crash" read, "You are two or three meters from the target. You can see clearly the muzzles of the enemy's guns. You feel that you are suddenly floating in the air. At that moment, you see your mother's face." These step-by-step instructions seem designed to increase the pilots' courage and preparations for death, reminiscent of the concept of resolved plans and preparations emphasized in Chapter 2.

Like suicide bombers, kamikaze pilots seem to calculate that their death is worth more to their community than their life. A relevant excerpt in this regard from the "how-to" manual read, "Sink the enemy and thus pave the road for our people's victory." Another read, "Transcend life and death. When you eliminate all thoughts about life and death, you will be able to totally disregard your earthly life. This will also enable you to concentrate your attention on eradicating the enemy with unwavering determination."

And also like the suicide bombers, high belongingness seemed to characterize the deaths of kamikaze pilots. A relevant excerpt from their manual read, "Remember when diving into the enemy to shout at the top of your lungs: 'Hissatsu!' ('Sink without fail!') At that moment, all the cherry blossoms at Yasukuni shrine in Tokyo will smile brightly at you." According to my model, one interpretation of this is that the pilots' need to belong has been met by death. Another interpretation, of course, is that their elevated sense of belongingness is a reason to define their deaths as other than suicides.

Menninger viewed deaths like these as nonsuicidal. In his 1938 book *Man Against Himself*, he wrote, "The heroic sacrifice of scientists who willingly incur the fatal risks incident to research, patriots who lay down their lives for freedom, saints of the church and other persons who give their lives for society, or for those they love, are usually not considered suicidal."[12] My claim is though no model of suicidality easily handles all of the definitional challenges presented by examples like kamikaze pilots, my framework, relative to others, provides more understanding of these complex phenomena.

Consider mass suicides in cults as another example. In both the Jonestown and Heaven's Gate incidents, people caused their own deaths, seemingly intentionally. In Jonestown, where 914 people died, the majority of people died from drinking a grape-flavored drink laced with cyanide and sedatives at the behest of leader Jim Jones; it should also be noted, however, that many people were murdered in the Jonestown tragedy, either by gunshot or the injection of poisons. In the Heaven's Gate event, which caused the deaths of thirty-nine people (two additional cult members died by suicide in the months following), people died by ingesting high doses of phenobarbital mixed with vodka, at the behest of leader Marshall Applewhite. The Heaven's Gate members believed that after death they would be transported to a spaceship that was following the comet Hale-Bopp, and that they would live on at higher evolutionary levels.

It is plausible to argue that these were not suicides but rather murders perpetrated by the cult leaders. Also, the same point regarding gender distribution in the World Trade Center deaths can be made regarding Jonestown and Heaven's Gate (more women than men died in the Heaven's Gate incident, for example). But if these deaths are to be characterized as suicides, how does the present framework explain them?

First, relevant to the acquired capability to enact lethal self-injury, there were numerous discussions about and explicit rehearsals for suicide in both the Jonestown and Heaven's Gate incidents, similar to the mental practice for suicide and aborted suicide attempts mentioned in Chapter 2. This was a harrowing aspect of Jonestown, in which Jones tested loyalty by telling members that a drink contained poison (when it did not) and asking them to drink it. In fact, habituation has been invoked as a factor at Jonestown: "Thus, with repeated incidents such as this, Jones was able to desensitize his followers regarding mass suicide."[13]

Also, people in both groups endured considerable pain and provocation. In Jonestown, in addition to the harrowing loyalty tests, people worked seventy-four hours per week in agricultural fields or construction in the searing heat of the South American jungle, and this was in the context of a sparse diet and lengthy and regular religious meetings.[14] Eight of the eighteen men who died in the Heaven's Gate incident had undergone voluntary castrations.[15]

But what about belongingness? Shouldn't the close ties among cult members offset suicide risk, according to the current model? It is an underappreciated fact that belongingness is low in many cults, particularly abusive ones.[16] To be sure, people in such cults work, live, and worship side by side (as people do in prisons, for example), but their connection to each other is not such that multiple meaningful and reciprocal relationships are cultivated; rather, their main interpersonal tie is to the cult leader, whose reciprocity is sporadic, one-sided, and often manipulative or abusive.

It is also common for people to forego deep and lifelong relationships when they join cults (for example, some of the Heaven's Gate members abandoned their children when they joined the cult).[17] Regarding feeling ineffective, people are routinely and severely subjugated in cults. If mass suicides in cults are suicides rather than murders, my model may explain more about them than can other theories of suicide.

Although very different in character from suicides in cults, physician-assisted suicide also presents definitional challenges. Recall the quotation that "if there were some little switch in the arm which one could press in order to die immediately and without pain, then everyone would sooner or later commit suicide." I think this view neglects how scary death is to most people, but the remark does convey the fact that, without such a "little switch," suicide is difficult. Physician-assisted suicide is perhaps as close to a "switch" as is possible.

According to my model, suicide involves the accrual of fearlessness about and the means for suicide (primarily involving habituation and opponent processes) as well as the desire for death (constituents of which are perceived burdensomeness and failed belongingness). The means for physician-assisted suicide are in a sense prearranged. Also, through a lengthy assessment and consultation process, death by physician-assisted suicide may become less and less fearsome. Therefore, competence and fearlessness may be implicated in choosing physician-assisted suicide.

There is evidence too that burdensomeness is involved. Researchers found that among amyotrophic lateral sclerosis (ALS) patients, those who were interested in assisted suicide had greater distress at being a burden than ALS patients not interested in assisted suicide.[18] Though the study does not precisely measure perceived burdensomeness or failed belongingness, researchers have also reported that, among hospice patients who refused food and fluids to hasten death, pointlessness and meaninglessness in life were main motivations. Patients in this group usually died within two weeks and nurses indicated that on average these were "good" deaths (relatively free of extreme pain and other discomfort).[19]

The author Caroline Knapp died this way. Knapp wrote honest and well-crafted memoirs, including the books *Drinking: A Love Story* in 1996 and *Appetites: What Women Want* in 2003. In each of these two books, two things about her become clear: first, she went through numerous provocative experiences related to her serious alcoholism and equally serious anorexia nervosa; second, she was a very strong person, as evidenced by her overcoming both alcoholism and anorexia. She was diagnosed with late-stage, terminal lung cancer in 2002 and decided to end her life by refusing food and fluids. She did this, her twin sister stated, as a way to take control.[20] Given what Knapp had been through, and given her strength, it does not seem surprising that she would have the wherewithal to take control like this.

Another phenomenon that presents definitional challenges is what might be termed "quasi-suicide." Consider for example a newspaper reporter who has covered many wars, and in each, has had a number of close calls, some due to recklessness. The reporter is killed by enemy fire in a war zone that he was explicitly forbidden to visit by military authorities. The model developed here applies at least with respect to the acquired ability to enact lethal behaviors—the reporter's repeated provocative experiences would have habituated him to injury or death. The relevance of the other two aspects of the model is less clear, however. It is possible that the reporter in the example would harbor feelings of perceived burdensomeness and failed belongingness, but it does not seem necessary; there is something incomplete in the reporter's resolve toward suicide.

In this connection, the concept of a "passive" suicide attempt should be noted. A passive attempt occurs when one takes no or minimal action but in so doing incurs risk. Refusing treatment for a life-threatening condition would be one example. Stepping off the sidewalk into a busy street without looking would count as a passive attempt also; here, minimal activity leads to someone else potentially being the agent of death—a passive suicide attempt.

In Chapter 2, I emphasized the distinction between the categories of suicidality—resolved plans and preparations versus suicidal desire. Interestingly, passive suicide attempts are grouped under the suicidal desire category. This suggests that passive suicide attempts are distinct from more active, resolved attempts.

Consider the example of those who refuse HIV testing, despite being at risk, and who thereby deny themselves potentially life-saving or -lengthening treatments. A situation like this was documented by Peter Cassels in the June 13, 2002 issue of *Bay Windows*, a gay and lesbian newspaper in New England. The mother of a man who had refused HIV testing and later died from complications arising from AIDS explained that her son was very affected by homophobia and never truly came out of the closet. She said, "On a subconscious level, his refusal to be tested for HIV when he could have been treated, the way homophobia affected him, maybe his death was a quasi-suicide." The man seemed to struggle with thoughts that his homosexuality was a burden to his family and himself, and his sense of connection seemed affected too. It is possible that he had the desire for death but had not developed a strong capacity for lethal, active self-injury, and instead used the passive means of HIV test refusal. The understudied phenomenon of "quasi-suicide" thus seems at the margin of what my framework would consider as truly suicidal, and needs more research attention.

The phenomenon of suicide-by-cop, however, seems explicable within my framework in that it shares many properties with other suicide methods. Suicide-by-cop occurs when a suicidal person aggressively provokes a law enforcement officer, who kills the person in self-defense. Though this has elements of a passive suicide attempt, in that the person is not the final agent of death, it also has active elements, in that the person has to engage and then actively and aggressively provoke a police officer. In a study of people involved in a standoff with police who acted provocatively toward them, those who died as a result were compared to those who survived.[21] Those who died had signatures of the acquired ability to enact lethal self-injury—for example, more previous suicide attempts—and also often voiced a desire to die. They thus seemed similar to those who die by suicide through other means. As to why someone would choose suicide-by-cop over other methods, we have very little systematic knowledge on method choice in general, and choice of suicide-by-cop in particular. One could invoke explanations like anger at law enforcement or at authority in general, but this seems a little unsatisfying.

Murder-suicide does not really present definitional challenges—the person has clearly died by suicide—but raises another question: Why murder someone first? Here again, relatively few systematic data are available, in part because the phenomenon is relatively rare.[22] Approximately 1.5 percent of all suicides occur in the context of murder-suicide.[23] A very interesting study determined whether the initiators of murder-suicides had profiles more like those who die by suicide or more like those who commit homicide. Seventy-five percent of the initiators of murder-suicide were depressed and 95 percent were men. In both these ways, they resemble those who die by suicide. By contrast, perpetrators of homicide were not depressed and one-half were women. The study concluded that the murder-suicide and homicide groups are distinct populations.[24]

But still, why murder someone before one's own death by suicide? One answer involves elderly, depressed men who are caretakers for impaired spouses. In a study comparing men who had died by suicide to those who first killed their spouse and then died by suicide, researchers found that half of the murder-suicide group were caretakers of an impaired spouse, as compared to 17 percent of the suicide group.[25] Depression was very common in both groups. A substantial number of murder-suicides involve older men who are depressed and confronted with the care of an impaired spouse. Some number of these murder-suicides likely involve suicide pacts, in which the spouse consents to joint suicide. Though the context and dynamics are different, this is reminiscent of the phenomenon mentioned earlier, in which people in Japan contacted one another over the Internet to plan their suicides.

A Comment on Method

The phenomena of suicide-by-cop and murder-suicide raise the more general issue of method choice in suicide. From the current perspective, choice of an especially lethal means of suicide should of course be more common among those who have acquired the ability to enact lethal self-injury than others. There is some evidence that this is the case. For instance, people who had engaged in repeated self-injury in the past reported that their current episode of self-harm was more aggressive and more lethal than first-time self-injury patients.[26] Similarly, among mood-disordered and borderline personality–disordered patients, number of previous suicide attempts is a strong predictor of the extent of medical damage resulting from the most serious lifetime suicide attempt.[27] Additionally, regarding perceived burdensomeness, my colleagues and I found that it was associated with more lethal (e.g., self-inflicted gunshot) as opposed to less lethal (e.g., overdose) means of completed suicide, consistent with the current theory.[28]

There are two ambiguities regarding suicide method, and indeed, the study on perceived burdensomeness illustrates one of them. In one of the two studies in that report, all participants had died by suicide, yet some did so by relatively less lethal means. The association between method choice and intent to die is thus complex, and in fact, some studies document a low association between intent and lethality of method.[29] A persuasive theory of suicide should be able to explicate, at least in part, the interrelations between method choice, intent to die, and death by suicide, as well as allow for complexities inherent in these interrelations; the current theory does so. A point prediction derived from the current theory is that those who choose especially lethal means of self-injury will be characterized by the theory's parameters (i.e., acquired ability, perceived burdensomeness, thwarted belongingness) regardless of whether they die or suffer extensive medical damage; those who choose a low lethality method will be characterized by the theory's parameters only if they die or suffer extensive medical damage.

The second complexity regarding method choice involves marked cross-cultural differences. In the United States, a country with high gun ownership, 55 percent of those who die by suicide do so by self-inflicted gunshot wound; the second leading method is hanging and other forms of suffocation (20 percent); and the third is poisoning (17 percent).[30] By contrast, poisoning is a more common means of suicide in England and China than in the United States.[31] The theory presented in this book has few predictions regarding which method would be chosen in which culture; rather, the theory attempts to explain which individuals will develop serious intentions to die by suicide, and which ones will act on them in serious ways (often by lethal means, but not always, because lethality of means differs cross-culturally and is not always a clear expression of intent to die). However, it is of interest that the most rare forms of suicide methods are also the most fearsome—for example, falls account for 2 percent of all deaths by suicide and fire, less than 1 percent. Thus, even among those who die by suicide and therefore by definition had developed the ability to enact lethal self-injury, the fearsome quality of some methods as compared to others seems to play a role in method choice.

Prevalence

In one sense, death by suicide is not rare. Around 30,000 people die by suicide in the United States each year, which translates to approximately eighty deaths by suicide every day—one person every eighteen minutes. Worldwide, approximately a million people die by suicide each year—one person every forty seconds. This rate means that more people are dying by suicide than in all of the world's armed conflicts combined; about as many people die by suicide as die in traffic accidents. Suicide is a leading cause of death.[32]

In another sense, however, suicide is a relatively rare occurrence. Expanding on the data presented in Chapter 1, in a U.S. city of 100,000 people, around ten will die by suicide each year (indeed, the usual metric for death rates is deaths per 100,000, and the U.S. rate is approximately 10 per 100,000 per year). Of all deaths in the United States, a little over 1 percent are due to suicide. Given that a person has died, the chance that the cause was heart disease or cancer is 52 percent. Whereas approximately eighty people per day die by suicide in the United States, approximately 1,900 U.S. people die from heart disease every day.

Many explanations for suicide fail fairly obviously in the face of prevalence rates. If suicide is due to factor X, it must be explained why this factor is fairly common and suicide less so. For example, mental illness is commonly invoked as an explanation for suicide. As will be detailed in the next chapter, there is no doubt whatsoever that mental illnesses play a role in suicidal behavior. But mental illness alone does not provide a satisfying explanation for suicide, because mental illness is much more common than suicide. How should we explain all those people with mental illness who do not die by suicide? Moreover, the absence of our hypothetical X factor in some suicides needs to be explained. Though it is rare for people without mental illness to die by suicide, it occasionally happens—a fact that an explanation centered around mental illness cannot account for.

By contrast, my theory is compatible with the epidemiology of suicide. Relatively few people have the experiences or opportunities to acquire the capability for lethal self-injury. Even among people who do have these experiences or opportunities, not all will necessarily fully acquire the capability, because some may have relatively mild experiences that do not lead to habituation. This capability is thus relatively rare and difficult to obtain. The other factors—perceived burdensomeness and failed belongingness—are relatively rare too. The confluence of these three factors, which according to my model is required for serious suicidal behavior, is more rare still. The current framework explains—indeed predicts—that death by suicide will be a relatively rare event.

Suicide rates are not evenly distributed across geographic regions, and a penetrating theory of suicidal behavior should have something to say about this. In certain regions of the United States, cultures of honor appear to reign. In these regions, the creed seems to be "give me honor or give me death." In fact, all fifteen of the states with the highest suicide rates are culture-of-honor states. A comprehensive theory of suicide thus must be able to incorporate the role of thwarted honor. The current theory does so by emphasizing one's standing vis-à-vis others, and proposing that if one's standing falls to the degree that one perceives oneself as a burden on others, risk for serious suicidal behavior is increased.

If suicide rates differ by state, such that culture-of-honor states have higher rates, rates may also differ within states, with higher rates occurring in rural counties where cultures of honor might be more influential than in urban areas. I examined this in my home state of Florida by randomly picking three rural counties and comparing them to counties in the urban areas of Miami and Tampa. The rural counties were Lake County (which is in the middle of the peninsula, northeast of Tampa, 2002 population 233,835), Calhoun County (which is in the panhandle west of Tallahassee, 2002 population 12,567), and Suwanee County (which is near where the panhandle and peninsula intersect, west of Jacksonville, 2002 population 36,121). The urban counties were Broward County (Miami, 2002 population 1,709,118), Dade County (Miami, 2002 population 2,332,599), and Hillsborough County (Tampa, 2002 population 1,053,864). The suicide rate per 100,000 in the rural counties was over fifteen. The comparable rate in the three counties in Miami and Tampa was just over nine.

These findings converge with those of a recent study that found that, from 1990 to 1997, the suicide rate in men was around 27 per 100,000 in rural U.S. counties, as compared to around 17 per 100,000 in urban areas.[33] A roughly similar pattern emerged for women as well. When interviewed about this finding by the *Atlanta Journal-Constitution*,[34] the study's lead author specifically invoked low belongingness. He said, "The usual explanations are that there are physical isolation and limited social interactions in rural areas. You have limited opportunity for social interaction and networks."

Indeed, a variety of explanations could account for this pattern, including more economic stress and less ethnic diversity in the rural counties (as will be discussed later in this chapter, white people in the United States have higher rates of suicide than nonwhite people). Nevertheless, it is an intriguing speculation that cultures of honor reign more in rural Florida than in places like Miami and Tampa, and in rural versus urban areas in general, and that this plays some role in the substantial difference in the suicide rate between rural and urban areas of the state.

As of 2001, the five countries with the highest suicide rates were Lithuania, Russia, Belarus, Latvia, and Ukraine. These countries are contiguous with each other, and all were formerly part of the Soviet Union. The suicide rates in these countries are staggering: In all five, the rate per 100,000 men is over fifty, and in Lithuania and Russia, the rate per 100,000 men is over seventy. For comparison's sake, the rate per 100,000 men in the United States is approximately sixteen. As many women die by suicide in Lithuania as men do in the United States.

It is not difficult to imagine these countries as typifying cultures of honor. Moreover, these countries have long histories of hardship (including in some cases brutal Soviet repression) and have undergone extremely fraught transitions from Soviet communism to independence with attendant crises of national identity and economy. That the acquired ability to enact lethal self-injury (developed through habituation to various hardships), perceived burdensomeness (due in part to economic stress), and failed belongingness (due in part to strains on societal integration) would occur at high rates in these countries provides one way of understanding their extremely high suicide rates.

Demographics

Gender

In the United States, men are approximately four times more likely than women to die by suicide, whereas women are approximately three times more likely than men to attempt suicide.[35] This pattern holds in most countries, with a ratio of at least four male suicides to every one female suicide. In the five countries with the highest suicide rates—Lithuania, Russia, Belarus, Latvia, and Ukraine—this ratio ranges from 4.69 (Lithuania) to 6.69 (Belarus). This pattern of male lethality is partly related to the tendency toward violent behavior in general, which is, of course, more common in men than women. Women's attempts are more frequent but less violent; vice-versa for men. For every three male suicide victims in the United States, two die by firearm, as compared to one of three for women. The most common method for U.S. female victims is overdose/poisoning.[36]

I believe that men are more lethal regarding suicide in part because they have acquired more of the ability to enact lethal self-injury. Men, more so than women, acquire this capability through an array of means. They have more exposure to guns, to physical fights, to violent sports like boxing and football, and to self-injecting drug use. They are, on average, more likely to be physicians. Moreover, men, more so than women, may struggle with belongingness. In this context, it has been suggested that women may die by suicide less frequently than men because women are less likely to abandon relational values that form part of their identities.[37] Perceived burdensomeness may also be more of an issue for men than women, given that traditional male gender roles include providing for others. Frustration of the breadwinner role may contribute to feelings of perceived burdensomeness in men, somewhat more so than in women.

A study comparing two models of the relation of previous to subsequent suicide attempt may also be relevant to gender differences. One model was called the "trait model," meaning that suicide attempts are, in a sense, predetermined by enduring dispositions—or traits—and are uninfluenced by intervening occurrences of suicidal behavior. The other model was called the "crescendo model," meaning that each occurrence of suicidal behavior increases the subsequent likelihood of suicidal behavior. The crescendo model bears similarities to my idea that various painful and provocative experiences increase the ability to enact lethal self-injury.

Data were equally consistent with both models.[38] The theory articulated here would more accurately be captured by an *amended* crescendo model, in which occurrences of suicidal behavior increase the likelihood of subsequent suicidal behavior *only if* the original behavior contains elements that approach or exceed previous worst-point suicidality. When this happens, habituation is furthered and opponent processes engaged. Relatively mild suicidality, on the other hand, may not increase the subsequent likelihood of severe or escalated suicidality. This may in part explain the empirical fact that women are more likely than men to experience mild suicidality, but less likely than men to escalate to completed suicide.

An important exception to the rule of more completed suicides in men than women occurs in China, where recent data show the rate for women to be 14.8 per 100,000 and the rate for men to be 13.0 per 100,000. The role of Confucianism in Chinese society and its view of the inferior position of women has been emphasized as one explanation,[39] one that is consistent with the current emphasis on effectiveness as a buffer against suicide.

An interesting speculation on the phenomenon of high suicide rates in Chinese women, consistent with the current theory, involves sports. In contrast to countries like the United States, Chinese women have performed considerably better than Chinese men in international sport competitions. It has been suggested that sport achievement contributes to an ethic among Chinese women of physicality, masculinity, and aggression, and that this may contribute to more lethality in women's suicidal behavior (perhaps via the acquired ability to enact lethal self-injury).[40] A survey of over 4,000 U.S. college students found evidence consistent with the possibility that sport-related masculinity and aggression in women may confer higher suicide risk. Women who engaged in vigorous athletic activity were at greater odds of reporting suicidal behavior than other women.[41] There is evidence, incidentally, of increased pain tolerance in women athletes,[42] which would also facilitate their acquisition of the ability to enact lethal self-injury.

A practice common in China from the 900s to the 1900s was described by M. Roach in her 2003 book *Stiff:* "adult children . . . were obliged to demonstrate filial piety by hacking off a piece of themselves and preparing it as a restorative elixir."[43] More often than not, the adult child was a daughter-in-law and the recipient her mother-in-law. One is tempted to speculate that traditions like these may have set in place a culture in which women habituate to pain and injury, including deliberate self-harm.

I pointed out earlier that the usual male:female ratio for suicide rates is at least 4:1 in most countries, often higher (for example, it is 6.69:1 in Belarus). China is clearly an exception to this rule, but interestingly, so are many Asian countries, as indicated by the following male:female ratios for suicide rates in Asian countries: 1.34 in India; 1.47 in the Philippines; 1.95 in Singapore; 2.27 in South Korea; 2.33 in Thailand; 2.59 in Japan; and 2.65 in Sri Lanka. The factors that have evened out the male:female ratio of suicide rates in China may be generalizable to other Asian countries as well.

Race and Ethnicity
A striking fact about U.S. suicide demographics is that African-Americans are, in general, protected from suicide as compared to Caucasians. Among African-American and Caucasian men, the suicide rates per 100,000 are 9.8 and 19.1, respectively; corresponding figures for women are 1.8 and 4.5.[44] Theorists have often explained this difference with regard to social support and religiosity, arguing that African-Americans experience more social support and are more religious, and as a function thereof, are protected from suicide.[45] On average, African-Americans do report more religiosity than Caucasians.[46] On measures like frequency of church attendance, frequency of prayer, closeness to God, and self-ratings of spirituality, African-Americans usually outpace Caucasians in the United States. Also, there is evidence that religiosity can buffer against suicidality.[47] In a national survey, it was found that African-Americans are more likely to attend church, pray, and feel more strongly about their reli-

gious beliefs than whites.[48] Regarding social support, there is little doubt that its absence constitutes a suicide risk factor.[49] However, it is less clear that African-Americans enjoy more overall social support than Caucasians, although there is some evidence to this effect.[50] Important in context of the current model, the possibility that African-American people in particular derive protection from suicide via contact with religious institutions and perhaps support from others is consistent with the assertion that the need to belong, when satisfied, can buffer from suicidality.

Another striking fact about suicide in African-Americans is the increased rates of death by suicide among African-American men in the last thirty years or so. This increase is accounted for mostly by the rise in suicides among young African-American males. During the 1980s and 1990s, African-American boys aged ten to fourteen demonstrated a 283 percent increase in suicide. A 165 percent increase was observed for adolescents aged fifteen to nineteen. While the risk for suicide increased among African-American men, the rate of suicide decreased for African-American women (19 percent decrease).[51]

My former student Rheeda Walker, who now teaches at the University of South Carolina, proposed a model geared toward explaining the increase in African-American male suicide. She focused on the idea of acculturative stress, which is the stress that someone experiences as they move from one cultural framework to another. She predicted that African-American men in particular would experience high levels of acculturative stress, because over the last thirty years or so, barriers to entry into mainstream education, employment, and the like have been reduced, perhaps more so for African-American men than African-American women. Further, she expected that this stress would be a risk for suicidality, especially if African-American men leave behind reliance on traditional suicide buffers among African-Americans; namely, close ties to extended family and to church. In her questionnaire study on 270 African-

American young adults, she found empirical evidence to support her expectations. Here again, this finding is consistent with this book's emphasis on failed belongingness as an important risk factor for serious suicidal behavior.[52]

In the months before his death by suicide, my dad (a Caucasian) occasionally attended African-American churches. I don't know for sure, but my suspicion is that feelings of failed belongingness were overtaking him, and that usual sources of solace, like his own church, were not adequate. I believe he reached out to African-American churches because he sensed the closeness that many African-American congregations enjoy. That this did not work for him is not surprising—my impression is that the churches were gracious to my dad, but that he never felt like he really belonged. Changing from one subculture to another and feeling a real part of the new subculture is always difficult—as Walker's study showed—and my dad was not up to this challenge, tragically.

Hispanics in the United States have fairly low rates of suicide—around 5 per 100,000, as compared to the national rate of approximately 10 per 100,000. Close contact with extended family is a plausible explanation for this low rate. However, it should be noted that Hispanics in the United States are a very diverse group, including Mexican Americans, Cuban Americans, Puerto Rican Americans, and others. People from Puerto Rico have higher rates of suicidal ideation and suicide attempts as compared to Mexican Americans and Cuban Americans.[53] More research is needed on differences among Hispanic groups in suicidality.

Just as it is important to differentiate among subgroups of Hispanics, it is necessary to couch findings on suicide in Native Americans in the context of tribal differences. Overall, Native Americans die by suicide at higher rates than other people in the United States—about 1.5 to 2 times the rate, depending on the year. Just as close family contacts appear to buffer African-American and Hispanic people from suicide, some have suggested that social disintegration related to the plight of Native American people is a factor in high rates of Native American suicide. Variations in social cohesion may play an important role in varying tribal suicide rates. Native American cultures of the Southwest, for instance, have a greater sense of social cohesion as compared to Native Americans of the Northern Plains; suicide rates are higher in the latter group, which is consistent with the current emphasis on belongingness as key in explaining suicidal behavior. Within individual southwestern tribes, social cohesion may also be explanatory. Higher suicide rates have been found in Apache as compared to Navajo or Pueblo people, and this difference may be attributable to higher tribal social integration among the Navajo and Pueblo.[54]

Within various ethnic groups and cultures, perceived burdensomeness might be more or less painful than failed belongingness. An important dimension on which cultures differ is the way their members construe the self. There are cultures in which an interdependent self-construal is normative (e.g., many Asian cultures); that is, people in these cultures see themselves as part of a larger whole, and do not emphasize their own personal autonomy and independence. People in cultures with autonomous self-construals take the opposite stance. They prioritize personal agency, control, and independence more than being part of a larger whole. The United States is an example of a culture with relatively autonomous self-construals.[55] One might speculate that, in cultures in which an interdependent self-construal is normative, failed belongingness may be particularly painful, whereas in cultures in which an autonomous self-construal is normative, perceived burdensomeness may be more painful. To my knowledge, no previous work has examined this possibility with regard to suicidality—a potential direction for future research.

Finally, it is interesting to note that pain tolerance appears to relate to race. In a study of chronic pain patients, Caucasian patients showed higher pain tolerance than African-American patients on a variety of experimental and questionnaire measures.[56] Other studies have affirmed this result in more general population samples.[57] In Chapter 2, I asserted that increased pain tolerance may be implicated in suicidal behavior. In this context, it is interesting that a relatively high-risk group, Caucasians, have higher pain tolerance than a relatively low-risk group, African-Americans.

Age

A very important factor in serious suicidality is the learned capability to, in Voltaire's words, "surmount the most powerful instinct of nature." The acquisition of this capability requires time and experience—it thus stands to reason that it would increase with age. According to the logic of my theory, if the acquired ability to enact lethal self-injury increases with age, so then should suicide.

In fact, in the vast majority of countries and cultures, suicide does increase with age. In the United States, suicide is most common in those who are sixty-five years old or older,[58] and this extends to virtually all countries with reliable suicide rates.[59] The ratio of attempted to completed suicide among adolescents is quite high (more than a hundred to one), whereas this ratio is around four to one among older people.[60] With age, then, suicidal behavior becomes increasingly lethal. Of course, there may be associations with age of the other two parts of the model as well—burdensomeness and thwarted belongingness. In our study of psychotherapy patients at the Florida State University Psychology Clinic, a measure of perceived burdensomeness was correlated with age, such that older people reported more perceived burdensomeness (the study did not include a measure of failed belongingness).

Although speculative, it seems plausible that over the last few decades exposure to violence has become more common through such means as violence in films, the media, and video games; weapon use; and drug use. Exposure to violence in general has increased markedly over the last fifty years. If it has become easier to acquire the capability for suicide, there should be some recent flattening of the age curve, such that suicides occur, on average, somewhat earlier in life in more recent cohorts. This does appear to be the case.[61]

It might be suggested that an important aspect of the current model, burdensomeness, seems mostly applicable to older people, and that despite the fact that suicide clearly increases with age, it remains true that some young people die by suicide. Indeed, in 2000, suicide was the third leading cause of death for young people in the United States, whereas it was the eleventh leading cause of death overall.[62] Why would burdensomeness be applicable to adolescents? In reply, the sense of being a burden is not limited to situations in which one feels like a failed breadwinner. One can feel a burden at any age, whether on one's family or on society. This is made clear by conceptual and empirical work on the "expendable child,"[63] mentioned in Chapter 3. Feelings of expendability, which explicitly include burdensomeness, are connected to suicidality in young people.[64]

Suicidal behavior is rare in young children, in part because they have not had the experiences and time to have acquired the ability to seriously injure themselves. Though rare, suicidality is occasionally observed in very young children. One study compared suicidal preschoolers, ages 2.5 to 5, to preschoolers who were not suicidal but who had serious psychiatric problems. The two groups of children were matched on age, sex, ethnicity, parental marital status, and socioeconomic status. The suicidal children differed from the comparison children in two relevant ways: they had higher pain tolerance, as indicated by fewer displays of pain and crying on injury; and they were more likely to be unwanted, abused, or neglected by parents.[65] Few models of suicidal behavior would claim to be able to explain suicidality in a three-year-old, yet the model developed here is consistent with data from preschoolers in that key aspects of the current model differentiate suicidal from other psychiatric inpatient preschoolers.

Depression is often viewed as a source for suicidality, with good reason. Depression exacerbates feelings of burdensomeness and disconnection. However, the view that depression is the main source for suicide does not square well with some epidemiological facts. Specifically, depression is, if anything, a young person's disease: the average age of onset is around twenty,[66] and rates of depression are highest in young adults.[67] On average, negative emotions are higher—and positive emotions lower—in young than in old people.[68] By contrast, despite some mild flattening of the age curve, suicide is much more a problem in older than in younger age groups. A simplistic framework that views depression as the main source for suicidal behavior has trouble grappling with these facts. By contrast, the model proposed in this book is compatible with the association between age and serious suicidal behavior.

To my knowledge, the only exception to the rule of increasingly serious suicidal behavior with increasing age occurs in Native American people. The peak for death by suicide among Native Americans is in young adulthood. Despite generally elevated rates of suicide among Native American people, older Native Americans are actually less likely to die by suicide than their U.S. Caucasian counterparts. This pattern may be attributable to tendencies toward passive acceptance by elderly Native Americans and traditional respect of the aged in Native American culture.[69] This seems plausible in terms of explaining low rates of suicide among older Native Americans, but why the very high rates of suicide among younger Native Americans (especially young men)? Far too little research has been conducted on this important question, but my prediction would be that young adult Native Americans confront conditions that drain them of feelings of belonging and effectiveness—experiences that older Native Americans, relatively speaking, may be buffered from.

In the United States, older, white men are most at risk for suicide. This stands to reason—on each dimension taken separately (age, gender, ethnicity), these men are in the at-risk group each time. One other factor is at play, I believe, and it is the tendency of this group in particular not to replenish their social connectedness as they age. U.S. men in general and white men in particular seem to form some close friendships in childhood and early and late adolescence, but the forming of new and deep friendships in adulthood is relatively rare. This is less the case for other groups (e.g., women in general; non-white men). Older white men in the United States thus may be particularly prone to feelings of failed belongingness as they age and as early friendships end for whatever reason; they are not buffered by the replenishment of new adult friendships, at least not to the degree of other groups.

This was clearly the situation for my dad at the time of his death. He had close friendships in early adulthood, but as they faded or failed for whatever reason, he did not form new ones. This was not the case for another man I knew who died in his eighties from natural causes. At his memorial service, I was impressed to learn of his constant social connectedness throughout his life. He made new sets of friends every decade, it seemed. He was a pretty gruff character, but he nonetheless had a habit of calling at least one friend a day just to chat for a few minutes. He worked at initiating and maintaining friendships, and this seemed to sustain him. If more older white men did this—indeed if more people did this—I would predict a decrease in the overall suicide rate.

The Clustering and "Contagion" of Suicide
As I mentioned in the Prologue, from time to time, completed suicides cluster in space and time. For example, in a high school of ap-

proximately 1,500 students, two students died by suicide within four days.[70] During an eighteen-day span that included the two completed suicides, seven other students attempted suicide. What is the mechanism underlying suicide clusters? Why are they relatively rare?

A possible explanation for the clustering of suicides is that assortative relating is involved. Specifically, people who are vulnerable to suicide may form friendships or romantic relationships with each other based in part on shared suicide risk factors (e.g., substance abuse)—that is, they relate assortatively, not randomly. This may have the effect of prearranging potential suicide clusters well in advance of any stimulus that might activate the cluster. When impinged upon by severe negative events, members of the cluster are at increased risk for suicidality. Severe negative events would include, but not be limited to, the suicidal behavior of one member of the cluster. An array of other negative events could activate the cluster as well.

According to this view, there are many potential clusters, but very few clusters involve any actual suicidal behavior, in part because of the "pulling together" effect noted earlier—if a member of a cluster attempts or dies by suicide, it is a local tragedy that can pull people together, increase belongingness, and buffer against suicidal behavior by other members of the cluster. Increased belongingness is viewed here as a braking mechanism in the phenomenon of suicide clusters.

This explanation is very challenging to test empirically, but I conducted a study that attempted to do so. I showed that, consistent with an assortative relating process, college roommates who *chose* to room together were more similar on a suicide index than were roommates who were *assigned* to room together. Stress in the roommate relationship amplified similarity in roommates' suicide levels. Results were consistent with the view that shared stress simultaneously affects the suicidality of people whose contiguity was prearranged by an assortative relating process.[71]

Case reports are also consistent with this perspective. A cluster of fourteen suicides among current patients of a London psychiatric unit took place during a one-year period. Thirteen of the fourteen patients suffered from severe, chronic mental illness (e.g., schizophrenia), and most had ongoing therapeutic contact with the psychiatric unit. One factor in the development of this cluster was the patients' valid perceptions that the future of the hospital was uncertain and that their access to medical staff was decreasing and ultimately threatened (a potential blow to the need to belong).[72] Victims were assortatively related (through contact with the same psychiatric unit) based, at least in part, on shared suicide risk factors (e.g., chronic mental illness). Vulnerable people were brought together (through contact with the agency), were exposed to a belongingness threat (potential for dissolution of the agency; lack of access to important caregivers; for some, suicides of peers), and may not have been well buffered by good social support (the chronically mentally ill often have low social support; a main source of support may have been the agency, which was threatened).

In a suicide pact among three adolescents, each was cocaine dependent (a possible assortative factor for this cluster), and each viewed the other two as the only source for a sense of belongingness. When the three were threatened with dissolution by trouble with the law and parents, their only source for belongingness was endangered. The three decided on suicide.[73]

Another consideration regarding suicide clusters involves the acquired ability to enact lethal self-injury, an emphasis of the theory proposed in this book. It was noted earlier that courage and competence regarding suicide may accrue ideationally through various forms of mental practice, including aborted suicide attempts.[74] It is possible that members of suicide clusters may habituate to the idea of suicide through frequent discussions of the topic with other members of the cluster.

This appears to occur on the disturbing "pro-suicide" website alt.suicide.holiday (or ASH), where suicide is construed favorably and where visitors are instructed on the best methods for suicide. For example, regarding self-poisoning, the site makes these points: "Most drugs cause vomiting. To help stop this, take one or two anti-histamine tablets . . . about an hour before" and "Use a large airtight plastic bag over your head, + something around your neck to hold it on. This transforms a 90% certainty method into a 99%." It is not difficult to see why many people feel rage and disgust at the activities of this website.

As many as twenty-four completed suicides have been linked to the site.[75] In a quotation that illustrates assortative relating, Andrew Kurtz, a visitor to the site, wrote in 1996, "I really like this site, because at least I know there are others out there who feel similar to me. Sometimes I feel so alone, but I feel a little better reading other people's posts." Kurtz died by self-inflicted gunshot wound a few days after posting these words to the site. His post can also be viewed as illustrating the merging of the need to belong and the wish for death. Just as young people in Japan have linked up over the Internet with the sole purpose of dying together, some people link up to this site and feel a kind of belongingness in their suicidality.

In Chapter 1, I recounted a story from Tad Friend's 2003 *New Yorker* article of a young girl who took a $150 taxi ride to the Golden Gate Bridge and jumped to her death. She had been visiting a how-to website about "effective" and "ineffective" suicide methods. The site states that poison, drug overdose, and wrist cutting are rarely fatal, and therefore recommends bridges, noting that "jumps from higher than . . . 250 feet over water are almost always fatal."

Pro-suicide group norms appear to attract people to the ASH website and to encourage suicidality among visitors. Researchers have experimentally evaluated the connection between group norms and self-aggression. They used a self-aggression paradigm, which involved self-administered shock during a task disguised as a reaction-time game, with self-aggression defined by the intensity of shock chosen. Their goal was to show that intensity of self-aggression is affected by social group norms.[76] In this research, high levels of self-administered shock occurred when group norms were manipulated to encourage self-aggression.

A tragic real-life version of this experiment occurred on January 12, 2003. Helen Kennedy reported in the *New York Daily News* on the death by overdose of a twenty-one-year-old man.[77] The particularly troubling aspect of his death was that many people witnessed it—he died as a group of virtual onlookers observed him via his webcam. As he took in more and more prescription and other drugs, comments like "That's not much. Eat more. I wanna see if you survive or if you just black out" and "you should try to pass out in front of the cam" were typed in by onlookers. Kennedy commented, "In the macho atmosphere of the druggie chat room, [the man who overdosed] seemed to have something to prove." The man's brother agreed, stating "It seems like the group mentality really contributed to it," adding that the transcript of the incident was "disgusting." Eventually, some of the onlookers came to understand the gravity of the situation and tried to intervene, but could not, because they had no way of finding out where the man was. He was found early in the afternoon of the next day by his mother. Here, as in the example of the ASH website, group mores normalizing risky behavior are encouraged, leading people to habituate to danger, which in turn leads to self-inflicted death in some cases.

Suicides do occasionally cluster. This phenomenon may be understood in part in terms of assortative relating, thwarted belongingness, and the accrual of suicide-related courage and competence via encouragement from those with "pro-suicide" views.

I was concerned about these phenomena recently when I served as a consultant to the city attorneys of St. Petersburg, Florida, who wanted to block the rock band Hell On Earth from staging a show featuring the public suicide of a terminally ill person. I emphasized two things in particular in my affidavit. First, I stated that there was potential for vulnerable people who see a public suicide to become further emboldened about their own plans for suicide—a vicarious accrual of the ability to enact lethal self-injury. Second, the terminally ill person had publicly committed to this incident, with plans for the concert dependent on his or her suicide. The public nature of the event may constrain the person from changing his or her mind. In Chapter 2, it was noted that people often do change their minds about suicide at the last minute. The city prevailed—the concert was cancelled and a judge banned further such displays.

Indeed, publicizing suicide in careless ways can be a menace to public health. In Tad Friend's 2003 *New Yorker* article, he wrote of the frenzy that occurred as the 1,000th suicide from the Golden Gate Bridge approached. He stated, "In 1995, as No. 1,000 approached, . . . a local disk jockey went so far as to promise a case of Snapple to the family of the victim." Friend noted that the California Highway Patrol halted its official count at 997, trying to quell attention to the countdown.

Specific media guidelines have been developed to decrease the pernicious effects of inappropriately publicizing deaths by suicide. A consortium of agencies, including the Centers for Disease Control and Prevention, the National Institute of Mental Health, and the American Association of Suicidology, came together to develop the guidelines. The recommendations include not portraying the person who died in romantic or heroic terms, reporting the death with few details about method and location of death, and not conveying that the suicide was an inexplicable act of an otherwise high-achieving person. In general, the guidelines are intended to minimize identification with the person who died.

The model described in this book exceeds, I believe, the ability of other frameworks to account for a diverse array of suicide-related facts. Regarding facts as disparate as mass suicides in cults, the high rate of suicide in Chinese women, the relative rarity of death by suicide, and the clustering and contagion of suicide, the model provides at least some explanatory power. In the next chapter, the applicability and compatibility of the model to the genetics and neurobiology of suicide, as well as the suicide risk factors of impulsivity, childhood adversity, and mental disorders, will be taken up.

WHAT ROLES
DO GENETICS,
NEUROBIOLOGY, AND
MENTAL DISORDERS
PLAY IN SUICIDAL
BEHAVIOR?

5

Suicidal behavior runs in families, and this fact has to do with genet-ics and neurobiology as well as genetically conferred personality traits like impulsivity. Families share genes and much else. They also share the family environment. Childhood adversity has been shown to be a risk factor for later suicidal behavior. Genetics, neurobiology, per-sonality, and early experience are each implicated in the development of mental disorders, which in turn confer substantial risk for suicide. In this chapter, I will review each of these topics as they link to sui-cide and examine the compatibility and relevance of my model to each of these topics.

In 1621, Robert Burton wrote in his massive *Anatomy of Melan-choly* that black bile is suicide's "shoeing horn." Burton was remark-able—almost four hundred years ago, he anticipated a lot of key findings about depression and suicide. Regarding suicide, he was right that there does appear to be a "shoeing horn," but black bile is not it. If there is a "shoeing horn" for suicide, it is the serotonin system.

Serotonin is a neurotransmitter that is key with regard to things like mood, sleep, and appetite. Understanding the role of serotonin requires more, however, than just knowing about this neurochemical. Serotonin is imbedded within a larger system, including specific genes that code for things like the serotonin transporter (which is responsible for "recycling" serotonin back up into neurons after it is released into the gap between neurons, called the synapse) and serotonin receptors (which receive serotonin from the synapse and thus transmit a signal). Of course, the transporter and receptors themselves, as well as serotonin itself, are important parts of the system. All of these interact with one another in intricate ways. Despite these complexities, the role of the system in suicide is becoming clearer. Since serotonin-system genes may play a role in suicide, I will start with a discussion of whether there is a genetic contribution in general to suicide, and then focus specifically on serotonin-system genes.

Genetics

In his 1936 book *Man against Himself*, Karl Menninger described several families in which suicide was common. For example, he wrote, "A highly regarded family contained five sons and two daughters; the oldest son killed himself at 35, the youngest developed a depression and attempted suicide several times but finally died of other causes at 30, a third brother killed himself in a manner similar to that of his older brother, still another brother shot himself to death, and the oldest daughter took poison successfully at a party. Only two children remain living of this entire family."[1] Incidentally, the gender difference in death by suicide can be discerned in this example. Of the brothers, 80 percent either died by or nearly died by suicide, as compared to 50 percent of the sisters—hugely elevated rates in both cases, but still, a gender effect of sorts.

Menninger continued, "There is no convincing scientific evidence that the suicidal impulse is hereditary and there is much psychoanalytic evidence to show that these cases of numerous suicides in one family may be explained on a psychological basis." The psychological basis, he believed, was unconscious death wishes toward loved ones. When a loved one dies by suicide, a relative's unconscious death wish is suddenly gratified, creating a wave of guilt that may culminate in the relative's suicide.

Menninger was working under an unfair disadvantage. Since the time of his 1936 book, an enormous amount of work has shown the clear involvement of genes in behavior in general and suicide in particular. Also since that time, psychoanalytic theories have not stood up well to scientific scrutiny.

A family history of suicide appears to contribute about a twofold increase in risk—a little more if there are multiple, close relatives who have died by suicide; a little less if there are relatively few and distant relatives. This rule of thumb can be very useful to people who have lost a loved one to suicide. In fact, I have had visits and calls from people around the United States about this very question.

Usually, the call or visit is from the wife of a man who has died by suicide, wanting to know the genetic risk to her children. Anecdotes like the family mentioned by Menninger in which five of seven siblings died by suicide can make people understandably anxious. It is often reassuring for people to hear that the risk for any given person walking down the street is 1 out of 10,000, or .0001. A child whose dad has died by suicide has a risk that is around 2 out of 10,000, or .0002—no higher than 5 out of 10,000, or .0005, in any event. The fact that I am a surviving child of a dad who died by suicide adds credibility, I think, to the reassurance.

Regarding the involvement of genes in behavior, twin samples are the most useful to study; they can help determine whether a genetic contribution to some trait or behavior exists. A usual strategy is to compare monozygotic, or identical, twin pairs, who share all of their genes, to dizygotic, or fraternal, twin pairs, who share on average half of their genes (as do any siblings who are not identical twins). If genes are involved, identical twins should share the trait or behavior more often than fraternal twins, because identical twins share all their genes, and fraternal twins share approximately half of their genes.

A potential complication is that the family environment may also be more similar for identical twins than it is for fraternal twins, because identical twins may be treated more similarly (e.g., dress alike) than fraternal twins. So, an even better strategy is to study twins separated at or near birth and reared apart from one another, as might happen when twins are adopted by different families. However, because the confluence of twinship, adoption, and later suicide is rare, no twin adoption study on suicide has been conducted, to my knowledge. There have been informative nontwin adoption studies, however.

Overall, twin studies have found that 13 to 19 percent of identical twin pairs were concordant for death by suicide as compared to less than 1 percent of the dizygotic (DZ) twin pairs, a significant difference.[2] Given that one twin has died by suicide, this means that the chances that the other will die by suicide are around 15 percent for identical twins and less than 1 percent for DZ twins. One percent is an elevated rate, it should be noted; the probability of any given individual in the United States dying by suicide is around .01 percent. Therefore, 15 percent is an extremely elevated rate.

Researchers in Denmark have used an adoption register to study the genetic aspects of suicide. From a register of thousands of adoptions, they identified fifty-seven who eventually died by suicide. These fifty-seven were compared to fifty-seven matched adopted controls who had not died by suicide, specifically with regard to family history of suicide among their biological relatives. Over 4 percent of the biological relatives of the suicide group had themselves died by suicide, as compared to well under 1 percent of the biological relatives of the control group.[3]

Further evidence of the role of genetics in suicide is shown through family studies. One early study examined the Old Order Amish over a hundred-year period. During this time there were twenty-six people who died by suicide, the majority of whom came from only four families. Interestingly, while these four families had a high genetic loading for depression in addition to suicide, other families had a similarly high loading for depression but no suicides. This suggests that the genetic component for suicide may be independent from the genetic component for depression.[4] Other studies, too, have pointed to a unique genetic contribution to suicide, over and beyond the genetic contribution to mental disorders like depression.[5] This is a key point about the relation of mental disorders to suicidality—mental disorders, though very important in understanding suicidality, do not fully explain it. Further, a simplistic view of the association between mental disorders and suicidality does not explain why most people with mental disorders do not attempt or die by suicide.

The twin and adoption studies converge to show that genes are involved in suicidal behavior. To return to the issue of the serotonin system, suicide's "shoeing horn," we are now honing in on specific genes that may confer risk for suicidal behavior. One gene that has received much attention is the serotonin transporter gene. As noted earlier, the neurochemical serotonin is important in mood, sleep, and appetite. The serotonin transporter maintains control over the availability of serotonin in the synapse, essentially by acting as its recycler—the transporter recycles serotonin back up into the neuron after serotonin is released into the synapse. SSRI drugs used to treat depression like Prozac, Zoloft, and Paxil exert their effects by shutting down or inhibiting the action of the transporter, one effect of which is to leave more serotonin "in play" in the synapse.

A single gene is responsible for encoding, or for the "architectural plans," of the transporter—the serotonin transporter gene. In humans, this gene is located on chromosome 17. A region of this gene has been identified as having what is called a "polymorphism" in it. A polymorphism just means that something can take multiple forms. In the case of the serotonin transporter gene, there are two possible forms, depending on the presence or absence of an additional string of gene building blocks in the gene sequence. Each of the two variations is referred to as an allele of that gene. If an allele has the insertion, it is called a long allele; if it does not, it is a short allele.[6] Since all humans carry two copies of each gene, there are three possible combinations of the two alleles: two long alleles (*l*/*l*), a long allele and a short allele (*l*/*s*), or two short alleles (*s*/*s*).

There is some emerging consensus that those with the *s*/*s* genotype have more dysregulated serotonin systems and thus are more prone to attendant problems. A recent study that followed 103 suicide attempters over the course of a year found that the *s*/*s* genotype was more common in people with higher numbers of suicide attempts.[7] A postmortem study found that the *s*/*s* genotype was more common among suicide victims than among others, although this difference did not reach statistical significance.[8] My colleagues and I reported that those with a significant family history of suicide were more likely to have the *s*/*s* genotype than were those without a family history.[9]

This latter study is of personal interest to me, not only because it was my study, but also because I have the *s*/*s* genotype and have a significant family history of suicide, having lost my dad to suicide. I do not know my dad's genotype, but he had to have had at least one *s* allele, because people get one allele from their mother and one from their father. Since I have two *s* alleles, my dad had to have had at least one himself, as must my mom, making both either *s*/*s* or *s*/*l*. It is not possible to know for sure which my dad was, though if I tested my sisters and both were, like me, also *s*/*s,* the likelihood increases that my dad was *s/s*. Given the research, my guess is that my dad did carry the *s/s* genotype.

There are other serotonin-system genes besides the serotonin transporter. Perhaps the one that has received the most overall attention is the tryptophan hydroxylase (TPH) gene. Tryptophan is a precursor, or ingredient, of serotonin. TPH breaks down tryptophan and thus serves as a kind of braking system in the making of serotonin. This gene is located on chromosome 11, and two polymorphisms in particular have been studied: *A218C* and *A779C*. The *A* and *C* represent different alleles (sort of like "long" and "short" on the serotonin transporter gene), and the numbers 218 and 779 represent locations on the chromosome.

A meta-analysis (pooled results across studies) of the association between the *A218C* polymorphism and suicidal behavior found that presence of the *218A* allele was significantly related to increased risk for suicide.[10] Other studies have examined the *A779C* polymorphism, and its relationship to suicide is less clear.[11]

One final gene that deserves mention is not a serotonin-system gene—the catechol-O-methyltransferase (COMT) gene has only recently been studied with regard to suicide. Somewhat similar to the relation of TPH to serotonin, COMT is responsible for breaking down neurochemicals like dopamine and norepinephrine, and thus can be viewed as a braking mechanism for these neurotransmitter systems. A gene on chromosome 22 codes for COMT activity and occurs in two variations, the *H* allele and the *L* allele, which trigger high or low COMT activity, respectively. As with most other research on candidate genes, results have been mixed. One study identified no difference in COMT genotype between patients at high risk for suicide and controls.[12] However, other studies have suggested that variations in the COMT gene are associated only with violent suicide. In one sample, the *L* allele was more frequent in violent suicide attempters versus nonviolent attempters and nonattempters. The nonviolent suicide attempters and nonattempters showed no difference in COMT genotype.[13] A similar study stratified the results by gender and found that the *L* allele was more frequent in males with a history of suicide attempts but not in females. Furthermore, males who carried the *L* allele were more likely to have made violent suicide attempts and more attempts overall, but this relationship did not hold for females.[14]

In summary, twin, adoption, and family studies of suicidality have clearly shown that there is a genetic component to suicidal behavior. This genetic risk for suicidality appears to be partly independent of risk for mental illness. Several candidate genes for the transmission of suicide risk have been identified. The serotonin transporter gene, the TPH gene, and the COMT gene have all shown links to suicidal behavior, at least in some studies. At the same time, it is important to note that suicidal behavior is too complex to be accounted for by any one gene; the analysis of the effects of multiple genotypes in combination may help to differentiate levels of genetic risk.

Neurobiology

Neurobiological variables also implicate the serotonin system in suicidal behavior. One of the most well-replicated findings involves 5-hydroxyindoleacetic acid (5-HIAA), which is the major metabolite of serotonin; that is, when the body breaks down serotonin, one of the main things it breaks it down into is 5-HIAA. Studies have found low levels of 5-HIAA in the spinal fluid of suicidal individuals. A meta-analysis (review of pooled studies) examining 5-HIAA, as well as metabolites of other neurotransmitters like dopamine and norepinephrine, found consistent evidence for lowered 5-HIAA in suicide attempters and completers but no evidence for consistent changes in other metabolites.[15] This suggests that the serotonin system specifically is linked to suicidality, whereas other neurotransmitter systems may not be, at least not as strongly. A subsequent review came to similar conclusions and also indicated that low levels of 5-HIAA in suicide attempters is predictive of subsequent attempts.[16]

Another approach to documenting abnormalities in the serotonin system is by administration of what is called a fenfluramine challenge. Fenfluramine stimulates serotonin release. Results have generally shown a decreased release of serotonin in suicide attempters versus depressed patients and controls, indicating less serotonin activity despite the fenfluramine challenge. It is noteworthy that this applies to suicidal patients specifically, even as compared to depressed patients.[17] Those who attempted suicide by more lethal means show decreased activity in an area of the brain called the prefrontal cortex, as compared to low-lethality attempters, and this was particularly apparent after the fenfluramine challenge.[18] The prefrontal cortex may be involved in impulse control. These high-lethality attempters also show decreased serotonin release in response to the fenfluramine challenge, as compared to low-lethality attempters.[19]

Still another method of evaluating the serotonin system's role in suicide is by postmortem analysis of the brains of individuals who have died by suicide. This area of research is not as clearly defined as the 5-HIAA and fenfluramine literature, as some have found no difference in important serotonin-system parameters between those who died by suicide and those who died by other means.[20] However, a postmortem study found decreased serotonin transporter binding in the prefrontal cortex of those who died by suicide.[21] This means that the serotonin transporter was not working optimally in those who died by suicide; note also that the relevant brain area, the prefrontal cortex, was the same as that identified in a previous study as important in suicide. In this study, as in others, results were specific to suicide as compared to major depression—emphasizing that the genetic vulnerability to suicide is distinct from the vulnerability to other conditions, even including depression.

Another interesting angle to the association of the serotonin system to suicidality involves sleep. Serotonin appears to play a significant role both in suicide and in the regulation of sleep.[22] The release of serotonin is highest during waking states, reduced during slow-wave sleep, and lowest during REM sleep. Interestingly, serotonin-system dysfunction, particularly a reduction in the synthesis of serotonin, is believed to promote wakefulness.[23]

Several studies have also demonstrated that disturbed sleep is related both to suicide attempts and to completed suicide.[24] One of the first studies to examine sleep, depression, and suicide over time found that symptoms of global insomnia were more severe among those who later completed suicide within a thirteen-month period.[25]

Depressed patients with self-reported repetitive and frightening dreams are more likely to be classified as suicidal compared to those without frequent nightmares.[26] A similar relationship recently emerged in an impressive study conducted in Finland. The study revealed a direct association between nightmare frequency at one point in time and completed suicides roughly fourteen years later. Compared to subjects reporting no nightmares, those reporting occasional nightmares were 57 percent more likely to die by suicide. Among those with frequent nightmares, the risk for suicide increased dramatically; individuals reporting frequent nightmares were 105 percent more likely to die by suicide compared to individuals reporting no frightening dreams.[27]

My colleagues and I recently studied this issue at the FSU Psychology Clinic. Among a large sample of psychotherapy outpatients, we assessed the associations of sleep problems to suicidal symptoms. Our results indicated that insomnia, nightmare symptoms, and sleep-related breathing problems collectively predicted suicidal ideation, but that nightmare symptoms were uniquely associated with suicidal ideation, whereas insomnia and sleep-related breathing problems were not. Put differently, nightmare problems were clearly related to suicidality; on the other hand, the only reason insomnia and breathing problems appeared to be related to suicidality is because they were more common in those who had frequent nightmares—they had no independent influence on suicidality.[28]

The specific association of nightmares to suicidality is interesting to consider in light of the framework developed in this book. People who have frequent nightmares, especially those in which they are subjugated or victimized, often have the thought, "I'm ineffective and powerless even in my sleep." Insofar as ineffectiveness is a general quality of which perceived burdensomeness is a severe subset, nightmares may relate to suicidality partly as a function of general feelings of ineffectiveness. Also, those who are having nightmares often disturb the sleep of their partners, which could have implications for belongingness. In fact, this seemed to have been an issue for my dad, whose snoring (a sleep-related breathing symptom) was problematic. In our study at the FSU clinic, sleep-related breathing symptoms were not uniquely associated with suicidality; however, that study used a very rough measure of sleep-related breathing problems, and so it would not surprise me if future research found a link between this variable and suicidality as well.

The literature is clear. Of all neurotransmitter systems, the serotonin system is the most important with regard to suicide risk. Metabolites of dopamine and norepinephrine are generally no different in those at risk for suicide than in others. However, one other brain system, the hypothalamic-pituitary-adrenal (HPA) axis, deserves mention.

The HPA axis is the body's main "stress reaction" system. Any stress lasting longer than a few minutes will stimulate release of a particular hormone by a structure in the brain called the hypothalamus. The released hormone then acts on the pituitary gland, causing it to release still another hormone. This in turn causes the adrenal cortex to release cortisol, often called the "stress hormone."

When this sequence works well and normally, it prepares the body for "fight or flight" responses to stress. But if stress is chronic and severe, cortisol is always circulating. The problem with this is that cortisol signals the hypothalamus and the pituitary gland to stop producing their respective hormones. Chronic signaling makes the system unresponsive, leaves too much cortisol circulating, and thus impairs the person's ability to respond to stress.

One way to measure HPA-axis activity is by administration of a substance called dexamethasone. Dexamethasone is a synthetic steroid similar to cortisol, which, in normal people, suppresses release of one of the hormones that leads up to cortisol release. Therefore, giving dexamethasone should reduce this hormone and thus reduce cortisol levels, as long as the HPA system is working well.

However, if the system has become dysregulated from chronic stress, it will not be sensitive to dexamethasone, and thus cortisol production will not be suppressed. Nonsuppression of cortisol in response to dexamethasone indicates an HPA system gone awry.

Nonsuppression of cortisol in response to dexamethasone may be predictive of later death by suicide. One study followed a group of patients over fifteen years and found that those with nonsuppression of cortisol at baseline went on to have a fourteenfold greater risk of death by suicide than those who did suppress cortisol output in response to dexamethasone.[29] These studies suggest that hyperactivity of the HPA system could be involved in suicidal behavior.

It even is implicated in self-wounding behaviors in monkeys. Rhesus monkeys who frequently and severely wound themselves (usually through biting) showed the same kinds of responses to dexamethasone as do humans whose HPA systems are dysregulated.[30]

In summary, neurobiological research to date has clearly shown that there are serotonin-related differences in suicidal individuals as compared to others. These differences appear to be specific to serotonin and may not involve other neurotransmitters. Studies of spinal fluid and fenfluramine challenge responses indicate decreased serotonin-system function in suicide attempters and completers. Research has also raised the possibility of involvement of the HPA system in suicidality.

Interestingly, many of the serotonin-system differences between suicidal people and others are also relevant to the personality variable of impulsivity. Serotonin-system problems may contribute to both suicidality and impulsivity. For example, differences between those who died by suicide and others regarding serotonin binding appear to be localized to an area of the prefrontal cortex, an area involved in impulse control.[31] Disruptions in serotonin-system functioning may predispose people to an array of impulsive behaviors, which, in turn, may reduce fear of provocative experiences, including suicidality.

Impulsivity and suicidality are not the only consequences of serotonin-system dysfunction. Another consequence involves tendencies toward negative emotion, depression, and anxiety. With regard to the theory proposed here, factors that increase negative emotionality may affect suicidality via impact on feelings of burdensomeness and failed belongingness.

Impulsivity

Impulsive personality characteristics are a well-documented risk factor for serious suicidality. To get a sense of what "impulsive" means, consider these items from a measure of impulsivity: "Have people told you that you're a daredevil type or that you take too many risks?" "Have you driven recklessly?" "Have you hurt yourself regularly, even if you didn't mean to (e.g., falling, bruising)?" "Have you stolen material goods (such as clothes or jewelry) from a store or vendor?" "Have you impulsively spent money on clothes, jewelry, or other items?" Answering "yes" to most of these questions would indicate an impulsive personality style.

Impulsivity can have serious negative consequences. Menninger wrote, "As for impulsiveness, a volume could be written about the disastrous consequences of this symptom. It has ruined many a business, many a marriage, and many a life."[32]

In a study of 529 mood-disordered patients, 36 participants died by suicide and 120 others attempted suicide during the fourteen years of the study. Impulsivity was among the variables that differentiated those who died by or attempted suicide from those who had no suicide attempt.[33] In a study of suicide attempts in 295 women with bulimia nervosa, the binge-purge syndrome, over a quarter of the women had attempted suicide, often including severe and multiple attempts. Those who had attempted suicide differed from those who had not with regard to frequency of impulsive behaviors.[34] These and other studies demonstrate that impulsivity is involved in suicidality.

But *how* is it involved? The literature on suicide often implies that a principal mechanism underlying the relation of impulsivity to suicide is "spur-of-the-moment" suicide—that is, someone deciding all of a sudden, perhaps in response to a serious disappointment or conflict, to die by suicide. I am very skeptical of this concept, and I doubt that true "spur-of-the-moment" suicides exist. Impulsivity is implicated not so much at the time of death, but beforehand, leading to experiences that allow people to get used to pain and provocation and engage opponent processes (e.g., impulsive people drink more and are injured in accidents more than others). Through repeated impulsive acts, suicidal and otherwise, impulsive people may become experienced, fearless, and competent regarding suicide and thus capable of forming plans for their own demise.

Musician Kurt Cobain's suicide is a very clear example of a planned suicide in someone who was viewed as impulsive and had clearly accrued an array of provocative experiences, including repeated self-injury. His impulsivity was involved in his death, but not in the sense of a "spur-of-the-moment" decision to die. Rather, his impulsivity led him to experiences that reduced his fear of death.

Alvarez was also skeptical of the phenomenon of "spur-of-the-moment" suicides, which he termed "so-called 'impetuous' suicides."[35] He says of them that, if they survive, they "claim never to have considered the act until moments before their attempt. Once recovered, they seem above all embarrassed, ashamed of what they have done, and unwilling to admit that they were genuinely suicidal . . . They deny the strength of their despair, transforming their unconscious but deliberate choice into an impulsive, meaningless mistake. They wanted to die without seeming to mean it." To Alvarez, "impetuous suicides" are ersatz; they are really usual suicide attempts with a posthoc, shame-saving explanation of impulsivity.

Menninger's book *Man against Himself* is packed with newspaper clippings and clinical anecdotes about suicidal behavior, but not one is a "spur-of-the-moment suicide," with one exception. The only exception is a fictional one, Shakespeare's Romeo.

Interestingly, the serotonin system, as was implied above, is implicated as a basis for impulsive personality style. For example, compared to others, people with impulsive/erratic personality disorders, people with histories of aggression, arsonists and other violent offenders, and people who have murdered a relationship partner all have lower levels of serotonin metabolites in their spinal fluid. In violent suicide attempters, those who were identified as having high impulsivity had significantly lower serotonin metabolites than non-impulsive attempters and controls.[36] Plasma blood levels of serotonin metabolites were lower in impulsive suicide attempters than non-impulsive attempters and controls.[37] Potentially lethal suicidal behavior, impulsivity, and disruptions in the serotonin system appear to be inter-related.

Fenfluramine challenge studies support this conclusion. As was noted earlier, fenfluramine stimulates serotonin release. A blunted response to fenfluramine challenge suggests less serotonin-system activity. Blunted response to the fenfluramine challenge is seen in impulsive people,[38] as it is in people at high suicide risk. One study examined the relationship of suicide attempt lethality as well as impulsive behaviors to fenfluramine challenge. Individuals with high lethality attempts and impulsive personality characteristics showed the lowest responses, indicating the most underactive serotonin systems.[39]

My claim is that impulsivity is associated with suicidal behavior, but indirectly. According to the model developed in this book, impulsivity only relates to suicidal behavior because impulsivity facilitates exposure to provocative and painful experiences. A similar statement could be made about the relation of serotonin-system problems to suicidality—the association exists only because serotonin-system problems tend to produce impulsivity (and negative emotion), which, in turn, increase the likelihood of provocative and painful experiences. The latter, according to my view, instills the acquired ability to enact lethal self-injury. Disruptions in serotonin-system functioning may predispose people to an array of impulsive behaviors, which, in turn, may reduce fear of provocative experiences. These experiences may lead to the acquired ability to enact lethal self-injury and thus to increased risk for completed suicide.

The definitive study to test this claim has not been conducted, to my knowledge. How would such a study look? I can think of two interesting strategies. The first would be to measure impulsivity, painful or provocative experiences, and suicidal behavior in a very large sample of people (a large sample is needed because of the relative rarity of suicidal behavior; one could also study a smaller, high-risk group in whom suicidal behavior is more likely). I predict that there would be a significant association between impulsivity and suicidal behavior; but crucially, I predict that this association would be reduced or eliminated when painful or provocative experiences were accounted for. This is a simplification, but generally, this pattern of results would indicate that impulsivity is associated with suicidality only because it facilitates exposure to painful or provocative experiences.

A second strategy would be to examine samples in which either impulsivity or painful or provocative experience was a constant. Imagine a sample selected so that everyone had the same level of impulsivity. I would predict an association between painful or provocative experiences and suicidality in this sample, because, according to my theory, painful or provocative experiences confer risk to suicide by dampening fear of self-injury, and this is the case regardless of the level of impulsivity. Now imagine a sample selected so that everyone had the same level of painful or provocative experiences. I would *not* predict an association between impulsivity and suicidal behavior in this sample, because, in my view, impulsivity only relates to suicidality through its relation to painful or provocative experiences. If the latter is held constant, impulsivity would have no "traction" through which to predict suicidality. My students and I are currently conducting experiments to test this claim.

Of all personality dimensions, impulsivity has the most clearly documented association with suicidal behavior. I believe this has provided the misleading suggestion that the act of suicide itself is an impulsive decision. I don't think so. Rather, there is a real and important association between impulsivity and suicidality, and it exists because impulsivity leads people to habituate to pain and provocation. They thus acquire the ability to enact lethal self-injury, and are thereby at increased risk for suicide, if the desire for death is in place. Impulsivity could relate to suicidality through increasing the desire for death as well. As Menninger noted, impulsivity can ruin lives. Accordingly, it would not be surprising if it tended to increase feelings of burdensomeness and failed belongingness.

Childhood Adversity

There is now little doubt of an association between childhood maltreatment and later suicidality—a real association not explained away by other variables. Other variables are important to consider. It could be, for example, that the same genes that predispose a parent to be abusive predispose the child to be suicidal. In fact, excellent candidates for such genes would be those that underlie impulsivity—an impulsive parent is more likely to abuse, and an impulsive child is more likely to attempt suicide. Under this scenario, there is no real association between child abuse and later suicidality. The real mechanism is genes and personality simultaneously raising risk for abuse by the parent and suicidality in the child.

This scenario appears to have been ruled out. There seems to be a direct link between childhood adversity and later suicidality, a link not explained by other variables. For example, as was noted earlier, feelings of expendability (including burdensomeness) have been empirically linked to suicide; it would not be at all surprising if the experience of childhood abuse and neglect were a main source of feeling expendable. A study of Eskimos in the Bering Strait region showed that the majority of a sample of suicide attempters had lost a parent during childhood.[40] Similar results were reported among patients with borderline personality disorder. Patients with borderline personality disorder who had died by suicide experienced more childhood losses such as death of a parent as compared to living control patients with borderline personality disorder.[41]

As noted in Chapter 3, neglectful parenting is an independent risk factor for adolescent suicidal ideation and attempts. This is true even after adjusting for other powerful variables like the presence of psychiatric disorder.[42] Childhood physical abuse differentiates adolescents who died by suicide from matched controls.[43] A study of over 3,000 female adolescent twins found that childhood physical abuse was one of the factors most associated with a history of attempting suicide.[44] Childhood physical abuse was also associated with lifetime suicide attempts in a study of people with alcohol-use disorders.[45]

A very persuasive study on this topic followed 776 randomly selected children from a mean age of five years to adulthood in 1975,

1983, 1986, and 1992 during a seventeen-year period. More than 95 percent of the sample was retained throughout the entire study period, a considerable achievement. The researchers ascertained the occurrence of abuse through official records as well as by participants' recall of abuse incidents. Results showed that childhood abuse conferred significant risk for suicidality in adolescence and adulthood, with the strongest and clearest effects for childhood sexual abuse in particular. Risk of multiple suicide attempts was eight times greater among those with a sexual abuse history than among others.[46]

As mentioned in Chapter 2, our study on data collected from the National Comorbidity Survey—a large project on the occurrence of mental disorders and associated variables in U.S. adults—told a similar story. Our analyses showed that some forms of abuse were more frequently linked to subsequent suicidality than were other forms; specifically, the effects for childhood physical abuse and sexual abuse on later suicidal behavior were relatively pronounced and similar to one another, and exceeded effects for molestation and for verbal abuse.

Various forms of injury and victimization may instill the ability to lethally harm oneself and increase risk for serious suicidal behavior. On the one hand, the experience of physical and sexual abuse could habituate people to self-injury. In fact, regarding childhood sexual abuse, there is evidence that more painful forms (e.g., severe forced abuse) are more associated with suicidality than less painful forms.[47] On the other hand, the model developed in this book posits that lethality combines with desire for death to result in serious suicidal behavior, and that desire for death stems from feeling a burden on loved ones and others, and feeling disconnected and alienated from others. As noted in Chapter 2, to the degree that any form of abuse facilitates either lethality (through habituation to pain and provocation) or desire for death (through increased feelings of burdensomeness or disconnection), it should, according to the current model, constitute a risk for later suicidal behavior. Childhood physical and sexual abuse may particularly confer risk, because they are both painful and imply burdensomeness and disconnection. In fact, there is evidence that increased alienation (similar to lack of belongingness) is a prevailing psychological link between childhood maltreatment and later suicidal behavior.[48]

What is the main neurobiological mechanism linking early abuse to later self-injury? There is intriguing evidence that the HPA axis is involved. Adults who have been abused as children appear to have a dysregulated HPA system.[49] Another effect of an HPA system gone awry is decreased volume of a brain region called the hippocampus, which is heavily involved in memory. Too much circulating cortisol seems to erode hippocampal cells. In one study, depressed women who had experienced childhood abuse had smaller hippocampal volume on brain scans as compared to depressed women who had not been abused.[50]

Childhood adversity harms the HPA axis and increases risk for adult suicidal behavior. As was noted earlier in this chapter, HPA problems may also increase risk for later suicidality. Putting these facts together, it is plausible that childhood adversity affects later suicidal behavior partly through its effects on the HPA system. This may be one neurobiological underpinning for the psychological effects of childhood adversity on suicide. Childhood adversity, especially when severe, impacts all aspects of my model. It familiarizes people with pain and provocation, and it makes them feel worthless and alienated—a lethal combination, according to the view developed here.

Mental Disorders

Approximately 95 percent of people who die by suicide experienced a mental disorder at the time of death.[51] As noted in the first chapter, I believe my dad had bipolar II disorder—serious depressions combined with hypomanic episodes—and this played a role in his death. Little is known about the other 5 percent, but most if not all of them likely experienced one or more "subsyndromal" mental disorders—

that is, they experienced many symptoms of, say, depression, but not quite enough symptoms to rise to the threshold of formal diagnosis according to the American Psychiatric Association's *Diagnostic and Statistical Manual of Mental Disorders, Fourth Edition (DSM-IV)*.

A brief side note on the *DSM* is in order. The manual has many merits, but one of them happens *not* to be an ultimate monopoly on truth—it is a work in progress, albeit a very reliable one. Despite the *DSM*'s imperfections, we must discount the views of some scholars who claim that mental disorders do not exist or represent social myths. A full discussion of this notion is beyond the scope of this book, but briefly, one profound problem with this idea is that it is an affront to people with mental disorders (indeed, people who have died from them), as well as to their loved ones. Imagine, as your loved one is dying from cancer, that someone smugly tells you, "Cancer doesn't really exist anyway." People with major mental disorders and their loved ones have suffered exactly this offense. Another problem with this idea is that it is highly implausible in light of current scientific knowledge. Writing specifically of schizophrenia, Seymour Kety summed up this issue succinctly: "If schizophrenia is a myth, it is a myth with a strong genetic component."[52]

The *DSM* has five axes, and the first two are relevant here. Axis I includes the major mental disorders like schizophrenia, mood disorders, anxiety disorders, substance-use disorders, and so on. Axis II includes the personality disorders. Several of these two categories of disorders (e.g., schizophrenia, bipolar-spectrum disorders, major depression, some anxiety disorders, some substance-use disorders, and some personality disorders) appear to play a role in the risk for suicide. In what follows, the relevance of the proposed model is evaluated with respect to suicidality in the context of several different mental disorders.

The anxiety disorders include panic disorder, social phobia, generalized anxiety disorder, post-traumatic stress disorder, obsessive-compulsive disorder, and specific phobia. Symptoms of some of the anxiety disorders have been repeatedly implicated in serious suicidality. For example, an analysis of the Food and Drug Administration (FDA) database of treatment outcome studies found a significant association between anxiety disorders and suicide.[53] Jan Fawcett and colleagues have repeatedly shown that severe anxiety is an important sign of acute suicide risk.[54]

Of all the anxiety disorders, panic disorder probably has received the most attention with regard to associations with suicidality. Panic disorder involves repeated experiences of severe panic attacks that often come "out of the blue"; people going through a panic attack often believe they are having a heart attack or that some other catastrophic thing is happening. Indeed, there does seem to be a significant association between panic disorder and suicidal symptoms,[55] although the connection may be explained mostly by the fact that panic disorder often co-occurs with mood disorders,[56] and of course suicidality often emerges in the context of mood disorders.

From the standpoint of the model developed in this book, it is interesting to note that there is a form of panic disorder, panic disorder with agoraphobia, that particularly affects the need to belong. People who experience this form of panic disorder are so concerned about experiencing panic attacks that they rarely leave their house and thus experience extreme reductions in social contact. By the logic of the current model, those who experience this form of panic disorder should be more prone to suicidality than those who experience panic disorder without agoraphobia. In fact, there is some evidence to this effect.[57]

Substance-use disorders confer risk for suicidality.[58] As has already been noted, according to the perspective proposed here, this association is mainly a result of substance abuse facilitating provocative experiences and thus the acquisition of the ability to enact lethal self-injury. In Chapter 2, for example, it was noted that heroin users are fourteen times more likely than peers to die from suicide, and that the prevalence of attempted suicide is also many orders of magnitude greater than that of community samples.[59]

Some people report feeling more courageous while intoxicated;[60] this sense of courage can be misdirected toward self-injury in some people. In a relevant study on this point, some participants were given alcohol to a blood alcohol level of .10 percent, and some were given a placebo drink. Then, all were provided the opportunity to self-administer shock during a task disguised as a reaction-time game, with self-aggression defined by the intensity of shock chosen. Men who had consumed alcohol self-inflicted more shock than those who did not.[61]

A recent example shows how substance abuse can facilitate painful and provocative experiences, including self-injury. On July 13, 2004, the Associated Press reported that in March of that year a man in England drank fifteen pints of beer, then got in an argument with a friend about whose turn it was to buy the next beer. Apparently the argument was unresolved, so the man went home to retrieve a sawed-off shotgun. He stuffed the gun in his pants. On the way back to the pub, the gun discharged. His lawyer stated, "He still feels quite severe pain" and added that some shotgun pellets remained lodged in the man's groin area, potentially rendering him infertile. To make it worse, the man was jailed for illegal possession of a firearm. In this example, substance use clearly led to a painful, self-injurious experience.

Prolonged substance abuse can certainly deteriorate social capital (leading to low belongingness) and diminish feelings of overall effectiveness (producing feelings of perceived burdensomeness). Indeed, a review of the literature on alcohol abuse and loneliness revealed that alcohol abusers experience more loneliness than do members of most other groups.[62] A series of phone interviews with a predominantly crack-cocaine-using sample found that those continuing to use the drug after treatment report lower self-efficacy.[63] Findings like these suggest additional points of consilience between parameters of substance-use disorders and the current model's emphasis on perceived burdensomeness and failed belongingness.

As was noted in Chapter 2, two mental disorders, borderline personality disorder and anorexia nervosa, are of particular interest, because they are among the most lethal of all psychiatric disorders (despite being more common in women than men), with the usual mechanism of death (including for anorexia nervosa) being suicide.[64] Borderline personality disorder is characterized by a longstanding pattern of stormy interpersonal relationships, self-destructive behaviors such as self-cutting or -burning, marked emotional lability and impulsivity, and an empty or diffuse sense of identity. Unfortunately, in some clinical settings, patients with the disorder have the reputation for manipulation, including manipulating others through self-destructive behaviors (e.g., "gesturing suicide"), as well as for "splitting" (e.g., pitting people, including clinicians, against one another); some people roll their eyes about such patients, take a subtly or overtly demeaning tone about them, and make disparaging comments.

In some clinical settings, mental health professionals harbor demeaning attitudes toward people with borderline personality disorder. I recently read a hospital progress note for a person with borderline personality disorder that stated, "This patient is certainly not getting treatment from *me.*" One reason for sentiments like these is the belief that many such patients merely "gesture" suicide. In other words, they engage in suicidal behaviors, such as cutting themselves, but do not really intend to kill themselves; instead, they only intend to provoke or manipulate others.

If only this were true. Those with borderline personality disorder have a 10 percent lifetime rate of death by suicide; at least 50 percent of people with borderline personality disorder have made a minimum of one very severe suicide attempt;[65] and among those with this syndrome, an average of over three lifetime suicide attempts has been reported.[66] Further, history of previous attempt among people with borderline personality disorder is a stronger predictor of completed suicides than for any other diagnostic group (e.g., 65 percent of suicides among those with borderline personality disorder have made a prior attempt; 33 percent of suicides among those with major depression have made a prior attempt).[67] Through repeated self-injury, people with borderline personality disorder become practiced regarding suicidal behavior and may thus become courageous and competent about suicide. Moreover, a common and pervasive sense of self-doubt and feelings of alienation and abandonment are very likely to instill perceptions of being a burden and create difficulty in belonging. As a consequence, suicide risk is usually elevated in patients with borderline personality disorder.

Women with anorexia, too, put themselves through a physical ordeal—namely, self-starvation. In addition, those with the binge-purge subtype of anorexia also endure various compensatory efforts like self-induced vomiting, ingesting agents like ipecac syrup that induce vomiting, repeated enemas, and so on. Through these provocative experiences, the theory proposed here suggests that women with anorexia may acquire the ability to enact lethal self-injury. Indeed, there is evidence that anorexic women have elevated pain thresholds,[68] as has also been shown in suicide attempters,[69] and suicide rates among women with anorexia are quite elevated. Over the course of a ten-year follow-up interval, the rate of death by suicide among 246 women with eating disorders was fifty-eight times the expected rate.[70] All of those who died were anorexic; no women with bulimia died (but see below).

Shneidman's case example of Beatrice represents an example of the co-occurrence of anorexia and suicidality.[71] Beatrice said of her suicide attempt by self-cutting, "The evening dragged on with me busy reopening the stubborn veins that insisted upon clotting up. I was patient and persistent, and cut away at myself for over an hour. The battle with my body to die was unexpected, and after waging a good fight, I passed out." She also said, "For the next two years . . . every night, before fading off to sleep, I imagined committing suicide. I became obsessed with death. I rehearsed my own funeral over and over, adding careful details each time." Beatrice later planned her suicide for three months and tried again to die by self-cutting; she survived.

Shneidman wrote something about Beatrice that is very revealing, I think. In her voice, he wrote, "I can try to control myself (and others) through controlling my body. My body is my only practical handle on the world, a rheostat (that I can turn up and down)—gain or lose the same 15 pounds—I can control my life by controlling my body. And if life gets too painful—I can turn it off completely." Through control of eating and body, she comes to the ability to beat down the self-preservation instinct. She has developed that "little switch"—the ability to turn life off—through the painful and provocative experiences of suicidality and anorexia. In her own words, Beatrice makes it plain: "For me, restricting my food intake is not about being fashionably thin, it's about my death wish."

As compared to women with anorexia, who may combine self-starvation with intermittent binges and severe compensatory behaviors, women with bulimia may not be at as high a risk, because their experiences are relatively less provocative (e.g., self-starvation is not present or not as extreme). Thus their activities may be less likely to produce habituation and engage opponent processes. Among women with bulimia, however, I would predict that those with purging behaviors (a provocative experience) would endorse more suicidal symptoms than those with nonpurging behaviors (e.g., excessive exercise, a relatively less provocative experience). In fact, a history of suicide attempt is more prevalent in purging bulimic women than in other bulimic women.[72]

As is the case for women with anorexia, women with bulimia have decreased pain sensitivity. In fact, their decreased sensitivity to pain may persist even after their eating disorder resolves. One study compared bulimic women who had recovered from bulimia at least a year ago to fifteen healthy volunteer women.[73] All women in the study received two pain evaluations. The first was a thermal pain stimulation test, which evaluates heat tolerance; the second was the submaximal effort tourniquet test, which assesses tolerance to pain induced by inflation of a blood pressure cuff. In general, recovered bulimic patients showed higher pain tolerance on both tests as compared to controls. To my knowledge, no study has examined the difference between purging and nonpurging women with bulimia regarding pain tolerance. Since purging bulimics have been through more provocation than nonpurging bulimics, I would predict higher pain tolerance in the former group. If true, their higher pain tolerance may play a role in their higher suicidality.

It is potentially important that high pain tolerance remains in women with bulimia, even well after they recovered. High pain tolerance in particular and the acquired ability to enact serious self-injury in general may be slow to fade. Once in place, these psychological features likely endure for quite some time. As will be pointed out in the next chapter, this has implications for prevention and treatment of suicidal behavior. The acquired ability to enact lethal self-injury may be resistant to change, more so than other aspects of the model (like perceived burdensomeness and low belongingness). These latter qualities thus may be more fruitful targets for treatment and prevention programs.

It is interesting to recall that, in general, women have low rates of completed suicide. Women who undergo an array of provocative experiences, however, may be exceptions to the general rule. Patients with borderline personality disorder, anorexia nervosa, and, perhaps to a lesser degree, bulimia nervosa may represent examples of such women.

Of course, mood disorders deserve consideration in any discussion of suicide. The rates of death by suicide in mood disorders are substantial, and this is true for major depression, bipolar I disorder (with clear manic and depressive phases), and bipolar II disorder (hypomanic and pronounced, recurrent depressive phases).[74] Viewed through the lens of the model proposed here, high suicide rates in mood disorders may be a function of the ability to enact lethal self-injury, which is acquired through repeated past experience with suicidality and through various provocative experiences associated with manic symptoms. Indeed, manic episodes frequently land people in jail, fights, or accidents. Moreover, mood disorders often include acute feelings of ineffectiveness and social isolation, a prominent symptom and associated feature, respectively, of major depression. Therefore, those suffering from mood disorders are vulnerable on all three of the dimensions emphasized in my model—acquired ability for lethality, perceived burdensomeness, and failed belongingness.

There is a form of major depression called the atypical subtype. This subtype's symptoms include oversleeping, overeating, and extreme interpersonal rejection sensitivity. The subtype is labeled "atypical" because the symptoms of oversleeping and overeating are unusual among depressed people; usually, depressed people lose their appetite and have insomnia. With regard to the rejection sensitivity symptom, it includes reactions to perceived criticisms or rebuffs that are so intense that it is difficult to maintain long-term relationships. New relationships are avoided for fear of potential rejection. Belongingness will therefore be a long-standing and vexed issue for people with the atypical subtype of depression. There is mixed evidence as to whether people with the atypical subtype experience higher risk for suicidal behavior than do other depressed people. One study found that people with the atypical subtype had more suicidal ideas and suicide attempts than other depressed people; atypical depressions also had earlier age of onset than other depressions.[75] Early age of onset is one marker of severity of a disorder, and this alone could explain why those with the atypical subtype had more suicidality than others. But if it is established that atypicality is associated with suicidal symptoms in a real way, my model would predict that this occurs, in part, because people with this syndrome struggle so intensely with rejection sensitivity and thus low belongingness.

Interestingly, rates of suicide are lower for people suffering from dysthymia (a low-grade but very chronic form of depression)[76] than from other depressions. Again viewed from the present perspective, this stands to reason, in that the feelings of ineffectiveness and social isolation in dysthymia may not reach the level of severity necessary to fully instill the desire for death.

Antisocial personality disorder is interesting to consider in light of the model proposed here. The disorder is characterized in the current psychiatric nomenclature as a long-standing pattern of aggressive behavior and reckless and impulsive disregard for others and for rules and norms. However, recent research, informed by classic work by the psychiatrist Hervey Cleckley,[77] suggests that there are two different kinds of antisocial personality. One type is characterized by emotional detachment (i.e., low anxiety; fake or shallow emotions; immunity to guilt and shame; callousness; and incapacity for love, intimacy, and loyalty). The other type is characterized by impulsive, reckless, and under-controlled behaviors.

Cleckley reserved the term "psychopath" for those with the cardinal feature of emotional detachment. Research has demonstrated that the two types of antisociality are separable.[78] One factor is currently emphasized by DSM and prioritizes antisocial behavior. The other factor was formerly emphasized in DSM to some degree and corresponds to Cleckley's emphasis on "emotional detachment." According to this research, there are two kinds of people with antisocial personality—those who are emotionally detached (and who are also prone to poor behavioral control, in part because of their emotional detachment), and those who are primarily impulsive, aggressive, and irresponsible but who are not emotionally detached (and actually may be especially emotionally reactive).

My colleagues and I predicted that this latter type of individual would be prone to suicidal behavior (due to the combination of impulsivity and emotional reactivity), but that emotionally detached, "Cleckley psychopaths" would not be, due in part to low emotional reactivity. Our study of 313 inmates supported this prediction: "antisocial behavior" was associated with history of suicide attempts; "emotional detachment" was not, and in fact, was negatively associated with suicide history, although to a nonsignificant degree. Moreover, we found that the link between "antisocial behavior" and suicidality occurred in part because antisocial characters were prone to the combination of negative emotionality and impulsivity.[79]

According to the model of suicidality described here, emotionally detached antisocial personalities may not be prone to suicide, because their callousness and incapacity for intimacy and loyalty would insulate them from perceived burdensomeness and disconnection from others. By contrast, antisocial personalities characterized by under-controlled behaviors would be at higher risk, because their recklessness gives them an opportunity to habituate to pain and injury, and because their negative emotionality increases the likelihood of a sense of burdensomeness and low belongingness.

Virtually everyone who dies by suicide experienced one or more mental disorders at the time of their death. Certain disorders are more associated with suicidal behaviors than others, and it is important to recall that relatively few people with a mental disorder die by suicide. My model explains these facts by arguing that some mental disorders are more likely than others to lay down the ability to enact suicide and to instill perceived burdensomeness and failed belongingness. Those with one of these suicide-related disorders who do not die by suicide have managed to avoid perceived burdensomeness, low belongingness, or acquiring the ability to seriously harm themselves, despite their mental disorder. Certain mental disorders substantially increase the likelihood but do not guarantee that the three conditions will be present that I propose are required for serious suicidality.

At the moment of conception, a baby's future is not fully plotted, but some of its general trajectories can be discerned. Genes influence neurobiology, including the serotonin system. Genes also influence personality traits like impulsivity, and this influence may occur mostly through genes' impact on the serotonin system. Genetics, neurobiology, and personality all interact in complex ways with an individual's life experience. Early adverse experience, including childhood abuse and neglect, heightens the risk for later problems, especially in vulnerable people. One set of such problems is mental disorders, which, in addition to the agony and impairment they cause, clearly confer risk to suicidal behavior. Genes, neurobiology, impulsivity, childhood adversity, and mental disorders are interconnected strands that converge and can influence whether people acquire the ability for lethal self-injury, feel a burden on others, and fail to feel that they belong. This lethal endpoint is the culmination of processes started at conception and furthered, biologically and through experience, over a person's lifetime.

6

Time and again, psychopathology theorists and researchers go to great lengths to develop theories and models of psychopathology, but then when it comes time to talk about applications like assessment, treatment, and prevention, there is a great disconnect between theory and application. I think this occurs in part because applications are often developed without theory in the clinic—on the fly, as it were. This is not all bad, because many treatments that are disconnected from theory are very good—and, it must be added, some treatments that are awash in theory are not very good at all.

Some examples of good treatments are interesting to consider. A first is called Interpersonal Psychotherapy (IPT) and it was developed in the 1970s by the late psychiatrist Gerald Klerman and colleagues. IPT is a down-to-earth, here-and-now kind of psychotherapy originally developed for depression but now used for other conditions too. Its central idea is that if a major interpersonal issue connected to symptom onset is worked out—say, a grief problem or a hostile standoff in a marriage—then that is bound to help relieve symptoms. IPT also recommends the sensible strategy of staying focused on one interpersonal issue, trusting that progress made on it will generalize to improve other areas too.

That IPT relieves symptoms is beyond doubt; randomized, controlled clinical trials have attested to the fact. In an intriguing study, IPT was assessed in rural Uganda.[1] Thirty Ugandan villages were studied. In each village, men or women who were self-identified and viewed by other villagers to have symptoms of depression were interviewed. In the local language, there is no single term to describe depression. Instead the interviewers asked for persons with *Yo'kwekyawa* or *Okwekubazida,* two depression-like syndromes well known to villagers. These two syndromes together include all the major depression symptom criteria in the *DSM-IV.* Approximately eight per village of the most depressed people were selected for participation, totaling around 250. Eight of fifteen male villagers and seven of fifteen female villagers were randomly assigned to the therapy and the remainder to a control group. People in the control villages did not receive the therapy; however, people in both control and intervention villages were free to seek whatever other interventions they wished throughout the study. The intervention villages received the depression therapy in group meetings for weekly ninety-minute sessions for sixteen weeks. Groups were led by a local person, of the same sex as the group, who had received brief training in the therapy. During each session, the group leader reviewed each participant's depressive symptoms, and participants described recent events and linked the events to his or her mood. The group leader then facilitated supportive statements and suggestions for change from other group members. The therapy was very effective. Among those who received the treatment, rates of severe depression went from around 90 percent before treatment to around 6 percent after treatment; by contrast, among those in the control groups, rates of severe depression went from around 90 percent before treatment to around 55 percent after treatment.

This and other studies show that IPT is effective. But it is remarkably theory-free. As IPT was being developed in the 1970s and thereafter, a scientific and theoretical literature on the interpersonal aspects of depression was developing too.[2] Strangely, these two strands of work rarely if ever intersected. IPT's relative lack of theory has not hamstrung it; it works, and additionally, no theoretical errors or obfuscations were introduced as part of the treatment description.

A second example of a good treatment being disconnected from theory is the Cognitive Behavioral Analysis System of Psychotherapy (CBASP).[3] This treatment relies heavily on past work by people like Aaron T. Beck and Albert Ellis on cognitive therapy, as well as on the field of applied behavior analysis. The gist of CBASP is, in ways, similar to IPT. The idea is to repeatedly focus on specific, discrete situations and then to mould one's thoughts and behaviors so that those situations tend to produce one's goals. Like IPT, the idea is down-to-earth, and like IPT, impressive clinical trial data support the treatment's effectiveness.[4]

The theory behind the treatment, however, is both flawed and largely irrelevant to the treatment. The theory makes unfortunate and unsubstantiated claims about the nature of depressed people— for example, that the chronically depressed individual is "a cognitive-emotionally retarded adult child who brings a negative 'snapshot' view of the world to the session. The chronic patient functions, at least in the social-interpersonal arena, with the structural mindset of a 4–6-year-old preoperational child."[5] I find this a ludicrous claim, and would feel even more strongly, I'm sure, if I were a chronically depressed adult. Moreover, the claim is not necessary or even very relevant to the treatment, which, far from being ludicrous, has been shown to be effective and useful.

The cognitive theorizing and treatment recommendations of Beck represent a good example of the coming together of theory and treatment. Beck and many other people working from a cognitive viewpoint have developed theories of psychopathology wherein a maladaptive schema for the understanding and making sense of one's role in the world confers vulnerability to various forms of psychopathology. The treatment revolves around correcting the maladaptive schema.

My goal in this chapter is to try to emulate Beck in a useful, relevant, and productive bringing together of theory and practice. The previous chapters have laid out the theory and its anecdotal and scientific support. This chapter attempts to use the theory to inform clinical practice regarding suicidal behavior, starting with the important area of suicide risk assessment.

Risk Assessment

Recall the distinction between the alarmist and the dismissive approach to suicide risk assessment. The alarmist position involves the idea that whenever someone mentions suicide, it is a life-threatening situation and alarms should be sounded. Those who take a dismissive approach make a mistake in the opposite direction. They become blasé about suicidal behavior, often attributing it to manipulation or gesturing on the part of the potentially suicidal person. A compromise is thus needed between the alarmist and dismissive approaches—one that is efficient and clinically useful, scientifically supported, and conceptually consistent with the model developed in this book.

Any risk assessment system has to grapple with the fact that there are dozens of suicide risk factors, some of which are associated with imminent risk (e.g., severe agitated anxiety), and others of which are important but are more distal and not clearly tied to imminent risk (e.g., family history of suicide). In fact, a quick survey of the websites of organizations like the American Association of Suicidology, the American Foundation for Suicide Prevention, and the American Psychological Association, among many others, shows that over seventy-five factors are listed as suicide risk factors or warning signs, including things as diverse and questionable as "loss of religious faith," "neurotransmitters," "perfectionism," and "loss of security." Given limited time, clinicians cannot thoroughly assess all of these various factors, and even if they could, how are they to organize the resulting mass of data?

Of all the numerous risk factors and warning signs, do any stand out as particularly important? If so, then a risk assessment approach might be built around them. Of course, based on the model developed in this book, the acquired ability to enact lethal self-injury deserves emphasis, as do perceived burdensomeness and low belongingness. To assess acquired ability, my colleagues and I argued that two factors deserve particular weight: a history of multiple suicide attempts and the specific nature of current suicidal symptoms, with specific reference to whether the symptoms include resolved plans and preparations or suicidal desire.

Multiple attempt status is emphasized because it is perhaps the clearest marker of the acquired ability for lethal self-injury. The distinction between resolved plans and preparations and suicidal desire is important too. Resolved plans and preparations includes the following symptoms: a sense of courage to make an attempt; a sense of competence to make an attempt; availability of means to and opportunity for attempt; specificity of plan for attempt; preparations for attempt; duration of suicidal ideation; and intensity of suicidal ideation. Suicidal desire includes a different set of symptoms: reasons for living, wish to die, frequency of ideation, wish not to live, passive attempt, desire for attempt, and talk of death or suicide.

Symptoms of the resolved plans and preparations cluster are evidence of the person's ability to lethally injure themselves, because the symptoms require a fearlessness and sense of resolve in order to formulate clear and actionable plans about death. My theory also suggests a broadening of the focus in suicide risk assessment from multiple attempters to anyone who has, through various means, acquired the capability for lethal self-injury. This capability is acquired by means of repeated practice or repeated exposure to self-injury. Practitioners should assess for instances in which a patient may have been able to practice self-harm, including aborted suicide attempts. Experiences like multiple surgeries and repeated tattooings and piercings represent other possible areas of inquiry. Various forms of exposure to violence, as well as other provocative experiences like self-injecting drug use, are other possible areas of investigation.

Another implication of the theory is that the desire for suicide may be most pernicious when it contains themes of both burdensomeness and thwarted belongingness. If suicidal desire in general is endorsed, it should be explored as to whether burdensomeness and thwarted belongingness undergird it. If so, risk may be more elevated; if not, risk may be more moderate. One complexity is that feelings of burdensomeness and low belongingness are not necessarily static; they are fluid and may vacillate in some people. A patient who has mild feelings of burdensomeness one week may have intense feelings the next day or the next week. A person who genuinely professes strong belongingness on one day may subsequently develop a sense of disconnectedness on another day, perhaps as a function of relationship conflict. Clinicians therefore have to monitor risk regularly, even in previously low-risk patients, and in particular need to monitor variables like perceived burdensomeness and failed belongingness, which are both central and fluctuating.

Returning to the overall risk assessment framework, it emphasizes two general domains—multiple attempt status and the two factors of suicidal symptoms described earlier (resolved plans and preparations and suicidal desire). For multiple attempters and those who indicate they have resolved plans and preparations for suicide, risk assessment proceeds differently than for everybody else. In these cases, risk is automatically viewed as elevated, especially in the presence of at least one other risk factor (e.g., burdensomeness, low belongingness, current and serious substance abuse, or severe negative life events). For those who are neither multiple attempters nor endorse symptoms of the resolved plans and preparations factor but who do have symptoms of suicidal desire, the threshold to establish elevated risk is set higher.

More specifically, here is how the framework is used: For multiple attempters, most *any* other additional risk factor (e.g., substance abuse) translates into *at least* moderate suicide risk. For nonmultiple attempters, those with resolved plans and preparations *and* most any other additional risk factor are at moderate suicide risk *at least.* For nonmultiple attempters with *no* resolved plans and preparations but who *do* voice suicidal desire, the presence of two or more additional risk factors translates into *at least* moderate suicide risk.

The framework is not a completely automated statistical prediction rule, but provides a relatively objective starting point for clinical decision-making in risk assessment. In Chapter 1, I mentioned my patient "Gayle," who had recurrent depressions and who had developed ideas about dying by severing her hand with a machete. She had acquired the ability to enact lethal self-injury not through previous suicidal behavior—she had never attempted suicide—but through severe substance abuse and an array of associated painful and provocative experiences in her past. When I saw her, she had been sober for many years, but there were residues of this past, and one was the acquired ability to lethally injure herself.

I wanted to hospitalize Gayle because of her clear and detailed suicide plan and perhaps especially because of her sense of calm and her lack of fear about the plan. But she was not at particularly high risk for suicide, because she did not report thwarted belongingness and perceived burdensomeness. On the contrary, Gayle was very connected to her son and had many friends. Also, she was a particularly capable woman, and there was no evidence that she felt ineffective, certainly not to the point that she believed she burdened others. The risk assessment framework described above clarifies clinical decision-making regarding a situation that would otherwise be very difficult to handle.

When combined with the current theory, an assessment approach like the one just described encourages scientifically and theoretically informed assessment and relatively routinized clinical decision-making and activity. This assessment approach also represents a satisfying integration of theory and application. This same kind of integration can be seen in the important area of crisis management and resolution, to be discussed next.

Crisis Intervention

As demonstrated by the case of Gayle, the acquired ability to enact lethal self-injury, once in place, does not fade quickly. It is a relatively static quality that does not come and go over time. It therefore would not be a particularly useful focus for crisis intervention, where the goal is to take the edge off the pain of the current crisis, so that it is within a tolerable range. Since acquired ability is unlikely to change much in the short-term, it does not provide any leverage to accomplish short-term reduction of distress.

By contrast, professionals who deal with suicidal crises would do well to focus on burdensomeness and belongingness. Unlike the acquired capability for serious suicidal behavior, burdensomeness and belongingness may be more malleable and thus more amenable to short-term crisis intervention. My colleagues and I have described techniques for in-session diminution of distress.[6] For example, techniques such as the symptom-matching hierarchy and development of a crisis card often take the edge off of intense negative moods. Each of these techniques is described next.

The symptom-matching hierarchy simply involves listing disruptive symptoms and feelings. The patient ranks these in terms of which are most upsetting (e.g., as rated on a one-to-ten scale). For the top two or three symptoms or feelings, very concrete recommendations are made (e.g., sleep hygiene for insomnia; relaxation for general emotional distress; pleasant activities for depressive symptoms). These recommendations are not intended or expected to solve the problem or to even change it very much; rather, they are intended to just take the edge off of the problem, so that the person is somewhat more comfortable and thus better able to tolerate the crisis and to start working toward solving the underlying problems.

Feelings of burdensomeness and low belongingness should routinely be targeted within this straightforward crisis-resolution approach. For example, a clinician might say, "I see that you perceive yourself a burden on your family, but do they see it the same way?"; or "Let's briefly review the relationships and groups, not just right now but in the past too, to which you felt a sense of belonging"; or "Let's review the ways you have contributed to people or society, not just right now but in the past too." The therapist could summarize the products of this discussion, perhaps in bulleted form on an index card, and give the summary to the patient, with instructions to expand and elaborate the list at home. Again, the point of this exercise is not to fully undo underlying feelings of burdensomeness and low belongingness, but to destabilize and reduce them slightly, so that the patient will be in a better position to handle the current crisis and build skills through therapy that will eventually target long-standing problems.

The crisis card is another simple technique designed to lessen the intensity of a crisis so that more clear-headed approaches can emerge. The crisis card simply involves the development of a straightforward crisis plan that can be written down on an index card or a sheet of paper. An example would be:

When I'm upset and thinking of suicide, I'll take the following steps:

1. Use what I've learned in therapy to try to identify what is upsetting me, focusing especially on feeling I'm a burden on others and like I don't belong;

2. Write down and review some reasonable, nonsuicidal responses to what is bothering me;

3. Try to do things that, in the past, have made me feel better (e.g., music, exercise, etc.);

4. If the suicidal thoughts continue and get specific, or I find myself preparing for suicide, I'll call the emergency call person at (phone number);

5. If I feel that I cannot control my suicidal behavior, I'll go to the emergency room or call 911.

Both the symptom-matching hierarchy and the in-session development of a crisis card may dilute intense distress then and there in the session. Both techniques should be focused on relieving feelings of burdensomeness and low belongingness. This, in turn, may decrease discomfort—not completely, but enough so that difficulties can be better tolerated and tackled with skill-based therapeutic techniques (to be discussed in the next section). A slight decrease in discomfort, incidentally, may also facilitate the occurrence of general positive moods, which my colleagues and I have shown improves treatment outcome in suicidal individuals.[7]

I recommend the use of a crisis card, as described above, instead of what are known as "no-suicide contracts." No-suicide contracts are written agreements that patients will not attempt suicide while under treatment. They usually are signed by both patient and therapist. One reason that I do not recommend them is that they apparently do not work very well. For example, a survey of Minnesota psychiatrists found that of those who used no-suicide contracts, over 40 percent reported that they had patients die by suicide or make a near-lethal attempt while under a contract.[8] In a study of self-harm incidents among psychiatric inpatients, some of whom were on no-suicide contracts, there was some indication that being under contract was associated with *more* self-harm.[9] This could be because the most seriously ill patients were put under contract, but nevertheless, it does not represent a ringing endorsement of no-suicide contracts.

Another reason that I do not use no-suicide contracts is that they only tell patients what not to do and neglect telling patients what they should do instead. Relatedly, no-suicide contracts ignore important aspects of the model developed in this book. Instead of advising patients not to try suicide, a better approach would be to advise them what to do in the event that suicidality in general escalates and that perceived burdensomeness and feelings of failed belongingness in particular intensify. The crisis card accomplishes this.

I borrow one last thought on crisis intervention from William James. He wrote that to persuade a suicidal person to live, one could "appeal—and appeal in the name of the very evils that make his heart sick—to wait and see his part in the battle out."[10] In their 1933 book on suicide, Dublin and Bunzel expand the point: "the consent to live on is a resignation based on manliness and pride" (pardon their politically incorrect use of "manliness," which I suppose was not politically incorrect in 1933). This perspective neglects the pain of perceived burdensomeness and failed belongingness; when these feelings are very intense, people do not want to continue living regardless of pride or manliness. However, it is an interesting idea to turn the very fearlessness that may facilitate self-injury against itself. Though not a routinely useful part of crisis interevention, this tactic may have promise for some patients, in that it redirects the resolve of the suicidal person on to fighting against evil on behalf of others, which in turn may alleviate low belongingness and perceived burdensomeness.

As with risk assessment, the theory of suicide developed in this book guides clinical activity in the realm of crisis intervention. Short-term interventions that target and take the edge off of perceived burdensomeness and feelings of failed belongingness are likely to contribute to crisis resolution.

Treatment and Prevention

William James wrote, "Be not afraid of life! Believe that life is worth living and your belief will help create the fact."[11] As was so often the case, James was ahead of his time. My colleagues and I have documented that psychotherapy that is focused on amending negative thoughts about self, others, and the future (cognitive therapy) is the leading treatment for suicidal behavior.[12] We also developed and described a particular form of cognitive therapy for suicidal behavior.

Two aspects of this therapy deserve emphasis here. The first is a technique for restructuring negative thoughts to which we gave the acronym ICARE. Each of the letters in the acronym stands for a step in the process of altering negative thoughts. "I" stands for identification of a particular negative thought. In context of my model of suicidal behavior, thoughts related to burdensomeness and low belongingness should be prioritized.

"C" stands for connection of the particular thought to general categories of cognitive distortion. There are numerous kinds of cognitive distortion. Some examples include all-or-nothing thinking, catastrophizing, disqualifying the positive, and overgeneralization. All-or-nothing thinking involves viewing a situation inflexibly, with only two extreme categories ("if everyone doesn't love me, then I'm unlovable"). Catastrophizing is predicting the future in a very negative way, without consideration of more likely outcomes ("I'll be so upset that I will be unable to function"). Disqualifying the positive means not counting positive qualities or experiences as real ("My success was just dumb luck"). Overgeneralization involves sweeping negative conclusions that go well beyond the data provided by a given situation ("I felt uncomfortable at a party, therefore I am socially defective").

The first two steps, identifying the thought and connecting it to a larger type of cognitive distortion, set up the third and fourth steps. "A" is for assessment of the particular thought, in light of tried and true cognitive therapy techniques. These techniques essentially involve questions like these: What is the objective evidence for the thought? Against the thought? How likely is it? Are there alternative explanations? Will it matter in a year?

"R" is for restructuring the thought, using information provided by the previous steps. A key process here is to use the assessment data to remove the cognitive distortion from the thought. For the thought "I felt uncomfortable at a party, therefore I am socially defective," the assessment data may include "my performance as a parent and a spouse shows that I'm not socially defective," and the category of distortion is overgeneralization. The task then is to use the assessment data to "degeneralize" the thought; for example, "my discomfort at the party was specific to that situation, and says little about me as a person."

"E" stands for execute—that is, act in ways that logically flow from the restructured thought. In the example of social discomfort at a party, this step may involve feeling free to act with confidence in other social domains, and exploring and if necessary remedying the reasons for discomfort in that one particular social situation.

In context of the theory developed in this book, it is important to focus the ICARE technique on thoughts and themes involving burdensomeness and failed belongingness. For example, the identified thought "I am a burden on my loved ones" could be connected to the distortion of labeling—putting a global, fixed label on oneself without considering evidence that would lead to a less negative label. Assessment data could include the ways that the person contributes to loved ones, but also more generally, to friends and to society. The thought would then be restructured, using the assessment data to make the label less global and more consistent with objective evidence, such as, "Though I feel a burden on others at times, the truth is that I contribute in multiple ways." The last step would involve acting in ways that logically flow from the restructured thought, for example, continuing contributing to others and noticing the rewarding qualities of doing so, and working in concrete ways to minimize feeling a burden and accepting that at times everyone comes up short.

Regarding low belongingness, the identified thought might be, "I'll never fit in." This thought could be connected to the distortion of catastrophizing—predicting the future in a very negative way, without consideration of more likely outcomes. Assessment data could emphasize the relationships and groups in which the person does experience or has experienced some sense of connection. The thought would then be restructured using the assessment data to decastrophize the thought, such as, "Though I may not fit in everywhere, the truth is that I belong to important relationships and groups." The last step would involve acting in ways that logically flow from the restructured thought, for example, further cultivating those connections that exist and systematically working to initiate new connections.

In addition to the ICARE technique, we emphasized some simple approaches to negative mood regulation—that is, better tolerating and handling of negative emotions. This is a weak spot for many people with suicidal symptoms. Consider these examples from individuals who had attempted suicide: "The situation was unbearable and I knew I had to do something but I didn't know what to do"; "I wanted to get relief from a terrible state of mind."[13] In a relevant study, researchers assessed therapist ratings of patients' mood regulation styles. The therapists rated suicidal patients as less likely to engage in active, healthy mood regulation strategies as compared to nonsuicidal comparison patients.[14]

One simple mood regulation technique is the drawing of mood graphs. These are simple charts, with an x-axis representing the passage of time and a y-axis representing the intensity of a negative mood. The task for the patient is to look for a time when negative moods are intense, and then to sit with a pencil and paper, make a mood graph, and simply chart the intensity of the mood over time, once every minute or two, usually for a total of around fifteen to twenty minutes. This exercise always results in some charted improvement in the negative mood. The improvement may not be extreme, but it is visible on the chart nonetheless, and this makes a powerful point. Specifically, the point is that by simply sitting down and making a chart and then rating mood periodically, negative moods lose some of their intensity. Negative moods are not unmanageable monsters; they are just unpleasant states that fade with time. Patients who absorb this lesson become better able to tolerate negative moods without resorting to extreme solutions like self-injury. Furthermore, the therapist is then positioned to make another important point: If the patient is able to gain detectable improvement just by sitting down and making a simple chart, much more improvement can be expected from more thoroughgoing techniques, like the ICARE approach.

The source of the negative emotion on a mood graph's y-axis is likely to consist of either feeling a burden or feeling a lack of belongingness. If patients chart these feelings over time, they will see that they lose their edge even over short periods of time. The understanding that these feelings, though intensely painful in the present, will not be permanent and pervasive, steels patients to ride out the wave of suicidal desire.

The therapeutic approach described thus far has focused on perceived burdensomeness and failed belongingness, because they are relatively fluid states and thus represent a therapeutic path of least resistance. The approach works because it systematically corrects and amends patients' views that they are a burden on others and that they do not belong to valued relationships and groups. However, because the approach emphasizes mindfulness, planning, and emotional and behavioral regulation, it may also inhibit the expression of the acquired capability for lethal self-harm and may discourage involvement in provocative experiences that strengthen this acquired capability. This would occur later in therapy, after self-control is well established. The therapeutic approach thus prioritizes perceived burdensomeness and low belongingness, on the theory that once suicidal desire is decreased, suicidal behavior will be less probable, even if a patient has acquired the ability for lethal self-injury. Over time, through repeated practice at things like ICARE and mood regulation, self-control increases to the point that the acquired ability for self-injury may gradually wane as well.

What about the role of medicines in the management of suicidal behavior? Over the last fifteen years or so, there have been periodic concerns that commonly prescribed antidepressant medicines like Prozac, Zoloft, Paxil, and their kind actually increase risk for suicidal behavior. Initial concerns that these medicines, called selective serotonin reuptake inhibitors (SSRIs), were associated with increased suicidality in adults were put to rest during the 1990s. In 2004, the concern resurfaced and intensified regarding antidepressants for childhood depression. There is some reason for concern. Reviews that examine both published and unpublished clinical trial data show increased suicidal ideation and behavior in depressed children on antidepressants compared to those on placebos, but this is true only for certain antidepressants like Paxil and Effexor.[15]

Oddly, it is not true regarding Prozac. Why would some compounds be associated with increased suicidality, when an extremely similar compound is not? I cannot think of a good answer for this, with one possible exception. Medicines like Paxil and Effexor have much shorter half-lives than does Prozac. In this context, half-life means the amount of time it takes for half the medicine to clear the body. Short-half-life medicines clear quickly and thus can shock the system if not taken very regularly, causing reactions like anxiety, insomnia, and agitation, which in turn have been linked to increased suicidality. If this is the explanation, then it is not the case that antidepressants are causing suicidality; rather, it is that some antidepressants need to be carefully managed, because their short half-lives increase risk for "system shock" and thus for suicidality. In my opinion, the upshot of this should simply be to focus on therapies that have been repeatedly and clearly shown to be both safe and effective for childhood depression—specifically, cognitive-behavioral psychotherapy and Prozac. From the perspective of my model, I doubt that antidepressants increase suicidality in children or in anyone. The majority of the record shows that they improve parameters associated with my model—things like feeling ineffective and socially isolated.

Prevention efforts too may be informed by the three components of the current model. As with treatment, the acquired ability to enact lethal self-injury may not be a wise focus for prevention efforts, because if someone has this quality, it is relatively static and there is not much to do about it in the short-term. By contrast, efforts that enhance belongingness and efficacy may be protective.

In an intriguing example, researchers studied over 3,000 people hospitalized because of depression or suicidality.[16] Thirty days after discharge from the hospital, patients were contacted about follow-up treatment. From those patients who refused follow-up care, a total of 843 patients were randomly divided into two groups. People in one group received a letter at least four times per year for five years. The other group received no further contact.

The letters received by the first group were simply brief expressions of concern and reminders that the treatment agency was there if needed. They were not form letters; the letters received by a given individual were always worded differently, and they included responses to any comments made to previous letters. The researchers always included a self-addressed, unstamped envelope. They provide this example of a contact letter: "Dear _____: It has been some time since you were here at the hospital, and we hope things are going well for you. If you wish to drop us a note we would be glad to hear from you."[17]

Results showed that patients who received the letter had a lower suicide rate in the five years after discharge than did patients in the control group. The researchers specifically attributed this finding to increased belongingness. Referring to belongingness, they described it as "a feeling of being joined to something meaningful outside oneself as a stabilizing force in emotional life . . . it is this force that we postulate as having exerted whatever suicide-prevention influence the contact program might have generated." They continued, "[an earlier paper][18] expressed this concept clearly after recounting suicide prevention measures over 600 years and contemplating what is really new, observing that 'there is surely at least one common theme through the centuries—it is the provision of human contact, the comfort of another concerned person, often authoritative but maybe not, conveying a message of hope consonant with the assumptions and values relevant to that particular time.'"

In the study just described, the prevention technique was targeted at those previously hospitalized for depression or a suicidal crisis. How might their success be generalized and presented to the public at large, or to segments thereof? I am not particularly adept at advertising, public service announcements, and the like, but if I were put in charge of developing a public service announcement, I think I might target it to older men—since they are a demographic with high suicide rates—and its gist might be something along the lines of "keep your friends and make new ones too—it's strong medicine." This idea reminds me of the man I mentioned in Chapter 4 who, despite a gruff exterior, called multiple friends each day for years and years, just to say hello and keep contact. He lived until he was almost ninety, died peacefully, and his memorial service was standing room only.

I noted earlier that the acquired ability to enact lethal self-injury may not be a useful target for prevention efforts, because this quality is relatively static and not very malleable, at least not over the short-term. But this ability is important to consider in planning preventions, because efforts that unintentionally foster habituation to suicidal stimuli may backfire. For example, I would not recommend a "scare tactic" intervention in which graphic pictures of those who died by suicide are shown, because this has the potential to further habituate at-risk people to the idea of death by suicide.

The idea that well-meaning prevention efforts can backfire and increase the behavior they try to prevent is not unheard of. For example, researchers evaluated an eating disorder prevention program in a sample of college women who were in their freshman year.[19] The intervention involved peers who had recovered from eating disorders describing their experiences and providing educational information about eating disorders; a control group who did not receive this intervention was also assessed. Results suggested that the intervention backfired: Those who received it had slightly *more* symptoms of eating disorders than did controls. In fact, I recently saw a specific example of this at the clinic I direct. A girl who was dissatisfied with her body but who had no frank symptoms of an eating disorder saw a prevention film at her school. The film discussed various aspects of eating disorders, including self-induced vomiting. According to the girl, the film produced in her the thought that "I'd like to try that to see if it helps me feel better about my body." Over the ensuing months, she developed a serious eating disorder, including self-induced vomiting multiple times per day.

A mild kind of backfiring has even been detected in some suicide prevention studies. For example, in an evaluation of a school-based suicide prevention program, it was found that the program increased relevant knowledge among girls, but that boys reported increased hopelessness and maladaptive coping responses upon exposure to the prevention program.[20]

The model of suicidal behavior developed in this book is intended as a comprehensive theory of suicidal behavior, not as a clinical description or as prelude to the introduction of some clinical technique. Nevertheless, one of the main benefits of a thoroughgoing theory is the clarification and illumination of clinically important and sometimes vexing topics. Indeed, a theory that has nothing to say about such things could rightly be viewed as suspect.

The theory developed here has substantive things to say about suicide risk assessment, crisis intervention, treatment, and prevention. Each of these areas is informed by the insight that those who do not desire death will be unlikely to pursue it. Therefore, reduced perceptions of burdensomeness and lowered feelings of belongingness represent key targets for clinical interventions from risk assessment on through to prevention. The acquired ability to enact lethal self-injury is important too, but its relatively static quality makes it a target mostly in risk assessment and intensive psychotherapy, and not as much in crisis intervention or in prevention.

7

In this book's opening chapter, I mentioned my own three connections to suicide—as survivor of my dad's death by suicide, as clinician, and as scientist. As perhaps has become clear in the previous chapters, the topic has become mostly scientific and professional for me, with the agenda of prevention and relief of suffering through the culmination of the slow labors of scientific understanding.

But it's still personal too. When I hear misinformation or ludicrous claims, like masturbation and nail biting as relevant to suicide, or the description of a depressed person as "a cognitive-emotionally retarded adult child," it's personal. Or when I am reminded that tomorrow, and the day after that, and the day after that, around 2,500 families worldwide will go through what my family went through, it's personal. And when people scramble to prevent death by lightning strike or death by bicycle accident on the Golden Gate Bridge, and yet are reticent about preventing death by suicide, it's personal.

And when friends and family looked me in the eye and expressed genuine sympathy and sadness about my dad's death—and when others did not do this—that was, and remains, personal. On this important point of support to those who have lost a loved one to suicide, I think my model has a few insights. The main contribution of the book, I hope, is to provide people with an understanding of death by suicide; despite the tragedy, shock, and pain of it, there are tractable and comprehensible reasons that people die by suicide, just as there are tractable and comprehensible reasons that people die by heart disease or cancer. My model emphasizes *perceived* burdensomeness and a *perceived* sense of low belongingness. It is painful for survivors to understand that their loved ones, lost to suicide, perceived these things about themselves; but it is helpful, I think, to understand that these were perceptions, not realities that should be blamed on survivors.

Indeed, if one insists on a special quality to the tragedy of suicide, this is it. These perceptions were lethal, but were changeable through proper treatment (as described in the previous chapter). In general, I believe that death by suicide should be viewed as death by any other means—a tragedy with painful and shocking though not mysterious or stigmatizing properties. Still, the process of death in some cancers, for instance, is simply not reversible with current treatments; that the process of death by suicide is reversible and yet so often is not reversed is a horrible tragedy.

Though my model has a few insights for those who have lost a loved one to suicide and for those who wish to support them, the model is mostly gainsaid by common sense on this point. My advice is to act like my Uncle Jim and my high school friends did for me: just act right. Look survivors in the eye, express sadness and sympathy, be there for them, support them, check in with them every so often, just as you would anyone who has lost a loved one. If you want to recommend a reliable resource for information, education, lists of support groups, and so forth, recommend www.suicidology.org, the website of the American Association for Suicidology, or www.afsp.org, the website of the American Foundation for Suicide Prevention. No lying, no tiptoeing around the subject, no whispering. And if you insist—wrongly, I believe—that suicide is a special case, not like other deaths, then that should make you more, not less, compassionate.

The confluence of the personal and the scientific has informed the model I developed in this book. My dad did not possess many of the characteristics that the public mind attributes to those who die by suicide—he was not timid or retiring; not prone to emotional outbursts or anger; not prone to substance abuse. He was generally an optimistic and hopeful character, though his periodic depressions tempered this. He had bipolar II disorder, but among the group of people with this disorder, I would estimate that my dad was in the top one or two percentiles in terms of functioning and accomplishment, and in the bottom half in terms of symptom severity. If you were looking at the charts of a hundred patients with bipolar II disorder, knowing that approximately ten may die by suicide in the ensuing years and trying to estimate risk for suicidal behavior based on symptoms and functioning, I do not think you would include my dad among the ten or even fifty most likely to die by suicide.

Yet he did. Why? By now, my answer should be familiar. Throughout his life, he had experiences and injuries that facilitated his acquisition of the ability to enact lethal self-injury. I mentioned several of these experiences in the opening chapter. Two others occur to me. In the late 1940s, he survived a hurricane. He told me that the wind blew the rain through the walls of the cinder block structure where he was, and his older brother later told me a similar story. In 1989, there was something wrong with one of my kidneys, and I needed to have surgery to have my kidney removed. My dad spent hours with me in the hospital as I recuperated, far more time than anyone else. This is a reflection of his caring nature, but also, I think, of his tolerance of pain and suffering—even that of his child. Add these experiences to all the others, and it is not hard to see why he had developed the capacity for lethal self-injury—he had numerous chances for habituation. He was as stoic a person in the face of pain as anyone I have met.

This makes suicide an option, an option that will only be accessed when the desire for death is present. My dad's desire for death, I believe, developed in the context of his losing touch with his professional identity, his marriage, and his church. He tried to compensate, for example, by visiting African-American churches, but his efforts were not sufficient. What he needed was to form new and deep friendships and to suffer the pain of rebuilding his professional identity. These things were beyond him, as they are to many men, particularly white men in their fifties and older. I believe this is a main reason that this demographic is at highest risk for death by suicide.

My theory is not only about my dad, however. It is intended to be comprehensive but succinct: to have at least something to say about all deaths by suicide worldwide, across cultures, by employing three simple concepts. I have attempted not only to explain facts, but also to produce new understanding with new ideas. For example, the erosion of fear and the attendant ability to tolerate and indeed engage in lethal self-injury may set into motion still other psychological processes that are important in suicidality; namely, the merging of death with themes of vitality and nurturance. Only when people have lost the usual fear and loathing of death do they become capable of construing it in terms related, ironically, to effectiveness and belongingness. Only those who desire death and have come not to fear it can believe that through death, their need to belong and to be effective will be met. Past researchers and theorists have remarked on attraction to death among suicidal people—my theory specifies the conditions under which it happens, as well as why it happens.

Where Do We Go From Here?

My theory leads to some as yet unanswered questions and suggests a number of avenues for future research. For example, do the rewarding properties of self-injury actually increase with repetition, as predicted in this theory? Is it defensible to view effectiveness and connectedness as the two key ingredients of the will to live? How are we to discriminate lethal, stable forms of burdensomeness and disconnection from less pernicious, more temporary forms? In cultures in which an interdependent view of the self is the norm, is disconnection more painful than burdensomeness, and in cultures in which an autonomous, individualist view of the self is the norm, is burdensomeness more painful than disconnection? What are the precise kinds of self-harm and other provocative behaviors that produce habituation and engage opponent processes? Are mechanisms like cognitive sensitization and cognitive deconstruction compatible with habituation and opponent processes?

Other directions for future research should be mentioned too. A basic but quite important agenda for future work involves measurement technology for each of the three main components of the model presented here. Reliable and valid self-report and clinician-rated measures would obviously benefit research on the model (as well as benefit clinical risk assessment). My students and I have a start on this; here are some of the items we are using to assess the three components of the model. The items are rated on a one-to-five scale. For belongingness, "These days I am connected to other people"; "These days I feel like an outsider in social situations" (this one is reverse scored); and "These days I often interact with people who care about me." For burdensomeness, "I give back to society" (reverse scored); "The people I care about would be better off if I were gone"; and "I have failed the people in my life." For acquired ability to enact lethal self-injury, "Things that scare most people do not scare me"; "I avoid certain situations (e.g., certain sports) because of the possibility of injury" (reverse scored); and "I can tolerate a lot more pain than most people."

A longitudinal study assessing acquired capability for self-harm, burdensomeness, and failed belongingness at baseline, with periodic assessments for changes in burdensomeness and belongingness, as well as for the development of suicidal behavior, would be of interest. In a study like this, it might be predicted that the combination of burdensomeness and failed belongingness should predict increases in suicidal desire, though it should not predict increases in the re-solved plans and preparations factor unless the acquired capability for self-injury is also present.

The various conditions and processes that lead up to the develop-ment of pernicious forms of burdensomeness and belongingness deserve study too. It has already been mentioned that one can poten-tially lead to the other, and that provocative experiences and behav-iors (e.g., repeated self-harm) can lay the groundwork for their de-velopment as well (e.g., through ostracization). Recurrent or chronic forms of mental disorders also seem likely to produce serious threats to the need to belong and to be effective.

By the logic of the current model, those who, through various means (especially deliberate self-injury), have acquired the ability for significant self-harm should be demonstrably different from others in many ways. In fact, as was reviewed earlier, extant data appear to support such differences. More research on this topic would be of in-terest, for example, in the area of neurobiology. Studies are needed on the neurophysiology and neuroanatomy of the acquired capabil-ity for lethal self-injury. Comparison of those who have acquired the capability for self-harm to those who have not on magnetic reso-nance imaging (MRI) and other scanning technologies may illumi-nate specific brain processes and areas that are implicated (for exam-ple, serotonin-related processes in the ventral prefrontal cortex, an area implicated in impulsivity).[1] The self-aggression paradigm de-scribed earlier, in which people self-administer shock,[2] may be useful in testing the present theory, especially with regard to the acquired ability to enact lethal self-injury. One prediction would be that those with substantial histories of provocative behaviors would self-ad-minister more shock as compared to others.

Psychological autopsy studies would also be useful tests of the theory presented here. These studies involve detailed interviews of relatives and reviews of documents regarding those who have recently died by suicide, as compared to those who have died by other means. Aspects of the three variables emphasized here—acquired capability for suicide, burdensomeness, and low belongingness—should all be demonstrable in such studies. A psychological autopsy that shows little evidence of one or more of these variables in those who have died by suicide would represent a grave challenge to the present theory.

Theorists and scientists who work on suicide are often asked why they have chosen their field of study. Isn't the topic morbid and depressing? My answer is probably predictable by now—there is nothing depressing about working to prevent and relieve the kind of suffering that my dad, my family, and millions of others go through. This alone is enough of a reason to study suicide.

But there are other reasons still. Artists and writers, for example, have long understood that the dysfunctional and moribund can inform us about human nature, including what is positive and good. Extreme states and conditions, including suicidal crises, have the potential not only to illuminate the nature of those experiencing suicidality, but to inform us about human nature in general. There are general psychological phenomena that may be invisible in the absence of dysfunction; for example, the study of people who have lost their memories through accidents has contributed greatly to the understanding of normal memory processes. Likewise, an understanding of why some people would wish to end their own lives must certainly contribute to an understanding of human nature in general. The need to belong and to contribute in some way to society seems to be an essential part of what it means to be human.

Voltaire anticipated aspects of the current model almost three hundred years ago in his description of Cato's suicide. I propose a rewording of Voltaire's statement: None but a fearless person—fearless at least about suicidal behavior—who also sees little to live for in terms of effectiveness and connectedness, can surmount the most powerful instinct of nature. This book has described the mechanisms that, tragically, allow some people to acquire the ability to enact lethal self-injury, and, more tragically still, to lose sight of reasons not to use it.

EPILOGUE

I dreamt about my dad as I was writing this book's last chapter; it's been fourteen years almost to the day since my dad died. In fact, this book was due to my editor on August 1, 2004, the fourteenth anniversary of my dad's death. After fourteen years, I still dream about him regularly. In my recent dream, he and I were in Atlanta—the place of my birth and of his death. We were looking together at some kind of construction—it wasn't finished yet, but we both thought it was already great and that once it was done it would be even better. To me, the dream is about my longing for him to see, share, and enjoy the ongoing construction of my personal and professional life.

Given my beliefs, this will never happen in any way. My dad is gone and it is my view that I will never see him again, in this life or the hereafter. This view entails agony for anyone who has lost a loved one, and death by suicide can exacerbate this agony for reasons articulated in my theory. With regard to my dad's death, I hate that he spent his last moments on Earth alone, in the back of a van in some parking lot. I hate that as he died, he must have held the (mistaken) view that he was forsaken by his loved ones and the world in general.

I hate that my mother, sisters, and I had to undergo the awful uncertainty of what happened to my dad, only to discover a truth that made the uncertainty seem easy. I shudder to imagine that in his last few moments of consciousness, he might have come to regret his decision, too late. And I regret that he did not say goodbye.

All of this is so painful that it is easy for me to understand why various views of the afterlife are common and comforting. I believe that these views and their comfort are illusory, but like any adequate scientist, I am aware of the possibility of being wrong. And if I am wrong, then I hope the afterlife is such that my dad is in his boat on Georgia's Lake Lanier, fishing for bass with his dad and my Uncle Jim (both now deceased). I hope the water is calm and that the bass are biting, and I hope my dad, my granddad, and my Uncle Jim know that, though I don't intend it to be anytime soon, I'll be there eventually, and when I arrive, I'll bring more beer and more bait.

NOTES

WORKS CITED

ACKNOWLEDGMENTS

INDEX

NOTES

Prologue

1. Range & Calhoun (1990).
2. Shneidman (1996), p. 15.
3. Menninger (1936), p. 13.
4. Ibid., p. 14.

1. What We Know and Don't Know about Suicide

1. Kellerman (1989), pp. 113–114.
2. Zanarini et al. (2003).
3. Lewinsohn et al. (2003).
4. Alvarez (1971), p. 167.
5. Joiner (1999).
6. Ibid. (2003).
7. Menninger (1936).
8. Sullivan (1953).
9. Menninger (1936), p. 61.
10. Ibid., p. 62.
11. Ibid., pp. 209–210.
12. Shneidman (1996), p. 4.
13. Ibid. (1985).
14. p. 20.
15. Shneidman (1996), p. 13.
16. For example, Beck et al. (1990).
17. Ibid. (1985).
18. Ibid. (1990).
19. Beck (1996).
20. See also Joiner & Rudd (2000); Joiner et al. (2000).
21. Baumeister (1990).
22. Shneidman (1996), p. 58.
23. For example, Linehan (1993).
24. Kirby (2002), p. 119.

2. The Ability to Enact Lethal Self-Injury Is Acquired

1. p. 78.
2. Shneidman (1996), p. 3.

3. Menninger (1936), p. 23.
4. Ibid., p. 66.
5. See Alvarez (1971), p. 158.
6. Ibid., p. 72.
7. Cross (2001).
8. *This American Life,* National Public Radio, Producer Ira Glass, May 11, 2003.
9. Knipfel (2000), pp. 13, 33.
10. Heckler (1994), p. 127.
11. Shneidman (1996), p. 76.
12. Rachman (1989).
13. Shneidman (1996), p. 133.
14. Menninger (1936), p. 23.
15. Sullivan (1953), pp. 48–49.
16. Menninger (1936), p. 64.
17. Reidel (2003).
18. Menninger (1936), p. 52.
19. Mariani (1999).
20. Alvarez (1971).
21. Meehl (1973), pp. 278–280.
22. Shneidman (1996), p. 42.
23. Solomon (1980).
24. Alvarez (1971), p. 108.
25. Rudd, Joiner, & Rajab (1996).
26. Forman et al. (2003); Gispert et al. (1987); Lewinsohn, Rohde, & Seeley (1996); Stein et al. (1998a).
27. Cavanagh, Owens, & Johnstone (1999).
28. Brown et al. (2000); see also Esposito, Spirito, Boergers, & Donaldson (2003).
29. Boardman et al. (1999).
30. Maser et al. (2002); Fawcett et al. (1990) obtained similar results; see also Nordstroem et al. (1995).
31. Joiner et al. (in press).
32. Mullen, Martin, Anderson, Romans, & Herbison (1993); Stepakoff (1998).
33. Glowinski et al. (2001).
34. O'Connor, Sheehy, & O'Connor (2000).
35. Pierce (1981).
36. Soloff et al. (2000); Soloff et al. (1994) reported similar results.
37. p. 269.
38. Dhossche, Snell, & Larder (2000).
39. Menninger (1936).
40. Rosenthal et al. (1972).
41. Veale et al. (1996); Phillips et al. (1993).
42. p. 183.
43. Whitlock & Broadhurst (1969).
44. Conner et al. (2001).
45. Brent et al. (1994).
46. Conner et al. (2003); DuRand et al. (1995).
47. Darke & Ross (2002).
48. Kidd & Kral (2002).
49. Yates, MacKenzie, Pennbridge, & Swofford (1991).
50. Gunderson (1984); Keel et al. (2003).
51. Menninger (1936), p. 69.
52. Ibid., p. 203.
53. Lindeman et al. (1996). A subsequent empirical study reached similar conclusions (Hawton et al., 2001).
54. Lindeman et al. (1996).
55. Grassi et al. (2001).
56. Lewinsohn, Rohde, & Seeley (1996) is one example.

57. Cross (2001). Knipfel (1999) described similar phenomena.
58. Orbach et al. (1996a, 1996b).
59. Ibid. (1997).
60. Ibid. (2002).
61. Rosenthal & Rosenthal (1984).
62. Levine et al. (1995).
63. Russ et al. (1999).
64. Nock et al. (2004).
65. Seguin et al. (1996).
66. For example, Beck, Kovacs, & Weissman (1979).
67. Joiner, Rudd, & Rajab (1997).
68. Joiner et al. (1997).
69. Joiner et al. (2003).
70. de Moore & Robertson (1998).
71. Maser et al. (2002).
72. Williams, Pennebaker, & Joiner (2005).
73. Pennebaker, Francis, & Booth (2001).
74. Isometsae & Loennqvist (1998).
75. Shneidman (1996), p. 75.
76. Cross (2001).
77. Colapinto (2000), p. 150.
78. Motto & Bostrom (1990).
79. Barber et al. (1998).
80. Beck (1996).
81. Joiner & Rudd (2000); Joiner et al. (2000).
82. Killias, van Kesteren, & Rindlisbacher (2001).
83. Lester (1999).
84. Brent et al. (2000).
85. p. 85.
86. Snow (2002) found that symptom relief was a main motivation for self-injury among prisoners; Haliburn (2000) reported a similar result among adolescents.
87. Kemperman, Russ, & Shearin (1997).
88. Similar to an earlier study by Stone & Hokanson (1969).
89. American Psychiatric Association (1994); cf. Brown et al. (2002).
90. Brain, Haines, & Williams (2002).
91. Shneidman (1996), p. 37.
92. Alvarez (1971), p. 47.
93. Heckler (1994), p. 81.
94. p. 48.
95. p. 239.
96. Shneidman (1996), p. 7.

3. The Desire for Death

1. Murray (1938).
2. Shneidman (1996).
3. From unpublished writings cited by Shneidman (1996), p. 29.
4. Ibid., p. 25.
5. Baumeister & Leary (1995), p. 497.
6. de Botton (2004).
7. Cohen (1998).
8. Seligman & Maier (1967).
9. Seligman (1974).
10. Kaplan et al. (1994).
11. Levy et al. (2002).
12. Described in Maris, Berman, & Silverman (2000).
13. Leighton & Hughes (1955).
14. Dublin & Bunzel (1933), p. 240.
15. Alvarez (1971), pp. 73–74.

16. Counts (1980).
17. Quoted in Tad Friend's (October 2003) *New Yorker* article.
18. Shneidman (1996), pp. 14–15.
19. Ibid., p. 94.
20. Heckler (1994), p. 64.
21. Alvarez (1971), p. 153.
22. See Segrin (2003), for a thorough review.
23. For example, Lewinsohn et al. (1980).
24. For example, Perez et al. (2001).

25. Segrin (1992).
26. Talavera, Saiz-Ruiz, & Garcia-Toro (1994).
27. Hautzinger, Linden, & Hoffman (1982).
28. Hinchliffe et al. (1977).
29. Segrin & Flora (1998).
30. Jacobson & Anderson (1982).
31. DeCatanzaro (1991).
32. Brown, Dahlen, Mills, Rick, & Biblarz (1999).
33. Joiner et al. (2002).
34. DeCatanzaro (1995).
35. Brown, Comtois, & Linehan (2002).
36. Filiberti et al. (2001).
37. Motto & Bostrom (1990).
38. O'Reilly, Truant, & Donaldson (1990).
39. Neuringer (1974).
40. Brown & Vinokur (2003).
41. Woznica & Shapiro (1990); see also Sabbath (1969).
42. Orbach, Gross, & Glaubman (1981).
43. Kaslow et al. (2002).
44. Motto & Bostrom (1990) also found that threat of financial loss was a risk factor for death by suicide.
45. Gargas (1932), p. 697.
46. Kennedy, Iveson, & Hill (1999).
47. Lester & Yang (1992).
48. Burr, Hartman, & Matteson (1999).
49. For example, one of the variables in Boardman et al.'s (1999) study that differentiated those who died by suicide from those who died by other causes was financial difficulty.
50. DeCatanzaro (1991).
51. Shneidman (1996), back cover copy.
52. Sullivan (1953), pp. 24–25.
53. McAllister, Roitberg, & Weldon (1990).
54. Poulin (1992).
55. O'Connor (1978).
56. Andrade (1996).
57. Perlson & Karpman (1943).
58. Magne-Ingvar & Oejehagen (1999).
59. Dublin & Bunzel (1933).
60. Eisenberger, Lieberman, & Williams (2003).
61. Hoyer & Lund (1993).
62. Shneidman (1996), pp. 14–15.
63. Colapinto (2000), p. 102.
64. Ibid., p. 127.
65. For example, Kazdin et al. (1985).
66. Troisi & Moles (1999).
67. Stirman & Pennebaker (2001).
68. Shneidman (1996), p. 12.
69. Williams & Joiner (2004).
70. DeCatanzaro (1995).

71. O'Reilly, Truant, & Donaldson (1990).
72. Rudd, Joiner, & Rajab (1995).
73. Conner, Duberstein, & Conwell (1999).
74. Boardman et al. (1999).
75. Magne-Ingvar & Oejehagen (1999).
76. Twomey, Kaslow, & Croft (2000).
77. Van Winkle & May (1993).
78. Compiled by McIntosh (2002).
79. Durkheim (1897).
80. Thorlindsson & Bjarnason (1998).
81. Hoyer & Lund (1993).
82. Leenaars & Lester (1999).
83. Qin & Mortensen (2003).
84. Marzuk et al. (1997).
85. Wagner et al. (1998).
86. Tomassini et al. (2003).
87. Gregory (1994).
88. Lester (1998).
89. Kjelsberg, Eikeseth, & Dahl (1991).
90. Yampey (1967).
91. Potter et al. (2001).
92. Biller (1977).
93. Rojcewicz (1971).
94. Dublin & Bunzel (1933), p. 110.
95. Fernquist (2000).
96. Steels (1994).
97. Trovato (1998).
98. Joiner, Van Orden, & Hollar (in press).
99. Kanner (2003).
100. Heckler (1994), p. 81.
101. From *The Letters of William James,* cited in Dublin & Bunzel (1933).
102. Freud (1929/1989).
103. Yen & Siegler (2003).
104. Maldonado & Kraus (1991).
105. Murray et al. (2002).

4. What Do We Mean by Suicide? How Is It Distributed in People?

1. Coudereau et al. (1997).
2. Barabasz (1981).
3. Magne-Ingvar & Oejehagen (1999).
4. Shneidman & Faberow (1961); see O'Carroll et al. (1996) for a leading treatment of this topic.
5. Lewinsohn, Rohde, & Seeley (1996) provided some evidence for this view.
6. Schmidt, Kotov, & Joiner (2004); Waller & Meehl (1998).
7. Cauchon & Moore (2002).
8. Post (2002).
9. Kamal & Lowenthal (2002).
10. Kelsay (2002).
11. Axell & Kase (2002).
12. p. 79.
13. Dickerson (2001).
14. Ibid.
15. Robinson (2001).
16. Hochman (1990).
17. Robinson (2001).
18. Ganzini et al. (2002).
19. Ibid. (2003).
20. Reported by David Meadow in *The Appian: The Student Publication of the Harvard Graduate School of Education,* March 1, 2004.

21. Lord (2000).
22. Cohen, Llorente, & Eisendorfer (1998).
23. Nock & Marzuk (1999).
24. Rosenbaum (1990).
25. Malphurs, Eisendorfer, & Cohen (2001).
26. O'Connor, Sheehy, & O'Connor (2000).
27. Soloff et al. (2000).
28. Joiner et al. (2002, Study 2).
29. For example, Eaton & Reynolds (1985).
30. McIntosh (2002).
31. He & Lester (1998); Snowden (1979).
32. McIntosh (2002).
33. Singh & Siahpush (2002).
34. June 28, 2002.
35. McIntosh (2002).
36. Ibid.
37. Kaplan & Klein (1989).
38. Clark et al. (1989).
39. Kok (1988); Pearson (1995).
40. Zhang (2000).
41. Brown & Blanton (2002).
42. Manning & Fillingim (2002).
43. p. 233.
44. McIntosh (2002).
45. Gibbs (1997).
46. Hunt & Hunt (2001).
47. Nisbet et al. (2000).
48. Taylor et al. (1996).
49. For example, Boardman et al. (1999).
50. Snowden (2001).
51. Statistics provided by the National Center for Injury Prevention and Control (1995).
52. Walker (2002).
53. Ungemack & Guarnaccia (1998).
54. Van Winkle & May (1993); May (1987).
55. Markus & Kitayama (1991).
56. Edwards et al. (2001).
57. Woodrow et al. (1972).
58. McIntosh (2002).
59. Cutright & Fernquist (2001).
60. Hendin (1982).
61. Cutright & Fernquist (2001).
62. McIntosh (2002).
63. Sabbath (1969).
64. Woznica & Shapiro (1990).
65. Rosenthal & Rosenthal (1984).
66. American Psychiatric Association (1994).
67. Blazer, Kessler, McGonagle, & Swartz (1994).
68. Mroczek (2001).
69. McIntosh (1983–1984).
70. Brent et al. (1989).
71. Joiner (2003).
72. Haw (1994).
73. Ryabik, Schreiner, & Elam (1995).
74. As described by Barber and colleagues (1998).
75. Scheeres (2003).
76. Berman & Walley (2003); Sloan, Berman, & Mae (2003).
77. Reported in the February 1, 2003 issue.

5. What Roles Do Genetics, Neurobiology, and Mental Disorders Play in Suicidal Behavior?

1. p. 53.
2. Roy (1992).
3. Kety (1986).
4. Egeland & Sussex (1985).
5. Statham et al. (1998).
6. Lesch et al. (1996).
7. Courtet et al. (2004).
8. Mann et al. (2000).
9. Joiner, Johnson, & Soderstrom (2002).
10. Rujescu et al. (2003a).
11. For example, Bennett et al. (2000); Pooley et al. (2003).
12. Russ et al. (2000).
13. Rujescu et al. (2003b).
14. Nolan et al. (2000).
15. Lester (1995).
16. Åsberg (1997).
17. Coccaro et al. (1989); Corrêa et al. (2000); Duval et al. (2001).
18. Oquendo et al. (2003).
19. Corrêa et al. (2000); Malone et al. (1996).
20. Arango et al. (2001); Du et al. (1999).
21. Mann et al. (2000).
22. Singareddy & Balon (2001).
23. Ursin (2002).
24. Sabo et al. (1990); Turvey et al. (2002).
25. Fawcett et al. (1990).
26. Agargun et al. (1998).
27. Tanskanen et al. (2001).
28. Bernert et al. (in press).
29. Coryell & Schlesser (2001).
30. Tiefenbacher et al. (2004).
31. Mann et al. (2000).
32. Menninger (1936), p. 280.
33. Maser et al. (2002).
34. Corcos et al. (2002).
35. Alvarez (1971), p. 155.
36. Cremniter et al. (1999).
37. Spreux-Varoquaux et al. (2001).
38. Sher et al. (2003).
39. Malone et al. (1996).
40. Gregory (1994).
41. Kjelsberg, Eikeseth, & Dahl (1991).
42. King et al. (2001).
43. Brent et al. (1994).
44. Glowinski et al. (2001).
45. Roy (2003); McHolm, MacMillan, & Jamieson (2003) reported similar results in depressed women, as did Anderson et al. (2002) in low-income African-American women.
46. Brown et al. (1999); Soloff and colleagues (2000) have reported similar results among women with borderline personality disorder—childhood sexual abuse was a strong predictor of adult suicide attempts among this group.
47. Mullen et al. (1993); Stepakoff (1998).
48. Twomey et al. (2000).
49. Newport et al. (2004).
50. Vythilingam et al. (2002).
51. Cavanagh et al. (2003).
52. Kety (1974), p. 961.

53. Khan et al. (2002).
54. For example, Busch, Fawcett, & Jacobs (2003).
55. Weissman et al. (1989).
56. Schmidt, Woolaway-Bickel, & Bates (2000).
57. Cox et al. (1994); Schmidt, Woolaway-Bickel, & Bates (2000).
58. American Psychiatric Association (1994).
59. Darke & Ross (2002).
60. Wall, Wekerle, & Bissonnette (2000).
61. McCloskey & Berman (2003).
62. Akerlind & Hoernquist (1992).
63. Coon, Pena, & Illich (1998).
64. Gunderson (1984); Keel et al. (2003).
65. Gunderson (1984).
66. Soloff et al. (1994).
67. Stone, Hurt, & Stone (1987).
68. Raymond et al. (1999).
69. Orbach et al. (1996a, 1996b).
70. Herzog et al. (2000).
71. Shneidman (1996), p. 76.
72. Favaro & Santonastaso (1997).
73. Stein et al. (2003).
74. Vieta et al. (1997).
75. Matza et al. (2003).
76. Spalletta et al. (1996).
77. Cleckley (1941).
78. Hare (1991).
79. Verona, Patrick, & Joiner (2001).

6. Risk Assessment, Crisis Intervention, Treatment, and Prevention

1. Bolton et al. (2003).
2. Joiner & Coyne (1999).
3. McCullough (2000).
4. Keller et al. (2000).
5. McCullough (2002), p. 246.
6. Rudd, Joiner, & Rajab (2000).
7. Joiner et al. (2001).
8. Kroll (2000).
9. Drew (2001).
10. Cited by Dublin & Bunzel (1933), p. 235.
11. Quoted by ibid., p. 236.
12. Rudd, Joiner, & Rajab (2000).
13. Quoted by DeCatanzaro (2000, p. 90).
14. Westen et al. (1997).
15. Jureidini et al. (2004).
16. Motto & Bostrom (2001).
17. Ibid., p. 829.
18. Morgan (1989).
19. Mann et al. (1997).
20. Overholser et al. (1989).

7. The Future of Suicide Prevention and Research

1. Oquendo et al. (2003).
2. Used by Berman and colleagues (for example, Berman & Walley, 2003).

WORKS CITED

Agargun, M. Y., Cilli, A. S., Kara, H., Tarhan, N., Kincir, F., & Oz, H. (1998). Repetitive and frightening dreams and suicidal behavior in patients with major depression. *Comprehensive Psychiatry, 39,* 198–202.

Akerlind, I., & Hoernquist, J. O. (1992). Loneliness and alcohol abuse: A review of evidences of an interplay. *Social Science & Medicine, 34,* 405–414.

Alvarez, A. (1971). *The savage god: A study of suicide.* New York: Norton.

American Psychiatric Association. (1994). *Diagnostic and statistical manual of mental disorders,* 4th ed. Washington, D.C.: American Psychiatric Association.

Anderson, P. L., Tiro, J. A., Price, A. W., Bender, M. A., & Kaslow, N. J. (2002). Additive impact of childhood emotional, physical, and sexual abuse on suicide attempts among low-income African American women. *Suicide & Life-Threatening Behavior, 32,* 131–138.

Andrade, M. C. B. (1996). Sexual selection for male sacrifice in the Australian redback spider. *Science, 271,* 70–72.

Arango, V., Underwood, M. D., Boldrini, M., Tamir, H., Kassir, S. A., et al. (2001). Serotonin 1A receptors, serotonin transporter binding and serotonin transporter mRNA expression in the brainstem of depressed suicide victims. *Neuropsychopharmacology, 25,* 892–903.

Åsberg, M. (1997). Neurotransmitters and suicidal behavior: The evidence from cerebrospinal fluid studies. *Annals of the New York Academy of Science, 836,* 158–181.

Axell, A., & Kase, H. (2002). *Kamikaze: Japan's suicide gods*. New York: Longman Publishing Group.

Barabasz, A. F. (1981). Effects of Antarctic isolation: EEG skin conductance and suggestibility and effects of laboratory controlled sensory restriction: Hypnotizability, pain tolerance, EEG and skin conductance. Research Project, 35-sup-36, pp. 1–172. University of Canterbury, New Zealand.

Barber, M. E., Marzuk, P. M., Leon, A. C., & Portera, L. (1998). Aborted suicide attempts: A new classification of suicidal behavior. *American Journal of Psychiatry, 155,* 385–389.

Bartels, S. J., Coakley, E., Oxman, T. E., Constantino, G., Oslin, D., Chen, H., Zubritsky, C., Cheal, K., Durai, U., Gallo, J. J., Llorente, M., & Sanchez, H. (2002). Suicidal and death ideation in older primary care patients with depression, anxiety, and at-risk alcohol use. *American Journal of Geriatric Psychiatry, 10,* 417–427.

Baumeister, R. F. (1990). Suicide as escape from self. *Psychological Review, 97,* 90–113.

——— (1996). *Evil.* New York: W. H. Freeman.

Baumeister, R. F., Campbell, J. D., Krueger, J. I., & Vohs, K. D. (2003). Does high self-esteem cause better performance, interpersonal success, happiness, or healthier lifestyles? *Psychological Science in the Public Interest, 4,* 1–44.

Baumeister, R. F., & Leary, M. R. (1995). The need to belong: Desire for interpersonal attachments as a fundamental human motivation. *Psychological Bulletin, 117,* 497–529.

Beck, A. T. (1996). Beyond belief: A theory of modes, personality, and psychopathology. In P. M. Salkovskis (Ed.), *Frontiers of cognitive therapy,* pp. 1–25. New York: Guilford.

Beck, A. T., Brown, G., Berchick, R. J., & Stewart, B. L. (1990). Relationship between hopelessness and ultimate suicide: A replication with psychiatric outpatients. *American Journal of Psychiatry, 147,* 190–195.

Beck, A. T., Kovacs, M., & Weissman, M. (1979). Assessment of suicidal intention: The scale for suicide ideation. *Journal of Consulting & Clinical Psychology, 47,* 343–352.

Beck, A. T., Steer, R., Kovacs, M., & Garrison, B. (1985). Hopelessness and eventual suicide: A 10-year prospective study of patients hospitalized with suicidal ideation. *American Journal of Psychiatry, 142,* 559–563.

Bennett, P. J., McMahon, W. M., Watabe, J., Achilles, J., Bacon, M., et al. (2000). Tryptophan hydroxylase polymorphisms in suicide victims. *Psychiatric Genetics, 10,* 13–17.

Berman, M. E., & Walley, J. C. (2003). Imitation of self-aggressive behavior: An experimental test of the contagion hypothesis. *Journal of Applied Social Psychology, 33,* 1036–1057.

Bernert, R., Joiner, T., Cukrowicz, K., Schmidt, N. B., & Krakow, B. (in press). Suicidality and sleep disturbances: Nightmares are uniquely associated with suicidal ideation. *Sleep.*

Biller, O. A. (1977). Suicide related to the assassination of President John F. Kennedy. *Suicide & Life-Threatening Behavior, 7,* 40–44.

Blazer, D. G., Kessler, R. C., McGonagle, K. A., & Swartz, M. S. (1994). The prevalence and distribution of major depression in a national community sample: The National Comorbidity Survey. *American Journal of Psychiatry, 151,* 979–986.

Boardman, A. P., Grimbaldeston, A. H., Handley, C., Jones, P. W., & Willmott, S. (1999). The North Staffordshire Suicide Study: A case-control study of suicide in one health district. *Psychological Medicine, 29,* 27–33.

Bolton, P., Bass, J., Neugebauer, R., Verdeli, H., Clougherty, K. F., Wickramaratne, P., Speelman, L., Ndogoni, L., & Weissman, M. (2003). Group interpersonal psychotherapy for depression in rural Uganda: A randomized controlled trial. *Journal of the American Medical Association, 289,* 3117–3124.

Brain, K. L., Haines, J., & Williams, C. L. (2002). The psychophysiology of repetitive self-mutilation. *Archives of Suicide Research, 6,* 199–210.

Brent, D. A., Baugher, M., Birmaher, B., Kolko, D. J., & Bridge, J. (2000). Compliance with recommendations to remove firearms in families participating in a clinical trial for adolescent depression. *Journal of the American Academy of Child & Adolescent Psychiatry, 39,* 1220–1226.

Brent, D. A., Johnson, B. A., Perper, J. A., & Connolly, J. (1994). Personality disorder, personality traits, impulsive violence, and completed suicide in adolescents. *Journal of the American Academy of Child and Adolescent Psychiatry, 33,* 1080–1086.

Brent, D. A., Kerr, M. M., Goldstein, C., & Bozigar, J. (1989). An outbreak of suicide and suicidal behavior in a high school. *Journal of the American Academy of Child & Adolescent Psychiatry, 28,* 918–924.

Bron, B., Strack, M., & Rudolph, G. (1991). Childhood experiences of loss and suicide attempts: Significance in depressive states of major depressed and dysthymic or adjustment disordered patients. *Journal of Affective Disorders, 23,* 165–172.

Brown, D. R., & Blanton, C. J. (2002). Physical activity, sports participation, and suicidal behavior among college students. *Medicine & Science in Sports & Exercise, 34,* 1087–1096.

Brown, G., Beck, A. T., Steer, R., & Grisham, J. (2000). Risk factors for suicide in psychiatric outpatients: A 20-year prospective study. *Journal of Consulting & Clinical Psychology, 68,* 371–377.

Brown, G. L., Ebert, M. H., Goyer, P. F., Jimerson, D. C., Klein, W. J., Bunney, W. E., & Goodwin, F. K. (1982). Aggression, suicide, and serotonin: Relationships to CSF amine metabolites. *American Journal of Psychiatry, 139,* 741–746.

Brown, J., Cohen, P., Johnson, J., & Smailes, E. M. (1999). Childhood abuse and neglect: Specificity and effects on adolescent and young adult depression and suicidality. *Journal of the American Academy of Child & Adolescent Psychiatry, 38,* 1490–1496.

Brown, M. Z., Comtois, K. A., & Linehan, M. M. (2002). Reasons for suicide attempts and nonsuicidal self-injury in women with borderline personality disorder. *Journal of Abnormal Psychology, 111,* 198–202.

Brown, R. M., Dahlen, E., Mills, C., Rick, J., & Biblarz, A. (1999). Evaluation of an evolutionary model of self-preservation and self-destruction. *Suicide & Life-Threatening Behavior, 29,* 58–71.

Brown, S. L., & Vinokur, A. D. (2003). The interplay among risk factors for suicidal ideation and suicide: The role of depression, poor health, and loved ones' messages of support and criticism. *American Journal of Community Psychology.*

Burr, J., Hartman, J., & Matteson, D. (1999). Black suicide in U.S. metropolitan areas: An examination of the racial inequality and social integration-regulation hypotheses. *Social Forces, 77,* 1049–1080.

Busch, K. A., Fawcett, J., & Jacobs, D. G. (2003). Clinical correlates of inpatient suicide. *Journal of Clinical Psychiatry, 64,* 14–19.

Catanzaro, S. (2000). Mood regulation and suicidal behavior. In T. Joiner & M. D. Rudd (Eds.), *Suicide science* (pp. 81–103). Boston: Kluwer.

Cauchon, D., & Moore, M. (2002, Sept. 2). Desperation forced a horrific decision. *USA Today* [On-line]. Available: http://www.usatoday.com/news/sept11/2002–09–02-jumper_x.htm [May 31, 2003].

Cavanagh, J. T. O., Carson, A. J., Sharpe, M., & Lawrie, S. M. (2003). Psychological autopsy studies of suicide: A systematic review. *Psychological Medicine, 33,* 395–405.

Cavanagh, J. T. O., Owens, D. G. C., & Johnstone, E. C. (1999). Suicide and undetermined death in southeast Scotland. A case-control study using the psychological autopsy method. *Psychological Medicine, 29,* 1141–1149.

Cherpitel, C. J. (1993). Alcohol, injury, and risk-taking behavior: Data from a national sample. *Alcoholism: Clinical & Experimental Research, 17,* 762–766.

Clark, D. C., Gibbons, R. D., Fawcett, J., & Scheftner, W. A. (1989). What is the mechanism by which suicide attempts predispose to later suicide attempts? A mathematical model. *Journal of Abnormal Psychology, 98,* 42–49.

Cleckley, H. (1941). *The mask of sanity.* St. Louis, Mo.: Mosby Co.

Coccaro, E. F., Siever, L. J., Klar, H. M., Maurer, G., et al. (1989). Serotonergic studies in patients with affective and personality disorders: Correlates with suicidal and impulsive aggressive behavior. *Archives of General Psychiatry, 46,* 587–599.

Cohen, D. (1998). Culture, social organization, and patterns of violence. *Journal of Personality & Social Psychology, 75,* 408–419.

Cohen, D., Llorente, M., & Eisendorfer, C. (1998). Homicide-suicide in older persons. *American Journal of Psychiatry, 155,* 390–396.

Colapinto, J. (2000). *As nature made him.* New York: Harper Collins.

Conner, K. R., Cox, C., Duberstein, P. R., Tian, L., Nisbett, P. A., & Conwell, Y. (2001). Violence, alcohol and completed suicide: A case-control study. *American Journal of Psychiatry, 158,* 1701–1705.

Conner, K. R., Duberstein, P. R., & Conwell, Y. (1999). Age-related patterns of factors associated with completed suicide in men with alcohol dependence. *American Journal on Addictions, 8,* 312–318.

Conner, K. R., Duberstein, P. R., Conwell, Y., & Caine, E. D. (2003). Reactive aggression and suicide: Theory and evidence. *Aggression & Violent Behavior, 8,* 413–432.

Coon, G., Pena, D., & Illich, P. (1998). Self-efficacy and substance abuse: Assessment using a brief phone interview. *Journal of Substance Abuse Treatment, 15,* 385–391.

Corcos, M., Taieeb, O., Benoit-Lamy, S., Paterniti, S., Jeammet, P., & Flament, M. F. (2002). Suicide attempts in women with bulimia nervosa: Frequency and characteristics. *Acta Psychiatrica Scandinavica, 106,* 381–386.

Corrêa, H., Duval, F., Mokrani, M-C., Bailey, P., Tremeau, F., et al. (2000). Prolactin response to d-fenfluramine and suicidal behavior in depressed patients. *Psychiatry Research, 93,* 189–199.

Coryell, W., & Schlesser, M. (2001). The dexamethasone suppression test and suicide prediction. *American Journal of Psychiatry, 158,* 748–753.

Coudereau, J-P., Monier, C., Bourre, J-M., & Frances, H. (1997). Effect of isolation on pain threshold and on different effects of morphine. *Progress in Neuro-Psychopharmacology & Biological Psychiatry, 21,* 997–1018.

Counts, D. A. (1980). Fighting back is not the way: Suicide and the women of Kaliai. *American Ethnologist, 7,* 332–351.

Courtet, P., Picot, M.-C., Bellivier, F., Torres, S., Jollant, F., et al. (2004). Serotonin transporter gene may be involved in short-term risk of subsequent suicide attempts. *Biological Psychiatry, 55,* 46–51.

Cox, B. J., Direnfeld, D. M., Swinson, R. P., & Norton, G. R. (1994). Suicidal ideation and suicide attempts in panic disorder and social phobia. *American Journal of Psychiatry, 151,* 882–887.

Cremniter, D., Jamain, S., Kollenbach, K., Alvarez, J.-C., Lecrubier, Y., et al. (1999). CSF 5-HIAA levels are lower in impulsive as compared to nonimpulsive violent suicide attempters and control subjects. *Biological Psychiatry, 45,* 1572–1579.

Cross, C. R. (2001). *Heavier than heaven: A biography of Kurt Cobain.* New York: Hyperion.

Cutright, P., & Fernquist, R. M. (2001). The age structure of male suicide rates: Measurement and analysis of 20 developed countries, 1955–1994. *Social Science Research, 30,* 627–640.

Darke, S., & Ross, J. (2002). Suicide among heroin users: Rates, risk factors and methods. *Addiction, 97,* 1383–1394.

de Botton, A. (2004). *Status anxiety.* New York: Pantheon Books.

DeCatanzaro, D. (1991). Evolutionary limits to self-preservation. *Ethology & Sociobiology, 12,* 13–28.

——— (1995). Reproductive status, family interactions, and suicidal ideation: Surveys of the general public and high-risk groups. *Ethology & Sociobiology, 16,* 385–394.

de Moore, G. M., & Robertson, A. R. (1998). Suicide in the 18 years after deliberate self-harm: A prospective study. In R. J. Kosky, H. S. Eshkevari, R. D. Goldney, & R. Hassan (eds.), *Suicide prevention: The global context,* pp. 79–85. New York: Plenum Press.

Dhossche, D., Snell, K. S., & Larder, S. (2000). A case-control study of tattoos in young suicide victims as a possible marker of risk. *Journal of Affective Disorders, 59,* 165–168.

Dickerson, T. (2001). People's Temple (Jonestown). University of Virginia, Religious Movements Web site. http://religiousmovements.lib.virginia.edu/nrms/Jonestwn.html.

Drew, B. L. (2001). Self-harm behavior and no-suicide contracting in psychiatric inpatient settings. *Archives of Psychiatric Nursing, 15,* 99–106.

Du, L., Faludi, G., Palkovits, M., Demeter, E., Bakish, D., et al. (1999). Frequency of long allele in serotonin transporter gene is increased in depressed suicide victims. *Biological Psychiatry, 46,* 196–201.

Dublin, L. I., & Bunzel, B. (1933). *To be or not to be.* New York: Harrison Smith & Robert Haas.

DuRand, C. J., Burtka, G. J., Haycox, J. A., & Smith, J. A. (1995). A quarter century of suicide in a major urban jail: Implications for community psychiatry. *American Journal of Psychiatry, 152,* 1077–1080.

Durkheim, E. (1897). *Le suicide: Etude de socologie.* Paris: F. Alcan.

Duval, F., Mokrani, M.-C., Correa, H., Bailey, P., Valdebenito, M., et al. (2001). Lack of effect of HPA axis hyperactivity on hormonal responses to d-fenfluramine in major depressed patients: Implications for pathogenesis of suicidal behaviour. *Psychoneuroendocrinology, 26,* 521–537.

Eaton, P., & Reynolds, P. (1985). Suicide attempters presenting at an emergency department. *Canadian Journal of Psychiatry, 30,* 582–585.

Edwards, R. R., Doleys, D. M., Fillingim, R. B., & Lowery, D. (2001). Ethnic differences in pain tolerance: Clinical implications in a chronic pain population. *Psychosomatic Medicine, 63,* 316–323.

Egeland, J., & Sussex, J. (1985). Suicide and family loading for affective disorders. *Journal of the American Medical Association, 254,* 915–918.

Eisenberger, N. I., Lieberman, M. D., & Williams, K. D. (2003). Does rejection hurt? An fMRI study of social exclusion. *Science, 302,* 290–292.

Esposito, C., Spirito, A., Boergers, J., & Donaldson, D. (2003). Affective, behavioral, and cognitive functioning in adolescents with multiple suicide attempts. *Suicide & Life-Threatening Behavior, 33,* 389–399.

Favaro, A., & Santonastaso, P. (1997). Suicidality in eating disorders: Clinical and psychological correlates. *Acta Psychiatrica Scandinavica, 95,* 508–514.

Fawcett, J., Scheftner, W., Fogg, L., Clark, D. C., Young, M. A., Hedeker, D., & Gibbons, R. (1990). Time-related predictors of suicide in major affective disorder. *American Journal of Psychiatry, 147,* 1189–1194.

Fernquist, R. M. (2000). An aggregate analysis of professional sports, suicide, and homicide rates: 30 U.S. metropolitan areas, 1971–1990. *Aggression & Violent Behavior, 5,* 329–341.

Filiberti, A., Ripamonti, C., Totis, A., Ventafridda, V., De Conno, F., Contiero, P., & Tamburini, M. (2001). Characteristics of terminal cancer patients who committed suicide during a home palliative care program. *Journal of Pain & Symptom Management, 22,* 544–553.

Forman, E. M., Berk, M. S., Henriques, G. R., Brown, G. K., & Beck, A. T. (2004). History of multiple suicide attempts as a behavioral marker of severe psychopathology. *American Journal of Psychiatry, 161,* 437–443.

Freud, S. (1929/1989). *Civilization and its discontents.* New York: W.W. Norton.

Ganzini, L., Goy, E. R., Miller, L., Harvath, T. A., Jackson, A., & Delorit, M. A. (2003). Nurses' experiences with hospice patients who refuse food and fluids to hasten death. *New England Journal of Medicine, 349,* 359–365.

Ganzini, L., Silveira, M. J., & Johnston, W. S. (2002). Predictors and correlates of interest in assisted suicide in the final month of life among ALS patients in Oregon and Washington. *Journal of Pain & Symptom Management, 24,* 312–317.

Gargas, S. (1932). Suicide in the Netherlands. *American Journal of Sociology, 37,* 697–713.

Gibbs, J. T. (1997). African-American suicide: A cultural paradox. *Suicide and Life-Threatening Behavior, 27,* 68–79.

Gispert, M., Davis, M. S., Marsh, L., & Wheeler, K. (1987). Predictive factors in repeated suicide attempts by adolescents. *Hospital & Community Psychiatry, 38,* 390–393.

Glowinski, A. L., Bucholz, K. K., Nelson, E. C., Fu, Q., Madden, P., Reich, W., & Heath, A. C. (2001). Suicide attempts in an adolescent female twin sample. *Journal of the American Academy of Child & Adolescent Psychiatry, 40,* 1300–1307.

Grassi, L., Mondardini, D., Pavanati, M., Sighinolfi, L., Serra, A., & Ghinelli, F. (2001). Suicide probability and psychological morbidity secondary to HIV infection: A control study of HIV-seropositive, hepatitis C virus (HCV)-seropostive and HIV/HCV-seronegative injecting drug users. *Journal of Affective Disorders, 64,* 195–202.

Gregory, R. J. (1994). Grief and loss among Eskimos attempting suicide in western Alaska. *American Journal of Psychiatry, 151,* 1815–1816.

Gunderson, D. (1984). *Borderline personality disorder.* Washington, D.C.: American Psychiatric Press.

Haliburn, J. (2000). Reasons for adolescent suicide attempts. *Journal of the American Academy of Child & Adolescent Psychiatry, 39,* 13–14.

Hare, R. D. (1991). *The Hare Psychopathy Checklist—revised.* Toronto: Multi-Health Systems.

Hautzinger, M., Linden, M., & Hoffman, N. (1982). Distressed couples with and without a depressed partner: An analysis of their verbal interaction. *Journal of Behavior Therapy & Experimental Psychiatry, 13,* 307–314.

Haw, C. M. (1994). A cluster of suicides at a London psychiatric unit. *Suicide & Life-Threatening Behavior, 24,* 256–266.

Hawton, K., Clements, A., Sakarovitch, C., Simkin, S., & Deeks, J. J. (2001). Suicide in doctors: A study of risk according to gender, seniority and specialty in medical practitioners in England and Wales, 1979–1995. *Journal of Epidemiology & Community Health, 55,* 296–300.

He, Z.-X., & Lester, D. (1998). Methods for suicide in mainland China. *Death Studies, 22,* 571–579.

Heckler, R. (1994). *Waking up, alive.* New York: Grosset/Putnam.

Hendin, H. (1982). *Suicide in America.* New York: Norton.

Herzog, D. B.,Greenwood, D. N., Dorer, D., Flores, A., Ekeblad, E., Richards, A., Blais, M., & Keller, M. (2000). Mortality in eating disorders: A descriptive study. *International Journal of Eating Disorders, 28,* 20–26.

Hinchliffe, M. K., Vaughan, P. W., Hooper, D., & Roberts, F. J. (1977). The melancholy marriage: An inquiry into the interaction of depression: II. Expressiveness. *British Journal of Medical Psychology, 50,* 125–142.

Hochman, J. (1990). Miracle, mystery, and authority: The triangle of cult indoctrination. *Psychiatric Annals, 20,* 179–184.

Hoyer, G., & Lund, E. (1993). Suicide among women related to number of children in marriage. *Archives of General Psychiatry, 50,* 134–137.

Hunt, L. L. & Hunt, M. O. (2001). Race, region, and religious involvement: A comparative study of Whites and African Americans. *Social Forces, 80,* 605–631.

Isometsae, E. T., & Loennqvist, J. K. (1998). Suicide attempts preceding completed suicide. *British Journal of Psychiatry, 173,* 531–535.

Jacobson, N. S., & Anderson, E. (1982). Interpersonal skill deficits and depression in college students: A sequential analysis of the timing of self-disclosure. *Behavior Therapy, 13,* 271–282.

Joiner, Jr., T. E. (1999). The clustering and contagion of suicide. *Current Directions in Psychological Science, 8,* 89–92.

———— (2000). Interpersonal aspects of depression and suicide. Paper presented at the annual conference of the American Psychological Association, Washington, D.C.

———— (2003). "Contagion" of suicidal symptoms as a function of assortative relating and shared relationship stress in college roommates. *Journal of Adolescence, 26,* 495–504.

Joiner, T., Conwell, Y., Fitzpatrick, K., Witte, T., Schmidt, N. B., Berlim, M., Fleck, M., & Rudd, M. D. (2005). Four studies on how past and current suicidality relate even when "everything but the kitchen sink" is covaried. *Journal of Abnormal Psychology, 114,* 291–303.

Joiner, T., & Coyne, J. C. (1999). *The interactional nature of depression.* Washington, D.C.: American Psychological Association.

Joiner, T., Johnson, F., & Soderstrom, K. (2002). Association between serotonin transporter gene polymorphism and family history of completed and attempted suicide. *Suicide & Life-Threatening Behavior, 32,* 329–332.

Joiner, Jr., T. E., Pettit, J. W., Perez, M., Burns, A. B., Gencoz, T., Gencoz, F., & Rudd, M. D. (2001). Can positive emotion influence problem-solving attitudes among suicidal adults? *Professional Psychology: Research & Practice, 32,* 507–512.

Joiner, T., Pettit, J. W., Walker, R. L., Voelz, Z. R., Cruz, J., Rudd, M. D., & Lester, D. (2002). Perceived burdensomeness and suicidality: Two studies on the suicide notes of those attempting and those completing suicide. *Journal of Social & Clinical Psychology, 21,* 531–545.

Joiner, T., & Rudd, M. D. (2000). Intensity and duration of suicidal crises vary as a function of previous suicide attempts and negative life events. *Journal of Consulting & Clinical Psychology, 68,* 909–916.

Joiner, Jr., T. E., Rudd, M. D., & Rajab, M. H. (1997). The Modified Scale for Suicidal Ideation among Suicidal Adults: Factors of suicidality and their relation to clinical and diagnostic indicators. *Journal of Abnormal Psychology, 106,* 260–265.

Joiner, Jr., T. E., Rudd, M. D., Rouleau, M., & Wagner, K. D. (2000). Parameters of suicidal crises vary as a function of previous suicide attempts in youth inpatients. *Journal of the American Academy of Child and Adolescent Psychiatry, 39,* 876–880.

Joiner, T., & Schmidt, N. B. (2002). Taxometrics can do diagnostics right. In L. Beutler & M. Malik (Eds.), *Rethinking the DSM: A psychological perspective,* pp. 107–120. Washington, D.C.: American Psychological Association.

Joiner, Jr., T. E., Steer, R. A., Brown, G., Beck, A. T., Pettit, J. W., & Rudd, M. D. (2003). Worst-point suicidal plans: A dimension of suicidality predictive of past suicide attempts and eventual death by suicide. *Behaviour Research & Therapy, 41,* 1469–1480.

Joiner, T., Van Orden, K., & Hollar, D. (in press). On Buckeyes, Gators, Super Bowl Sunday, and the Miracle on Ice: "Pulling together" is associated with lower suicide rates. *Journal of Social and Clinical Psychology.*

Joiner, T., Walker, R., Rudd, M. D., & Jobes, D. (1999). Scientizing and routinizing the outpatient assessment of suicidality. *Professional Psychology: Research & Practice, 30,* 447–453.

Jureidini, J. N., Doecke, C. J., Mansfield, P., Haby, M., Menkes, D., & Tonkin, A. (2004). Efficacy and safety of antidepressants for children and adolescents. *British Medical Journal, 328,* 879–883.

Kamal, Z., & Lowenthal, K. M. (2002). Suicide beliefs and behaviour among young Muslims and Hindus in the UK. *Mental Health, Religion & Culture, 5,* 111–118.

Kanner, B. (2003). *The Super Bowl of advertising: How the commercials won the game.* New York: Bloomberg Press.

Kaplan, A. G., & Klein, R. B. (1989). Women and suicide. In D. H. Jacobs &

H. N. Brown (Eds.), *Suicide: Understanding and responding,* pp. 257–282. Madison, Conn.: International Universities Press.

Kaplan, R. M., Ries, A. L., Prewitt, L. M., & Eakin, E. (1994). Self-efficacy expectations predict survival for patients with chronic obstructive pulmonary disease. *Health Psychology, 13,* 366–368.

Kaslow, N. J., Thompson, M. P., Okun, A., Price, A., Young, S., Bender, M., Wyckoff, S., Twomey, H., Goldin, J., & Parker, R. (2002). Risk and protective factors for suicidal behavior in abused African American women. *Journal of Consulting & Clinical Psychology, 70,* 311–319.

Kazdin, A. E., Sherick, R. B., Esveldt-Dawson, K., & Rancurello, M. D. (1985). Nonverbal behavior and childhood depression. *Journal of the American Academy of Child Psychiatry, 24,* 303–309.

Keel, P. K., Dorer, D. J., Eddy, K. T., Franko, D., Charatan, D. L., & Herzog, D. B. (2003). Predictors of mortality in eating disorders. *Archives of General Psychiatry, 60,* 179–183.

Keller, M., McCullough, J., Klein, D., Arnow, B., Dunner, D., Gelenberg, A. J., Markowitz, J., Nemeroff, C., Russell, J., Trivedi, M. H., & Zajecka, J. (2000). A comparison of nefazodone, the cognitive behavioral-analysis system of psychotherapy, and their combination for the treatment of chronic depression. *New England Journal of Medicine, 342,* 1462–1470.

Kellerman, J. (1989). *Silent partner.* New York: Bantam Books.

Kelsay, J. (2002). Suicide bombers. *The Christian Century, 119,* 22–26.

Kemperman, I., Russ, M. J., & Shearin, E. (1997). Self-injurious behavior and mood regulation in borderline patients. *Journal of Personality Disorders, 11,* 146–157.

Kennedy, H. G., Iveson, R. C. Y., & Hill, O. (1999). Violence, homicide and suicide: Strong correlation and wide variation across districts. *British Journal of Psychiatry, 175,* 462–466.

Kety, S. (1974). From rationalization to reason. *American Journal of Psychiatry, 131,* 957–963.

——— (1986). Genetic factors in suicide. In A. Roy (Ed.), *Suicide.* Baltimore: Williams and Wilkins.

Khan, A., Leventhal, R. M., Khan, S., & Brown, W. A. (2002). Suicide risk in patients with anxiety disorders: A meta-analysis of the FDA database. *Journal of Affective Disorders, 69,* 183–190.

Kidd, S. A., & Kral, M. J. (2002). Suicide and prostitution among street youth: A qualitative analysis. *Adolescence, 37,* 411–430.

Killias, M., van Kesteren, J., & Rindlisbacher, M. (2001). Guns, violent crime, and suicide in 21 countries. *Canadian Journal of Criminology, 43,* 429–448.

King, R. A., Schwab-Stone, M., Flisher, A. J., Greenwald, S., Kramer, R. A.,
Goodman, S. H., Lahey, B. B., Shaffer, D., & Gould, M. S. (2001).
Psychosocial and risk behavior correlates of youth suicide attempts and
suicidal ideation. *Journal of the American Academy of Child & Adolescent
Psychiatry, 40,* 837–846.

Kirby, D. (2002). *What is a book?* Athens, GA: University of Georgia Press.

Kjelsberg, E., Eikeseth, P. H., & Dahl, A. A. (1991). Suicide in borderline patients—predictive factors. *Acta Psychiatrica Scandinavica, 84,* 283–287.

Knipfel, J. (1999). *Slackjaw: A memoir.* New York: Berkley Books.

Knipfel, J. (2000). *Quitting the Nairobi Trio.* New York: Berkley Books.

Kok, L-p. (1988). Race, religion and female suicide attempters in Singapore. *Social Psychiatry & Psychiatric Epidemiology, 23,* 236–239.

Kroll, J. (2000). Use of no-suicide contracts by psychiatrists in Minnesota.
American Journal of Psychiatry, 157, 1684–1686.

Leenaars, A. A., & Lester, D. (1999). Domestic integration and suicide in the
provinces of Canada. *Crisis, 20,* 59–63.

Leighton, A. H., & Hughes, C. C. (1955). Notes on Eskimo patterns of suicide.
Southwestern Journal of Anthropology, 11, 327–338.

Lesch, K.-P., Bengel, D., Heils, A., Sabol, S. Z., Greenberg, B. D., Petri, S.,
Benjamin, J., Muller, C. R., Hamer, D. H., Murphy, D. L. (1996). Association of anxiety-related traits with a polymorphism in the serotonin transporter gene regulatory region. *Science, 274,* 1527–1531.

Lester, D. (1992). State initiatives in addressing youth suicide: Evidence for their
effectiveness. *Social Psychiatry & Psychiatric Epidemiology, 27,* 75–77.

——— (1995). The concentration of neurotransmitter metabolites in the
cerebrospinal fluid of suicidal individuals: A meta-analysis.
Pharmacopsychiatry, 28, 45–50.

——— (1998). Experience of loss in famous suicides. *Psychological Reports, 82,*
1090.

——— (1999). Gun deaths in children and guns in the home. *European Journal
of Psychiatry, 13,* 157–159.

Lester, D., & Heim, N. (1992). Sex differences in suicide notes. *Perceptual & Motor Skills, 75,* 582.

Lester, D., & Yang, B. (1992). Social and economic correlates of the elderly suicide rate. *Suicide & Life-Threatening Behavior, 22,* 36–47.

Levine, A. D., Abramovich, Y., Stein, D., & Newman, M. (1995). Differences in
psychological reactions to an experimental "suicide experience" between
suicide attempters, suicide contemplaters, and nonsuicidal patients. Paper
presented at Israel Association of Suicidology Conference, Tel-Aviv, Israel.

Levy, B. R., Slade, M. D., Kunkel, S. R., & Kasl, S. V. (2002). Longevity increased by positive self-perceptions of aging. *Journal of Personality & Social Psychology, 83,* 261–270.

Lewinsohn, P. M., Mischel, W., Chaplin, W., & Barton, R. (1980). Social competence and depression: The role of illusory self-perceptions. *Journal of Abnormal Psychology, 89,* 203–212.

Lewinsohn, P. M., Pettit, J. W., Joiner, T., & Seeley, J. R. (2003). The symptomatic expression of major depressive disorder in adolescents and young adults. *Journal of Abnormal Psychology, 112,* 244–252.

Lewinsohn, P. M., Rohde, P., & Seeley, J. (1996). Adolescent suicidal ideation and attempts: Prevalence, risk factors, and clinical implications. *Clinical Psychology: Science & Practice, 3,* 25–46.

Lindeman, S., Laeaerae, E., Hakko, H., & Loennqvist, J. (1996). A systematic review on gender-specific suicide mortality in medical doctors. *British Journal of Psychiatry, 168,* 274–279.

Linehan, M. M. (1993). *Cognitive-behavioral treatment of Borderline Personality Disorder.* New York: Guilford Press.

Lord, V. B. (2000). Law enforcement–assisted suicide. *Criminal Justice & Behavior, 27,* 401–419.

Magne-Ingvar, U., & Oejehagen, A. (1999). Significant others of suicide attempters: Their views at the time of the acute psychiatric consultation. *Social Psychiatry & Psychiatric Epidemiology, 34,* 73–79.

Maldonado, G., & Kraus, J. F. (1991). Variation in suicide occurrence by time of day, day of the week, month, and lunar phase. *Suicide & Life-Threatening Behavior, 21,* 174–187.

Malone, K. M., Corbitt, E. M., Li, S., & Mann, J. J. (1996). Prolactin response to fenfluramine and suicide attempt lethality in major depression. *British Journal of Psychiatry, 168,* 324–329.

Malphurs, J. E., Eisendorfer, C., & Cohen, D. (2001). A comparison of antecedents of homicide-suicide and suicide in older married men. *American Journal of Geriatric Psychiatry, 9,* 49–57.

Mann, J. J., Brent, D. A., & Arango, V. (2001). The neurobiology and genetics of suicide and attempted suicide: a focus on the serotonergic system. *Neuropsychopharmacology, 24,* 467–477.

Mann, J. J., Huang, Y-y., Underwood, M. D., Kassir, S. A., Oppenheim, S., Kelly, T. M., Dwork, A. J., & Arango, V. (2000). A serotonin transporter gene promoter polymorphism (5-HTTLPR) and prefrontal cortical binding in major depression and suicide. *Archives of General Psychiatry, 57,* 729–738.

Mann, J. J., Malone, K. M., Sweeney, J. A., Brown, R. P., Linnoila, M., Stanley, B.,

& Stanley, M. (1996). Attempted suicide characteristics and cerebrospinal fluid amine metabolites in depressed inpatients. *Neuropsychopharmacology, 15,* 576–586.

Mann, T., Nolen-Hoeksema, S., Huang, K., Burgard, D., Wright, A., & Hanson, K. (1997). Are two interventions worse than none? Joint primary and secondary prevention of eating disorders in college females. *Health Psychology, 16,* 215–225.

Manning, E. L., & Fillingim, R. B. (2002). The influence of athletic status and gender on experimental pain responses. *Journal of Pain, 3,* 421–428.

Mariani, P. (1999). *The broken tower: The life of Hart Crane.* New York: Norton.

Maris, R., Berman, A., & Silverman, M. (2000). *Comprehensive textbook of suicidology.* New York: Guilford Press.

Markus, H. R., & Kitayama, S. (1991). Culture and the self: Implications for cognition, emotion, and motivation. *Psychological Review, 98,* 224–253.

Marzuk, P., Tardiff, K., Leon, A. C., & Hirsch, C. (1997). Lower risk of suicide during pregnancy. *American Journal of Psychiatry, 154,* 122–123.

Maser, J., Akiskal, H., Schettler, P., Scheftner, W., Mueller, T., Endicott, J., Solomon, D., & Clayton, P. (2002). Can temperament identify affectively ill patients who engage in lethal or near-lethal suicidal behavior? A 14-year prospective study. *Suicide & Life-Threatening Behavior, 32,* 10–32.

Matza, L., Revicki, D., Davidson, J. R., & Stewart, J. (2003). Depression with atypical features in the National Comorbidity Survey: Classification, description, and consequences. *Archives of General Psychiatry, 60,* 817–826.

May, P. (1987). Suicide and self-destruction among American Indian youths. *American Indian & Alaska Native Mental Health Research, 1,* 52–69.

McAllister, M., Roitberg, B., & Weldon, K. L. (1990). Adaptive suicide in pea aphids: Decisions are cost sensitive. *Animal Behaviour, 40,* 167–175.

McCloskey, M. S., & Berman, M. E. (2003). Alcohol intoxication and self-aggressive behavior. *Journal of Abnormal Psychology, 112,* 306–311.

McCullough, J. P. (2000). *Treatment for chronic depression: Cognitive behavioral analysis system of psychotherapy.* New York: Guilford Press.

McCullough, J. P., Jr. (2002). Treatment for chronic depression: Cognitive Behavioral Analysis System of Psychotherapy (CBASP). *Journal of Psychotherapy Integration, 13,* 241–263.

McHolm, A. E, MacMillan, H. L., & Jamieson, E. (2003). The relationship between childhood physical abuse and sucidality among depressed women: Results from a community sample. *American Journal of Psychiatry, 160,* 933–938.

McIntosh, J. L. (2002). *U.S.A. suicide statistics for the year 1999: Overheads and a presentation guide.* Washington, D.C.: American Association of Suicidology.

Meehl, P. (1973). Why I do not attend case conferences. In *Psychodiagnosis: Selected papers,* pp. 225–302. Minneapolis: University of Minnesota Press.

Menninger, K. A. (1936). Purposive accidents as an expression of self-destructive tendencies. *International Journal of Psycho-Analysis, 17,* 6–16.

Morgan, H. G. (1989). Suicide and its prevention. *Journal of the Royal Society of Medicine, 82,* 637.

Motto, J. A., & Bostrom, A. (1990). Empirical indicators of near-term suicide risk. *Crisis, 11,* 52–59.

——— (2001). A randomized controlled trial of postcrisis suicide prevention. *Psychiatric Services, 52,* 828–833.

Mroczek, D. K. (2001). Age and emotion in adulthood. *Current Directions in Psychological Science, 10,* 87–90.

Mullen, P. E., Martin, J. L., Anderson, J. C., Romans, S. E., & Herbison, G. P. (1993). Childhood sexual abuse and mental health in adult life. *British Journal of Psychiatry, 163,* 721–732.

Murray, H. (1938). *Explorations in personality.* New York: Oxford University Press.

Murray, S. L., Rose, P., Bellavia, G. M., Holmes, J. G., & Kusche, A. G. (2002). When rejection stings: How self-esteem constrains relationship-enhancement processes. *Journal of Personality & Social Psychology, 83,* 556–573.

National Center for Injury Prevention and Control (1995). *Suicide in the United States, 1980–1992,* vol. 1. Atlanta: U.S. Department of Health and Human Services.

Neuringer, C. (1967). Rigid thinking in suicidal individuals. *Journal of Consulting Psychology, 28,* 54–58.

——— (1974). Attitudes toward self in suicidal individuals. *Life-Threatening Behavior, 4,* 96–106.

Newport, D. J., Heim, C., Bonsall, R., Miller, A. H., & Nemeroff, C. B. (2004). Pituitary-adrenal responses to standard and low-dose dexamethasone suppression tests in adult survivors of child abuse. *Biological Psychiatry, 55,* 10–20.

Nisbett, P. A., Duberstein, P. R., Conwell, Y., & Seidlitz, L. (2000). The effect of participation in religious activities on suicide versus natural death in adults 50 and older. *Journal of Nervous & Mental Disease, 188,* 543–546.

Nock, M., & Marzuk, P. (1999). Murder-suicide: Phenomenology and clinical implications. In D. G. Jacobs (Ed.), *The Harvard Medical School guide to suicide assessment and intervention*, pp. 188–209. San Francisco, Calif.: Jossey-Bass.

Nock, M., Prinstien, M., Gordon, K., & Joiner, T. (2005). *Self-Mutilation, Suicide Attempts, and the Experience of Physical Pain among Adolescents.* Manuscript under editorial review.

Nolan, K. A., Volavka, J., Czobor, P., Cseh, A., Lachman, H., et al. (2000). Suicidal behavior in patients with schizophrenia is related to COMT polymorphism. *Psychiatric Genetics, 10,* 117–124.

Nordstroem, P., Asberg, M., Aberg-Wistedt, A., & Nordin, C. (1995). Attempted suicide predicts suicide risk in mood disorders. *Acta Psychiatrica Scandinavica, 92,* 345–350.

O'Carroll, P. W., Berman, A., Maris, R. W., & Moscicki, E. K. (1996). Beyond the tower of Babel: A nomenclature for suicidology. *Suicide & Life-Threatening Behavior, 26,* 237–252.

O'Connor, R. C., Sheehy, N. P., & O'Connor, D. B. (2000). Fifty cases of general hospital parasuicide. *British Journal of Health Psychology, 5,* 83–95.

O'Connor, R. J. (1978). Brood reduction in birds: Selection for fratricide, infanticide and suicide? *Animal Behaviour, 26,* 79–96.

Oquendo, M. A., Placidi, G. P. A., Malone, K. M., Campbell, C., Keilp, J., Brodsky, B., Kegeles, L. S., Cooper, T. B., Parsey, R. V., Van Heertum, R. L., & Mann, J. J. (2003). Positron emission tomography of regional brain metabolic responses to a serotonergic challenge and lethality of suicide attempts in major depression. *Archives of General Psychiatry, 60,* 14–22.

Orbach, I., Gilboa-Schechtman, E., Sheffer, A., Meged, S., Har-Even, D., & Stein, D. (2002). The suicidal "bodily self." Manuscript under editorial review.

Orbach, I., Gross, Y., & Glaubman, H. (1981). Some common characteristics of latency-age suicidal children: A tentative model based on case study analyses. *Suicide & Life-Threatening Behavior, 11,* 180–190.

Orbach, I., Mikulincer, M., King, R., Cohen, D., & Stein, D. (1997). Threshold for tolerance of physical pain in suicidal and nonsuicidal adolescents. *Journal of Consulting & Clinical Psychology, 65,* 646–652.

Orbach, I., Palgi, Y., Stein, D., & Har-Even, D. (1996a). Tolerance for physical pain suicidal subjects. *Death Studies, 20,* 327–341.

Orbach, I., Stein, D., Palgi, Y., Asherov, J., Har-Even, D., & Elizur, A. (1996b). Perception of physical pain in accident and suicide attempt patients: Self-preservation vs. self-destruction. *Journal of Psychiatric Research, 30,* 307–320.

O'Reilly, R. L., Truant, G. S., & Donaldson, L. (1990). Psychiatrists' experience of suicide in their patients. *Psychiatric Journal of the University of Ottawa, 15,* 173–176.

Overholser, J., Hemstreet, A. H., Spirito, A., & Vyse, S. (1989). Suicide awareness programs in the schools: Effects of gender and personal experience. *Journal of the American Academy of Child and Adolescent Psychiatry, 28,* 925–930.

Pearson, V. (1995). Goods on which one loses: Women and mental health in China. *Social Science & Medicine, 41,* 1159–1173.

Pennebaker, J. W., Francis, M. E., & Booth, R. J. (2001). *Linguistic inquiry and word count,* 2nd ed. Mahwah, N.J.: Erlbaum.

Perez, M., Pettit, J. W., David, C. F., Kistner, J. A., & Joiner, T. (2001). The interpersonal consequences of inflated self-esteem in an inpatient youth psychiatric sample. *Journal of Consulting & Clinical Psychology, 69,* 712–716.

Perlson, J., & Karpman, B. (1943). Psychopathologic and psychopathic reactions in dogs. *Journal of Criminal Psychopathology, 4,* 504–521.

Phillips, K. A., McElroy, S. L., Keck, P. E., & Pope, H. G. (1993). Body dysmorphic disorder: 30 cases of imagined ugliness. *American Journal of Psychiatry, 150,* 302–308.

Pierce, D. W. (1981). The predictive validation of a suicide intent scale: A five year follow-up. *British Journal of Psychiatry, 139,* 391–396.

Pooley, E. C., Houston, K., Hawton, K., & Harrison, P. J. (2003). Deliberate self-harm is associated with allelic variation in the tryptophan hydroxylase gene (TPH A779C), but not with polymorphisms in five other sertonergic genes. *Psychological Medicine, 33,* 775–783.

Popper, K. R. (1959). *The logic of scientific discovery.* New York: Basic Books.

Post, J. (2002). Killing in the name of God. *By George,* September 6. http://www.gwu.edu/~bygeorge/sept6ByG!/drpost.html.

Potter, L. B., Kresnow, M., Powell, K. E., Simon, T. R., Mercy, A. J., Lee, R. K., Frankowski, R. F., Swann, A. C., Bayer, T., & O'Carroll, P. W. (2001). The influence of geographic mobility on nearly lethal suicide attempts. *Suicide & Life-Threatening Behavior, 32(Suppl),* 42–48.

Poulin, R. (1992). Altered behaviour in parasitized bumblebees: Parasite manipulation or adaptive suicide? *Animal Behaviour, 44,* 174–176.

Qin, P., & Mortensen, P. B. (2003). The impact of parental status on the risk of completed suicide. *Archives of General Psychiatry, 60,* 797–802.

Rachman, S. J. (1989). *Fear and courage.* New York: W. W. Freeman.

Range, L. M., & Calhoun, L. G. (1990). Responses following suicide and other types of death: The perspective of the bereaved. *Omega, 21,* 311–320.

Raymond, N. C., Faris, P. L., Thuras, P. D., Eiken, B., Howard, L. A., Hofbauer,

R. D., & Eckert, E. D. (1999). Elevated pain threshold in anorexia nervosa subjects. *Biological Psychiatry, 45,* 1389–1392.

Reidel, J. (2003). *Vanished Act: The life and art of Weldon Kees.* Lincoln, Nebr.: University of Nebraska Press.

Reuter, C. (2004). *My life is a weapon.* Princeton, N.J.: Princeton University Press.

Roach, M. (2003). *Stiff.* New York: W. W. Norton.

Robinson, B. A. (2001). *Heaven's gate.* Ontario Consultants on Religious Tolerance Web site. http://www.religioustolerance.org/dc_highe.htm.

Rojcewicz, S. J. (1971). War and suicide. *Life-Threatening Behavior, 1,* 46–54.

Rosenbaum, M. (1990). The role of depression in couples involved in murder-suicide and homicide. *American Journal of Psychiatry, 147,* 1036–1039.

Rosenthal, P. A., & Rosenthal, S. (1984). Suicidal behavior by pre-school children. *American Journal of Psychiatry, 141,* 520–525.

Rosenthal, R. J., Rinzler, C., Wallsh, R., & Klausner, E. (1972). Wrist-cutting syndrome: The meaning of a gesture. *American Journal of Psychiatry, 128,* 1363–1368.

Roy, A. (1992). Are there genetic factors in suicide? *International Review of Psychiatry, 4,* 169–175.

——— (2003). Distal risk factors for suicidal behavior in alcoholics: Replications and new findings. *Journal of Affective Disorders, 77,* 267–271.

Rudd, M. D., Joiner, Jr., T. E., & Rajab, M. H. (1995). Help negation in suicide. *Journal of Consulting & Clinical Psychology, 63,* 499–503.

——— (1996). Relationships among suicide ideators, attemptors, and multiple attemptors in a young-adult sample. *Journal of Abnormal Psychology, 105,* 541–550.

Rudd, M. D., Joiner, T., & Rajab, M. (2000). *Treating suicidal behavior.* New York: Guilford.

Rudd, M. D., Rajab, M. H., Orman, D. T., Stulman, D. A., Joiner, Jr., T. E., & Dixon, W. (1996). Effectiveness of an outpatient problem-solving intervention targeting suicidal young adults: Preliminary results. *Journal of Consulting and Clinical Psychology, 64,* 179–190.

Rujescu, D., Giegling, I., Gietl, A., Hartmann, A. M., & Moeller, H.-J. (2003a). A functional single nucleotide polymorphism (V158M) in the COMT gene is associated with aggressive personality traits. *Biological Psychiatry, 54,* 34–39.

Rujescu, D., Giegling, I., Sato, T., Hartmann, A. M., Moller, H.-J. (2003b). Genetic variations in tryptophan hydroxylase in suicidal behavior: Analysis and meta-analysis. *Biological Psychiatry, 54,* 465–473.

Russ, M. J., Campbell, S. S., Kakuma, T., Harrison, K., & Zanine, E. (1999). EEG theta activity and pain insensitivity in self-injurious borderline patients. *Psychiatry Research, 89,* 201–214.

Russ, M. J., Lachman, H. M., Kashdan, T., Saito, T., & Bajmakovic-Kacila, S. (2000). Analysis of catechol-O-methyltransferase and 5-hydroxytryptamine transporter polymorphisms in patients at risk for suicide. *Psychiatry Research, 93,* 73–78.

Ryabik, B., Schreiner, M., & Elam, S. M. (1995). Triple suicide pact. *Journal of the American Academy of Child & Adolescent Psychiatry, 34,* 1121–1122.

Sabbath, J. C. (1969). The suicidal adolescent: The expendable child. *Journal of the American Academy of Child Psychiatry, 8,* 272–285.

Sabo, E., Reynolds, C. F., Kupfer, D. J., Berman, S. R. (1990). Sleep, depression, and suicide. *Psychiatry Research, 36,* 265–277.

Scheeres, J. (2003). Suicide 101: Lessons before dying. *Wired News,* February 3. http://www.wired.com/news/print/0,1294,57444,00.html.

Schmidt, N. B., Kotov, R., & Joiner, T. (2004). *Taxometrics.* Washington, DC: APA.

Schmidt, N. B., Woolaway-Bickel, K., & Bates, M. (2000). Suicide and panic disorder: Integration of the literature and new findings. In T. Joiner & M. D. Rudd (Eds.), *Suicide science: Expanding the boundaries,* pp. 117–136. Boston: Kluwer.

Segrin, C. (1992). Specifying the nature of social skill deficits associated with depression. *Human Communication Research, 19,* 89–123.

——— (2003). *Interpersonal processes in psychological problems.* New York: Guilford.

Segrin, C. & Flora, J. (1998). Depression and verbal behavior in conversations with friends and strangers. *Journal of Language & Social Psychology, 17,* 492–503.

Seguin, J. R., Pihl, R. O., Boulerice, B., & Tremblay, R. E. (1996). Pain sensitivity and stability of physical aggression in boys. *Journal of Child Psychology & Psychiatry & Allied Disciplines, 37,* 823–834.

Seligman, M. E. (1974). Submissive death: Giving up on life. *Psychology Today, 7,* 80–85.

Seligman, M. E., & Maier, S. F. (1967). Failure to escape traumatic shock. *Journal of Experimental Psychology, 74,* 1–9.

Sher, L., Oquendo, M. A., Li, S., Ellis, S., Brodsky, B. S., et al. (2003). Prolactin response to fenfluramine administration in patients with unipolar and bipolar depression and healthy controls. *Psychoneuroendocrinology, 28,* 559–573.

Shneidman, E. S. (1985). *Definition of suicide.* New York: Wiley.
——— (1996). *The suicidal mind.* New York: Oxford University Press.
——— (1998). Perspectives on suicidology: Further reflections on suicide and psychache. *Suicide & Life-Threatening Behavior, 28,* 245–250.
Shneidman, E. S., & Faberow, N. L. (1961). Statistical comparisons between attempted and committed suicides. In N. L. Faberow & E. S. Shneidman (Eds.), *The cry for help,* pp. 19–47. New York: McGraw-Hill.
Singareddy, R. K., & Balon, R. (2001). Sleep and suicide in psychiatric patients. *Annals of Clinical Psychiatry, 13,* 93–101.
Singh, G. K., & Siahpush, M. (2002). Increasing rural-urban gradients in U.S. suicide mortality, 1970–1997. *American Journal of Public Health, 92,* 1161–1167.
Sloan, P., Berman, M. E., & Mae, L. (2003). Effects of group norms on self-aggressive behavior. Manuscript under editorial review.
Snow, L. (2002). Prisoners' motives for self-injury and attempted suicide. *British Journal of Forensic Practice, 4,* 18–29.
Snowden, L. (2001). Social embeddedness and psychological well-being among African-Americans and Whites. *American Journal of Community Psychology, 29,* 519–536.
Soloff, P. H., Lis, J. A., Kelly, T., & Cornelius, J. R. (1994). Risk factors for suicidal behavior in borderline personality disorder. *American Journal of Psychiatry, 151,* 1316–1323.
Soloff, P. H., Lynch, K. G., Kelly, T. M., Malone, K. M., & Mann, J. J. (2000). Characteristics of suicide attempts of patients with major depressive episode and borderline personality disorder: A comparative study. *American Journal of Psychiatry, 157,* 601–608.
Solomon, R. L. (1980). The opponent-process theory of acquired motivation: The costs of pleasure and the benefits of pain. *American Psychologist, 35,* 691–712.
Spalletta, G., Troisi, A., Saracco, M., & Ciani, N. (1996). Symptom profile, Axis II comorbidity and suicidal behaviour in young males with DSM-II-R depressive illnesses. *Journal of Affective Disorders, 39,* 141–148.
Spreux-Varoquaux, O., Alvarez, J. C., Berlin, I., Batista, G., Despierre, P. G., et al. (2001). Differential abnormalities in plasma 5-HIAA and platelet serotonin concentrations in violent suicide attempters: Relationships with impulsivity and depression. *Life Sciences, 69,* 647–657.
Statham, D. J., Heath, A. C., Madden, P. A. F., et al. (1998). Suicidal behaviour: An epidemiological and genetic study. *Psychological Medicine, 28,* 839–855.

Steels, M. D. (1994). Deliberate self poisoning—Nottingham Forest Football Club and F. A. Cup defeat. *Irish Journal of Psychological Medicine, 11,* 76–78.

Stein, D., Apter, A., Ratzoni, G., Har-Even, D., & Avidan, G. (1998). Association between multiple suicide attempts and negative affects in adolescents. *Journal of the American Academy of Child and Adolescent Psychiatry, 37,* 488–494.

Stein, D., Kaye, W., Matsunaga, H., Myers, D., Orbach, I., Har-Even, D., Frank, G., & Rao, R. (2003). Pain perception in recovered bulimia nervosa patients. *International Journal of Eating Disorders, 34,* 331–336.

Stepakoff, S. (1998). Effects of sexual victimization on suicidal ideation and behavior in U.S. women. *Suicide & Life-Threatening Behavior, 28,* 107–126.

Stirman, S. W., & Pennebaker, J. W. (2001). Word use in the poetry of suicidal and nonsuicidal poets. *Psychosomatic Medicine, 63,* 517–522.

Stone, L. J., & Hokanson, J. E. (1969). Arousal reduction via self-punitive behavior. *Journal of Personality & Social Psychology, 12,* 72–79.

Stone, M., Hurt, S., & Stone, D. (1987). The PI 500: Long-term follow-up of borderline inpatients meeting DSM-III criteria: I. Global outcome. *Journal of Personality Disorders, 1,* 291–298.

Sullivan, H. S. (1953). *Conceptions of Modern Psychiatry: Collected Works of Harry Stack Sullivan,* vol. 1. New York: Norton.

Talavera, J. A., Saz-Ruiz, J., Garcia-Toro, M. (1994). Quantitative measurement of depression through speech analysis. *European Psychiatry, 9,* 185–193.

Tanskanen, A., Tuomilehto, J., Viinamaki, H., Vartiainen, E., Lehtonen, J., & Puska, P. (2001). Nightmares as predictors of suicide. *Sleep, 24,* 844–847.

Taylor, R., Chatters, L., Jayakody, R., & Levin, J. (1996). Black and White differences in religious participation: A multisample comparison. *Journal for the Scientific Study of Religion, 35,* 403–410.

Thorlindsson, T., & Bjarnason, T. (1998). Modeling Durkheim on the micro level: A study of youth suicidality. *American Sociological Review, 63,* 94–110.

Tiefenbacher, S., Novak, M. A., Marinus, L. M., Chase, W. K., Miller, J. A., & Meyer, J. S. (2004). Altered hypothalamic-pituitary-adrenocortical function in rhesus monkeys *(Macaca mulatto)* with self-injurious behavior. *Psychoneuroendocrinology, 29,* 501–515.

Tomassini, C., Juel, K., Holm, N. V., Skytthe, A., & Christensen, K. (2003). Risk of suicide in twins: 51 year follow up study. *British Medical Journal, 327,* 373–374.

Troisi, A., & Moles, A. (1999). Gender differences in depression: An ethological study of nonverbal behavior during interviews. *Journal of Psychiatric Research, 33,* 243–250.

Trovato, F. (1998). The Stanley Cup of hockey and suicide in Quebec, 1951–1992. *Social Forces, 77,* 105–126.

Turvey, C. L., Conwell, Y., Jones, M. P., Phillips, C., Simonsick, E., Pearson, J. L., & Wallace, R. (2002). Risk factors for late-life suicide. *American Journal of Geriatric Psychiatry, 10,* 398–406.

Twomey, H. B., Kaslow, N. J., & Croft, S. (2000). Childhood maltreatment, object relations, and suicidal behavior in women. *Psychoanalytic Psychology, 17,* 313–335.

Ungemack, J. A., & Guarnaccia, P. J. (1998). Suicidal ideation and suicide attempts among Mexican Americans, Puerto Ricans and Cuban Americans. *Transcultural Psychiatry, 35,* 307–327.

Ursin, R. (2002). Serotonin and sleep. *Sleep Medicine Reviews, 6,* 57–69.

Van Winkle, N. W., & May, P. (1993). An update on American Indian suicide in New Mexico, 1980–1987. *Human Organization, 52,* 304–315.

Veale, D., Boocock, A., Gournay, K., & Dryden, W. (1996). Body dysmorphic disorder: A survey of fifty cases. *British Journal of Psychiatry, 169,* 196–201.

Verona, E., Patrick, C., & Joiner, T. (2001). Psychopathy, antisocial personality, and suicide risk. *Journal of Abnormal Psychology, 110,* 462–470.

Vieta, E., Benabarre, A., Colom, F., & Gasto, C. (1997). Suicidal behavior in bipolar I and bipolar II disorder. *Journal of Nervous & Mental Disease, 185,* 407–408.

Vythilingam, M., Heim, C., Newport, J. M., Andrew, H., Anderson, E., Bronen, R., Brummer, M., Staib, L., Vermetten, E., Charney, D. S., Nemeroff, C. B., & Bremner, J. D. (2002). Childhood trauma associated with smaller hippocampal volume in women with major depression. *American Journal of Psychiatry, 159,* 2072–2080.

Wagner, K. D., Berenson, A., Harding, O., & Joiner, Jr., T. E. (1998). Attributional style and depression in pregnant teenagers. *American Journal of Psychiatry, 155,* 1227–1233.

Walker, R. L. (2002). An investigation of acculturative stress and ethnic identification as risk factors for suicidal ideation in African-American vs. Anglo-American men and women. Ph.D. diss., Florida State University.

Wall, A-M., Wekerle, C., & Bissonnette, M. (2000). Childhood maltreatment, parental alcoholism, and beliefs about alcohol: Subgroup variation among alcohol-dependent adults. *Alcoholism Treatment Quarterly, 18,* 49–60.

Waller, N. G., & Meehl, P. E. (1998). *Multivariate taxometric procedures.* Thousand Oaks, Calif.: Sage.

Weissman, M., Fox, K., Klerman, G. L. (1973). Hostility and depression associated with suicide attempts. *American Journal of Psychiatry, 130,* 450–455.

Weissman, M. M., Klerman, G. L., Markowitz, J. S., & Ouellette, R. (1989). Suicidal ideation and suicide attempts in panic disorder and attacks. *New England Journal of Medicine, 321,* 1209–1214.

Westen, D., Muderrisoglu, S., Fowler, C., Shedler, J., & Koren, D. (1997). Affect regulation and affective experience: Individual differences, group differences, and measurement using a Q-sort procedure. *Journal of Consulting & Clinical Psychology, 65,* 429–439.

Whitlock, F. A., & Broadhurst, A. D. (1969). Attempted suicide and the experience of violence. *Journal of Biosocial Science, 1,* 353–368.

Williams, F., & Joiner, T. (2004). How do linguistic patterns change as one approaches suicide? A psychological analysis of Quentin's and Jason's linguistic patterns in *The Sound and The Fury. Proteus: A Journal of Ideas, 22,* 8–12.

Williams, F., Pennebaker, J. W., & Joiner, T. (2005). Linguistic Inquiry and Word Count (LIWC) comparison of notes from those who died by suicide versus from those who attempted suicide and survived. Manuscript in preparation.

Williams, K. D., Cheung, C. K. T., & Choi, W. (2000). Cyberostracism: Effects of being ignored over the Internet. *Journal of Personality & Social Psychology, 79,* 748–762.

Woodrow, K. M., Friedman, G. D., Siegelaub, A. B., & Collen, M. F. (1972). Pain tolerance: Differences according to age, sex, and race. *Psychosomatic Medicine, 34,* 548–556.

Woznica, J. G., & Shapiro, J. R. (1990). An analysis of adolescent suicide attempts: The expendable child. *Journal of Pediatric Psychology, 15,* 789–796.

Yampey, N. (1967). Epidemiological considerations on suicide in Buenos Aires. *Acta Psiquiatrica y Psicologica de America Latina, 13,* 39–44.

Yates, G. L., MacKenzie, R. G., Pennbridge, J., & Swofford, A. (1991). A risk profile comparison of homeless youth involved in prostitution and homeless youth not involved. *Journal of Adolescent Health, 12,* 545–548.

Yen, S., & Siegler, I. C. (2003). Self-blame, social introversion, and male suicides: Prospective data from a longitudinal study. *Archives of Suicide Research, 7,* 17–27.

Zanarini, M. C., Frankenburg, F. R., Hennen, J., & Silk, K. R. (2003). The longitudinal course of borderline psychopathology: 6-year prospective follow-up of the phenomenology of Borderline Personality Disorder. *American Journal of Psychiatry, 160,* 274–283.

Zhang, J. (2000). Gender differences in athletic performance and their implications in gender ratios of suicide: A comparison between the USA and China. *Omega: Journal of Death & Dying, 41,* 117–123.

ACKNOWLEDGMENTS

As it happens, I am the sort of professor who does not need match-
ing furniture or really hardly any furniture in the office, or for that
matter, an office at all. I could have written this book in my front
yard, and in fact I did write it with my two sons at their computer
three feet from mine, regularly shouting with glee, defeat, or at each
other. I revised it with a cat in my lap whose presence in our family
I protested and lost in a 3–1 vote, and who, ironically, chose me as
her favorite human. I have a sort of disdain for material things, a result, perhaps, of my dad's experience, and a corresponding love for
ideas—especially ones that are true, virtuous, and compassionate—
and for the interpersonal, psychological, and other environments
that foster them.

In this connection, I want to thank two organizations that set the
interpersonal and psychological tone for this book. The first is the
Department of Psychology at Florida State University (FSU) in Tallahassee, Florida. I have lived in Tallahassee for eight years now, and
periodically hear comments along the lines of "Tallahassee is no New
York City." And I answer, thank god (no offense to residents of New

York). Thank god for its lack of pretense, its lushness, and its warmth (and I'm not just talking about the weather). FSU's Psychology Department has these same qualities—lush with ideas and interpersonally warm. For an academic department, it has a lack of pretense and absence of interpersonal irritants that, though not total, may be unrivalled in an accomplished department. I would particularly like to mention colleagues and graduate students who were in some way especially helpful. My own Ph.D. students, past and present, have regularly refined and challenged my thinking—they are Rebecca Bernert, Jessica Brown, Kelly Cukrowicz, Jill Denoma, Katie Gordon, Daniel Hollar, Katie Merrill, Marisol Perez, Jeremy Pettit, Nadia Stellrecht, Kim Van Orden, Zach Voelz, Rheeda Walker, Foluso Williams, Ricki Wingate, and Tracy Witte. Other Ph.D. students at FSU have also been engaging, thoughtful, and thought-provoking: Andrea Burns, Kiara Cromer, Keith Donohue, Kim Driscoll, Jenn Minnix, Maureen Lyons Reardon, Lorraine Reitzel, Karla Repper, Edelyn Verona, and Brad White. Supportive colleagues at FSU are abundant; I am especially grateful to Ellen Berler, Rob Contreras, John Corrigan, Anders Ericsson, Don Foss, Frank Johnson, Neil Jumonville, Janet Kistner, Al Lang, Jon Maner, Dianne Tice, and Rick Wagner. Special mention needs to be made of my closest colleagues and best friends at FSU, Roy Baumeister, Natalie Sachs-Ericsson, and Brad Schmidt.

The second organization I would like to thank for setting a particular psychological context for the book is the John Simon Guggenheim Memorial Foundation. For a professor who tries to live the life of the mind and who admires and respects excellence across academic disciplines, a Guggenheim Fellowship is a unique recognition, inspiration, and responsibility. If my tone in the book becomes overconfident at times, I apologize up front, and wonder whether it has to do with the Guggenheim imprimatur, though of course I absolve them of any of my offenses, and thank them for an honor that has changed me for the better.

I have received other generosities too. People like Lyn Abramson, Aaron T. Beck, Jim Coyne, and Pete Lewinsohn were under no obligation to me and yet have set a standard for me and many others on how to encourage and cultivate younger colleagues. David Rudd and Lanny Berman have included me in stimulating meetings of the American Association of Suicidology, allowing me to give a keynote address on the ideas in this book in April 2004 in Miami. The questions and discussion that followed my address were the most insightful and helpful of any that I have received. I also gave talks on this material at the University of North Dakota School of Medicine, the University of Georgia, and the Centers for Disease Control and Prevention in Atlanta, and in each case, received encouragement and thought-provoking reactions. David Rudd deserves special recognition, as so much of my thinking and work in suicide research have been in collaboration with him. Others who have supported me and the development of the ideas in this book in one way or another are Julianna Baggott, Steve Beach, Sheila Curran, Marty Franklin, Todd Heatherton, Barry Krakow, Rich McNally, Matt Nock, Ainhoa Otamendi, Dave Scott, Karen Wagner, Mark Winegardner, and Steve Wonderlich. Elizabeth Knoll at Harvard University Press deserves her consensus reputation for excellence and gentle rigor.

Finally, to my mother and sisters, I say, "I'm just *so* sorry we had to go through that." To my lovely wife, Graciela Marquina, I say *"Te amo mi amor, siempre."* And as I put this book to bed, it reminds me of the routine that has developed in my family as I put our sons, Malachi and Zekey, to bed—I say, "I love you, I'm proud of you, and I'm happy to be your dad." It is so true.

INDEX